THROUGH AMERICAN AND IRISH WARS

The Irish Abroad

GENERAL EDITOR: RUAN O'DONNELL, UNIVERSITY OF LIMERICK

This new series aims to publish short biographies of Irish men and women who made their mark outside their native country. Accounts of those who settled permanently overseas will be published along with the life stories of temporary residents and involuntary emigrants. Expatriates of all types will be considered whether explorers, travellers, military personnel, colonial pioneers, members of religious orders, professionals, politicians, revolutionaries, exiles or convicts. While it is envisaged that the majority of the subjects would have gone overseas during the early modern and modern period, persons from different times may also be deemed appropriate for inclusion. Most titles will concern the Irish in North America, the former territories of the British Empire (including Australasia) and Great Britain, although it is intended that biographies of those who journeyed to Spanish America, the West Indies, Africa, continental Europe and other non-English speaking sectors will form part of the series. Men and women of Irish extraction will also merit inclusion if it is evident that their perceived ethnicity and family origins played a significant part in their careers. A number of autobiographies will be selected for republication with critical introductions by leading scholars.

Also from the Irish Abroad series from Irish Academic Press:

Thomas Francis Meagher
The Making of an Irish American
John M. Hearne and Rory T. Cornish (Eds)

Through American and Irish Wars
The Life and Times of General Thomas W. Sweeny
Jack Morgan

Bishop in the Dock
The Sedition Trial of James Liston
Rory Sweetman

THROUGH AMERICAN AND IRISH WARS

The Life and Times of General Thomas W. Sweeny 1820–1892

Jack Morgan
University of Missouri–Rolla

IRISH ACADEMIC PRESS
DUBLIN • PORTLAND, OR

First published in 2006 by
IRISH ACADEMIC PRESS
44, Northumberland Road, Dublin 4, Ireland

and in the United States of America by
IRISH ACADEMIC PRESS
c/o ISBS, Suite 300, 920 NE 58th Avenue
Portland, Oregon 97213–3644

***WEBSITE*: www.iap.ie**

British Library Cataloguing in Publication Data
A catalogue entry is available on request

ISBN 0–7165–3323–5 (cloth)
ISBN 0–7165–3324–3 (paper)

Library of Congress Cataloging-in-Publication Data
A catalog entry is available on request

Typeset by Carrigboy Typesetting Services, County Cork
Printed by in Great Britain by MPG Books Ltd, Bodmin, Cornwall

Contents

For my father,
farther along

List of illustrations

I see they are making another movement for Irish Independence. I hope it will amount to something this time. Ell, how would you like me to embark on such an undertaking? . . . We might accomplish great things – do deeds that our children could point at on the page of history with pride: perhaps help to pull a sinewy tyrant from his throne, and raise a prostrate people from chains to liberty. Let me know what you think of it, Ell. There's much excitement here on the subject.

TWS to his wife from Sioux Territory, 1856

Acknowledgements

The phrase 'Life and Times' is not used here merely as a biographical title convention. The attempt in this book is to represent the historical period and Thomas Sweeny's life as they were intertwined, and the aspects of the times especially focused upon, readers will note, are those related to the story of the Irish in the nineteenth-century United States. A paper on General Sweeny, written originally for a conference at the University of Prince Edward Island, and subsequently published in the series 'Working Papers in Irish Studies', edited by Jim Doan, represented the start of what became the present book.

I wish to thank firstly and sincerely John Bradbury, Western Historical Manuscripts, University of Missouri–Rolla, for his unstinting help and his unfailing generosity, scholarly and in general, over the years. Also: my daughter, Jennifer Olson, for assistance at the New York Public Library; Deborah McWilliams for her kindness and valuable research help in California; Mona Schulman and the Huntington Library staff for their helpfulness. Thanks are due as well to Larry Vonalt, Anne Peterson, Trent Watts, Michael Ruddy, Linda Sands, Dr Tom Sweeney, Kris Swenson, Scott Peterson, Nick Knight, Moya O'Berry and the late Timothy Sarbaugh.

Foreword

Thomas Sweeny left Cork in 1832 and was one of millions of Irish emigrants who settled in the United States during the nineteenth century. Sweeny's martial disposition induced him to volunteer for the American army in which he served with distinction during the Mexican War. Although severely wounded, he became a commissioned officer and enjoyed a highly successful and eventful military career. Sweeny rose to the rank of Brigadier General during the catastrophic American Civil War and played a notable role in the Battle of Shiloh.

Recent scholarship has emphasized the extensive Irish participation in such campaigns and this book is an important contribution to the field. Sweeny was by no means the only Irishman to attain high rank in the American forces in the 1860s but his experience was untypical in several respects. In the first instance, he belonged to a pre-Famine immigrant wave which in the late 1840s was inundated by an unprecedentedly large influx of their desperate countrymen. Sweeny, a man of modest means, had long assimilated into American society and witnessed the uneven reception encountered by later Irish migrants and refugees. If anything, the plight of such persons and the context in which it occurred accentuated his radical inclinations. Sweeny readily took a major part in one of the most enduring and significant post-Famine phenomena: the revival of the physical force tradition.

Sweeny was arguably the most important Civil War general to align himself with the Irish Republican Brotherhood (Fenians) and became a prime mover in the conspiracy to invade Canada in 1866. A family relation to John Sweeny, a prominent Cork United Irishman of 1798 and 1803, may have had bearing on this activism but General Sweeny was certainly a militant revolutionary prior to leaving the army in 1870. Like many Irishmen of his generation, Sweeny saw no conflict of interest between military service in his adopted country and offering leadership to a revolutionary movement focused on that of his birth. He was simultaneously an American patriot willing to suppress Mexican and Sioux insurgency and an Irish republican who promoted assaults on British interests in Canada.

Jack Morgan has drawn heavily and with great effect on Sweeny's family papers, journals and contemporary sources to reconstruct the life and career of a fascinating Irish–American. The biography covers Sweeny's adolescence in New York, soldiering in Mexico, campaigns against Native Americans on the western frontier, travels in South America and service in the American Civil War. Morgan's work on Sweeny's Fenian activities is a marked advance on earlier treatments and explores hitherto ignored or suppressed issues. By chance and design, Sweeny participated in many of the key events of the late nineteenth century Hibernian world. Morgan's detailed and illuminating account of that life is the first to date.

DR RUAN O'DONNELL
History Department
University of Limerick

1

'Whistle Up the Marching Tune'

> The excitement of danger, the bravery of defying it, the triumph and glory of overcoming it.
>
> Sweeny, *Journal*[1]

When Thomas Sweeny died at his residence in Astoria, Long Island, on 10 April 1892, the newspaper obituaries of the following few days carried biographical sketches presenting details of his extraordinary life and military career. Born in Dunmanway, County Cork, he had come to the United States in 1832 at the age of 12, a pre-Famine Irish immigrant, and worked as a compositor in the printing trade in Brooklyn until the Mexican War, at which time he volunteered and lost his right arm in the conflict. He later served for five years as a lieutenant in the 2nd Infantry in the desert wilds of the California–Arizona territory. At the onset of the Civil War he oversaw protection of the critical St Louis Arsenal until it could be fortified properly, his decisive actions preventing that installation from falling into the hands of the secessionist state militia. Appointed Brigadier General, Missouri Volunteers, he was a key player in the Civil War in Missouri and at the Battle of Wilson's Creek, the first major Civil War battle fought after Bull Run. There he was wounded again, and yet again at Shiloh where he led one of the largest Union brigades in the field.

There were typically a few final remarks in these obituaries noting his outstanding generalship at Corinth and around Atlanta at the war's end. At the conclusion of their summaries of Sweeny's military accomplishments, some of the newspaper reports tended to make tactfully brief mention of one thing more. The *New York Herald*, for example, noted that Sweeny was an 'active Irish Nationalist', and the *New York Times* mentioned laconically that he had 'participated in the Fenian invasion of Canada'.[2] Even some twenty-six years after the event, the Canadian affair was apparently still a touchy subject, and the obituaries understated matters. Sweeny had in fact been the Fenian Secretary of War and, in the 1860s, was a particular object of the *Times*' anti-Fenian editorial ire. Along with William Randall Roberts, he was leader of the Brotherhood's militant, direct-action wing in the United States which faction ultimately deposed the O'Mahony wing, and he was the architect of the Canadian invasion – plans for which he presented to the Pittsburgh Fenian Convention in February 1866. (He would ultimately resign his position at the discordant Troy, New York, convention of September 1866.) Indeed, his extensive papers and correspondence have been a documentary mainstay for studies of the American

Fenian movement from Joseph Denieffe's *A Personal Narrative of the Irish Revolutionary Brotherhood* (1906)[3] to William D'Arcy's classic *The Fenian Movement in the United States: 1858–1886* (1947), and beyond.

Even the *Irish World* in its editorial at the time of Sweeny's death in 1892, underplayed his Fenian connections and emphasized instead his service to the US, mentioning the Fenian invasion only in the obituary's conclusion:

> The year after the war General Sweeny's intense Irish sympathies were aroused by the Fenian agitation, and he risked everything to join in the invasion of Canada. He was often a visitor to the office of the *Irish World*, and we loved him for his honest straightforward manner and his high sense of honour. He was a man of whose memory his adopted and his native land may well be proud.[4]

The writer of this editorial said nothing to the effect that Thomas Sweeny would be long remembered. If he had, events would by now have proven him wrong. To the extent that aspects of Sweeny's life are referenced at all, it is in a fragmentary fashion; the biographical dots have not been connected. In *The St Louis Irish*: *An Unmatched Celtic Community* (2001) Jesuit historian William Barnaby Faherty mentions no Sweeny connection to Fenianism, concluding in a footnote on Sweeny's role at St Louis' Camp Jackson, that Sweeny 'retired from the army in 1870 and had no further relationship with St Louis'.[5] Nor did Arthur Woodward, in his 1956 'Introduction' to Sweeny's *Journal* – the diary of his California years – mention his post-Civil War Fenian activities.[6] Prominent mention of him might also have been expected in a 1991 special issue of the magazine *Civil War*,[7] one given over to the role of the Irish in that conflict, but the issue somehow managed entirely to overlook this particular one-armed general, the first Irish-born officer to be placed on the US Army's retired list. The article, like most studies of the Irish in the Civil War, tended to emphasize the Potomac sector of the engagement, in which Generals Corcoran and Meagher and the New York Irish Brigade were involved, to the neglect of the western theatre in which Sweeny and many other Irish officers and enlisted men served. In fact, among the first 'Irish Brigades' to see action in the Civil War were Captain Patrick Naughton's dragoons and Colonel James Mulligan's 23rd Illinois Regiment, both in Missouri in 1861 at the battles of Wilson's Creek and Lexington respectively.

George Potter, to cite another example of Sweeny neglected, in his *To the Golden Door: The Story of the Irish in Ireland and America* (1960), considers the Irish in the Mexican War at some length, but does not mention Sweeny. A few paragraphs in Alan Axelrod's *Chronicle of the Indian Wars from Colonial Times to Wounded Knee* (1993) are given over to Sweeny's pre-Civil War years in Indian territory, however, and he is, of course, mentioned in the copious historical literature devoted to American Fenianism, but there, on the other hand, his life and wide-ranging military experience prior to 1866 are usually given short shrift. In addition, treatments of American Fenianism typically set forth a narrative that privileges those who were involved in the Young Ireland movement and the 1848 uprising, a narrative in which James Stephens, John O'Mahony, Michael Doheny, John Mitchel, Thomas Francis Meagher, Terence Bellew McManus, et al., are the starring figures. Sweeny, having emigrated young, was not part of that group, or at least entered it late, somewhat marginally, and from another, more American direction. The renewed interest in the US Civil War and the concurrent interest in Irish immigration studies, however, may serve to rescue Sweeny from the historical shadows. During the time the present book was being written, for example, he came in for significant mention in the History Channel television presentation *The Irish in America*.[8]

Viewed as a whole, his life would seem to belong in a novel; he emerges as a remarkably colourful and controversial personality, a man whose picaresque American journey typified the Irish experience in the US at its boldest and most romantic, particularly from the Famine decade through the 1860s when he found himself deeply involved in the defining geopolitical events of the mid-century – the opening of the west, the Mexican War, the discovery of gold in California and the Civil War. In his 'introduction' to the journal Sweeny kept during his years in southwest Indian territory, 1849–53, the historian Woodward remarks that Sweeny provides physical descriptions and character sketches of the Yuma Indian leaders 'as no other writer has done'.[9] He was aboard the first steamer to go up the Gila River, knew Geronimo personally, participated in the Sioux Expedition of 1855–56, was present at major peace councils with the Yuma and the Sioux, and was a member of the Guard of Honour when Lincoln's remains lay in state in New York in 1865.[10] Physically, as described by an officer in 1862, Sweeny was '5 ft. 9 inches tall with black hair and whiskers, dark eyes, straight, slim, and very quiet'.[11] As will become evident, however, he was not always so quiet when his nerves were frayed or when he had a drop taken, or – as was often the case when he was in the midst of the horrors of the Civil War – both. The American western historian, Robert G. Cleland, has described Sweeny as:

> brave, often to the point of rashness, efficient, resourceful, well-educated, self-confident, careful of the safety and comfort of his men, capable of enduring the most trying hardships, skillful in dealing with the crafty, unpredictable Indians both in negotiation and the art of merciless desert war, quick to damn incompetence or veniality in his superiors, quicker still to resent any slight, real or imaginary . . .[12]

His bold character fitted the image often projected upon the Irish by journalists of the period. In a recent biography of General Philip Sheridan, for instance, the author notes the way in which the northern press tended to characterize Sheridan according to their stock Hibernian model whereas actually, 'far from being the apotheosis of Celtic dash . . . he was instead the most deliberate and careful of commanders'.[13] The mercurial, defiant and oft-court-martialed Sweeny was perhaps closer to the swashbuckling Irish rogue those writers had in mind – this officer who rode during drills and reviews with the horse's reins in his mouth and his sword in his only hand.[14] Indeed, his life was arguably one long expression of precisely that 'Celtic dash' for which the nineteenth-century American journalists had such a fondness.[15]

Though perhaps a little overdrawn, Arthur Woodward's characterization of Sweeny in his introduction to Sweeny's frontier journal would seem not inappropriate given its subject's dramatic later life:

> The essence of traditional Irish blarney and the strength of the native Irish stone were in the blood and bone of Thomas William Sweeny . . . the youngest of four sons of William and Honora Sweeny. The elder Sweeny died in 1827, and was interred alongside the remains of countless forbears in the cemetery of Macroon in County Cork.[16]

If Tom Sweeny was not aware of his family genealogy, the Fenian leader and Irish historical scholar, John O'Mahony, during the brief time the two were on friendly terms, could have, and probably did, fill him in regarding the Sweeny ancestry:

> The McSweenys were standard bearers and marshals of the O'Donnells. They were famous throughout Ireland as leaders of those heavy-armed soldiers called gallowglasses. A Branch of the family settled in the county of Cork in the thirteenth century.[17]

The New York *Irish-American* would later point out that a relative of Tom Sweeny's, John Sweeny,

> was a prominent member of the United Irishmen, and an intimate and confidential friend of Robert Emmet. He was confined, along with Thomas Addis Emmet, William James MacNevin, Arthur O'Connor, and others in Fort George, for the part he took in the insurrection of 1798.[18]

Five years after her husband's death, Honora Sweeny, with two of her sons – her daughter Sarah would come over later – departed Ireland by way of Liverpool aboard the ship *Augusta* for the United States. Thomas Sweeny was 12 years old. In mid-voyage, according to Sweeny's account, he was washed overboard in a sudden storm and all but drowned, spending over half an hour in the ocean before being rescued. The near drowning would prove to be in keeping with the tenor of much of his life thereafter; his lifelong inclination to brashness and derring-do would perhaps account for his being up on deck in a fierce Atlantic storm and perhaps also for his later coolness in the face of death:

> It was a stormy, tempestuous day, and the waves broke over, sweeping everything before them. I was caught by one and borne along, but saved myself by grasping at the ratlines, where I clung, half-stunned, until a second

> wave, more powerful than the first, struck me and bore me away. In a moment I found myself lying on my back and tossed hither and thither like a chip. My first feeling was one of utter loneliness, and I felt that I should never see land again or meet those I loved, and yet, thinking it might attract attention from the ship and being the means of letting them know on board that I was overboard – for none had seen me swept off – I untied my cap – a sealskin one – and threw it into the air. I then folded my arms across my breast, and as a weary child might, rocked to slumber in his cradle, said my prayers, and almost sunk into insensibility. I felt perfectly resigned, and as calm as ever I was in my life. It was only when I caught sight of a small boat, with three men in it . . . coming down upon me from the top of a wave, that I found voice to shout . . . They, after much difficulty and risk, had been able to find me. With considerable skill, they managed to pick me up without running me under, and . . . I sunk insensible into their arms.
>
> As we neared the vessel, which the captain had wore to when my sudden exit was discovered, one of the men whispered to me. 'Tommy, do you think you can stand up and show them on the ship that you're alive?' 'I guess so', I answered, and being lifted up I stood in the bows of the boat and looked up at the faces peering over the side of the ship.[19]

His schooling in New York, while probably not extensive, seems to have been enough to make a more than competent writer of him, as is attested to by his letters, reports and journals, which are, as Woodward notes, sprinkled with quotations from the Romantic poets. Early on he became a printer's apprentice in the New York City publishing house of Alfred Pell and Company and then moved to the law publishers Gould, Banks and Company. In the Irish 'Wild Geese' tradition, however, he was drawn toward the military. Marching societies, drill clubs and parading associations of various types were popular during the early to mid-nineteenth century, particularly in New York, and Sweeny was a member of a number of them incuding the 'Paul Jones Parading Club' and 'The Independent Tompkins Blues'.[20] Such clubs afforded those of martial spirit an opportunity to don uniforms and become weekend warriors in peacetime. They also spawned a variety of honorary 'colonels' and 'captains' – often ones with dubious credentials. Years later, looking back on these societies from the vantage point of a seasoned soldier, Sweeny was scornful of their pseudo-military pretensions. On Independence Day in 1851, while stationed in southwest Indian territory, he imagined that day's New York parade disdainfully:

> What holiday crowds are thronging the sidewalks of Broadway, and what endless parade of belaced and weaponed butchers, bakers, and tailors are moving down the street, fancying themselves in the martial glow of their suffocating uniforms, to be soldiers. God save the mark! A few long marches in the desert would tame them down.[21]

His early experience with amateur military units might explain Sweeny's tendency in later years to hold in similar disdain comparable Canadian organizations when he was estimating, and perhaps underestimating, the likely resistance Fenian raiders would encounter on crossing the border. As Hereward Senior has pointed out, the Canadian military picture in 1866 included a considerable element of such questionable military units, ones of the kind Sweeny had been in as a young man: 'The male population was enrolled in militia regiments, which held annual parades. Officers were appointed for their social influence rather than their military talents'.[22]

One military club of which he was a member had a real influence on Tom Sweeny, however: the Scott Cadets – later the 'Independent Tompkins Blues' – commanded by Charles Baxter. From Baxter Sweeny derived a love of the codes, protocols and traditions of soldiering.[23] Many years later he would name one of his sons, Charles Baxter Sweeny, in tribute to this early military mentor.

The year of 1846 was marked by some significant events in American history. Francis Parkman set out on his journey west along the Oregon Trail, the Donner Party cannibalism horror occurred in the Sierras, and major Mormon adventuring in the West commenced. It was also the year in which a devastating blight was working its way through the potato fields in Ireland – something that would soon occasion massive Irish emigration to the United States. By this point it had become evident that the volatility that had characterized US–Mexican relations in Texas and California for over a decade could not be contained. Following the Texas declaration of independence in 1836, events such as the fall of the Alamo and the terrible massacre at Goliad, wedded to inflammatory editorial urges toward war and annexation, resulted in popular – though far from unanimous – support for a full-scale assault on Mexico.[24] With the election in 1844 of James K. Polk, a president who harboured expansionist inclinations toward the Canadian part of the Oregon territory as well as toward Mexican California and Mexico itself, the die had been cast. According to Bernard DeVoto, 1846 was the year that provided the political template for the rest of the nineteenth century – there was 'a turning point in American destiny within the limits of [this] one year'.[25] An aggressive, expansionist period of major military initiatives was underway – the Manifest Destiny political vision that would dominate American foreign policy at least until the war in the Philippines in 1898.

When war with Mexico was declared on 13 May 1846, it was the first war, aside from the Seminole campaigns, in which the United States had been involved since the war of 1812. Preparations were under way for putting Mexico City itself under siege. Colonel Stephen Kearney proceeded south from Fort Leavenworth, Missouri, captured Santa Fe and drove west to San Diego. Zachery Taylor struck across the border into northern Mexico, captured Monterrey and prepared to engage Santa Anna at Buena Vista. At this point, however, the US administration revised its invasion plans, abandoning the idea of invading along the Rio Grande in favor of another strategy. Taylor was replaced by General Winfield Scott, and an invasion from the east was to replace the western campaign already under way. Taylor's 6,000 troops left the border region bound east and south for the new site of attack on Mexico – the Gulf port of Vera Cruz. There they were to be joined by numerous regiments of volunteers, among whom was 26-year-old Thomas Sweeny.

He was one of 800 men who had enlisted with the 1st Regiment, New York Volunteers, that year, and one of the 4,811 Irish-born soldiers who were to fill the US Army ranks in Mexico.[26] He would spend most of the next five years in the southwest, in Mexico and on the US–Mexican border. At the age of 26, he was embarking upon a military career that would entail a full measure of adventure before his retirement, at the rank of general, in 1870. He would achieve that rank despite his Irish-immigrant background, his lack of an extensive formal education, much less a West Point one, and the formidable handicap of a missing right arm. It was a career that would take him to Mexico, Brazil, around the horn to California, into the barely explored depths of the American desert and Indian territories, through many of the Civil War's bloodiest battles, and ultimately into his role in the Fenian movement. He later recalled with bemused irony the romantic zeal which had led him as a young man into an army career:

> It was the dash, gallantry, and *éclat* of the military profession that roused my youthful enthusiasm and seduced me from the peaceful calling for which I was designed . . . The excitement of danger, the bravery of defying it, the triumph and glory of overcoming it . . . these with the gaiety, glitter, reckless revelry and daring of martial life, were the excitements once presented to my imagination![27]

Such a romantic–martial imagination was not an idiosyncratic quirk of Sweeny's, however; his personality and career can be viewed very much in the light of the prevailing mindset of his era; his life was lived more in the active mode than the philosophical – or, better put perhaps, his philosophy was actional, Kiplingesque. His personality would seem to bear comparison to Melville's, Crane's, Jack London's, or Ambrose Bierce's, to cite only literary comparisons. Though exceptionally family-oriented and highly intelligent, Sweeny was very much an adventurer. He had grown up on the romantic Irish nationalist narrative, and the period of his schooling in America was filled with the romanticizing of warfare and adventure with their potential glories. The United States, as noted, had not been engaged in a war since that of 1812, and the country cherished images of the exciting feats of John Paul Jones and the heroes of the Revolution, Washington being a particular historical icon. A high-quality education system had produced a population given to reading, and the works of Sir Walter Scott, historical romances informed by neo-Arthurian values, were especially popular and influential.[28] Prescott's *Conquest of Mexico* (1843) had sparked interest in Spanish/Aztec history in the United States and spawned a popular genre of adventurous tales of conquest. When Gothic novelist Charles Maturin's Irish-born son, Edward, for example, published

Montezuma: The Last of the Aztecs late in 1845, the *New York Mirror* hailed it as 'a sensation'. Robert W. Johanssen argues that this species of literature had a significant impact in the United States, shaping the American imagination to a point where citizens could 'view their own expedition into Mexico in a heroic context . . . in the reflected light of romance and history'. Critics of the Mexican war, he notes, 'were dismayed by the martial literature that formed so large a part of the nation's reading'. The result was that, as the war approached, the volunteer ranks were packed by ardent young men anxious to march bravely to the Halls of the Montezumas. They would do so with, for the most part, the enthusiastic support of everyday Americans. 'In every section of the country, the volunteers became the object of adulation as communities vied with one another in their show of support for the country's cause'.[29] Young ladies were particular enthusiasts and admirers of the dashing volunteers setting out upon a grand, chivalric enterprise south of the border. Professional groups such as printers, of whom Sweeny was one, also vied with one another to supply the war effort with manpower. As he prepared for departure to the warfront, the printers for whom he worked, Gould, Banks and Company, gave him a party and presented him with 'a handsome pair of revolving pistols as a token of esteem and regard'.[30]

Holding a second lieutenant's commission owing to his popularity among his fellow militiamen – volunteer officers were elected – he left New York harbour with the 1st New York on 8 January 1847, bound for the seat of war. After two weeks at sea, his 800-strong regiment reached the Lobos Islands, two miles from Vera Cruz, the rendezvous point to drill and coordinate with volunteer regiments from Massachusetts, Pennsylvania, South Carolina and Louisiana. On 9 March, Sweeny's unit joined General William J. Worth's command. Sweeny would be part of the more than 12,000 aboard a fleet of 100 ships to land just down the coast from Vera Cruz and take part in the siege of the port.[31] This landing, conceived by Naval Commodore David Connor, was historically the first successful amphibious landing by US troops. Because of the formidable fortress castle of San Juan de Ulua, however, with its batteries set on an off-shore coral reef protecting the city's harbour, the American Army attacked Vera Cruz indirectly, from beaches down the coast, with the intention of encircling the city from the south, the US Navy meanwhile shelling from the sea. Sweeny's regiment was in the main strike force attacking from the southeast. He was felled by sunstroke for a while during the ensuing siege, but recovered.[32]

On 27 March, after eighteen days of concerted artillery bombardment, the Mexican command at Vera Cruz was forced to capitulate. On 8 April 1847, Sweeny's unit joined the American march into Mexico's interior. US troops anticipated that their next engagement would be at Jalapa. A mere thirty miles inland, however, in the hills around Cerro Gordo, entrenched artillery units awaited the American advance, and it was there that Sweeny was to get his first taste of genuine combat. It was here, he wrote, on 17 and 18 April 1847, that in real terms he first 'smelt powder'. While the main American force engaged the

Mexican defenders, it was decided that a unit would attempt to flank the enemy position – Santa Anna had assumed the prohibitive terrain would prevent any advance on his left flank. Under the direction of engineers, Sweeny's company, as part of General Shield's brigade, was involved in the difficult effort to do just that – advance on the Mexican left flank, taking a strategic hill in the process:

> We cut a road through the chaparral for the artillery, to the left of the enemy's position, in order to turn it. After reaching the base of the hill . . . we were exposed to a raking fire by the Mexican batteries. During the night of the 17th we were ordered to drag the artillery and ammunition to the top of the hill, a very laborious work, but it was accomplished by three o'clock on the morning of the 18th. Although not obliged to do so, I carried balls with the men, in order to encourage them in their arduous work. So thoroughly broken down were some of the men on its completion that they dropped where they stood and in the cold night air enjoyed a sound repose for a couple of hours. I lay down between two men who, I supposed, were members of my company, but on awakening in the morning, I found they were dead Mexicans, killed in taking the heights the evening before.[33]

Nearby at the time but less immediately involved in the Cerro Gordo fighting, was Nathaniel Lyon, a regular army lieutenant from Connecticut with whom Sweeny would cross paths significantly many years later in Missouri; and among the numerous US Army wounded at Cerro Gordo was Samuel Spear, an enlisted man who would later be promoted to colonel and finally brevet brigadier general in the Civil War and who would twice lead Fenian Army wings into Canada – in 1866 under Sweeny's command and in 1870 under the command of Colonel John O'Neill. Sweeny's regiment here was attached to regular units commanded by officers such as Colonel Riley, the son of Irish immigrants, and even more notably, General Shields, an Irishman born in County Tyrone in 1810, who emigrated in 1826, and became a lawyer and ultimately judge of the Illinois Supreme Court before entering the military as a brigadier general at the outbreak of the war with Mexico. Shields was wounded at Cerro Gordo and later at Chapultepec, but lived to have an extensive political career later on in Illinois and Missouri.[34] The example of Irish-born role models such as Shields, whose 'activity, zeal, and talent'[35] Winfield Scott praised, may have impressed upon Sweeny, as another Irish immigrant, the correctness of his choice of a military career.

When the critical battle at Cerro Gordo concluded in an American victory, Scott's invasion proceeded inland through Jalapa and Puebla, with a two-month pause for regrouping and supply at the latter location. In Puebla, despite the dangers, American troops took time on 4 July for an incongruous Independence Day celebration with fireworks. Sweeny recalled the partying and pyrotechnics and, in retrospect, considered how dangerous an indulgence the festivity could have proven:

> Those who like myself had entered the city with the advance guard of the army under General Worth, and held possession until the arrival of the main body under General Scott two weeks after, were not so 'profoundly inspired' as the rest, for the paucity of our number (2,500 men) had compelled us to be constantly under arms, knowing as we all did, that Santa Anna, with about 4,000 men, after disputing our entrance, was hovering about the suburbs, waiting for the advantage, and the inhabitants of the city itself, a population of 90,000 of the most warlike of the Mexican people, were ready and instructed by their chief to overwhelm us, a favorable chance occurring. I did not know if the Pueblans were too much taken aback by the suddenness of our transition from rigid sobriety to overflowing and vociferous jollity, whether they regarded it as a miracle, or as a *ruse de guerre*, but certain it is, they lost the best opportunity of exterminating a hostile army ever presented to an invaded people.[36]

Things were not to remain light-hearted and celebratory for long, however. On 8 August the march inland along the national road toward the capital proceeded, and Shield's brigade, of which Sweeny's regiment was a part, after battling through Contreras and San Geronimo, prepared to close on Churubusco and its heavily fortified bridge and convent, the latter having adobe walls four feet thick and twelve feet high with emplacements for seven artillery pieces.[37] There a decisive and bloody battle loomed. Santa Anna's troops dug in and threw up a fierce resistance, defending the fortified convent and the key bridge over the Rio Churubusco canal, which, if they fell, would leave US troops effectively at the gates of Mexico City. Directing the Mexican artillery from the convent was John Riley, chief officer of the Mexican St Patrick's Battalion. When the fortress eventually fell, sixty-five members of this perdominantly Irish battalion, who had opted to fight for Catholic Mexico, were captured by US troops, and most of them were later tortured and hanged.[38] Nor was it a fortunate day for Sweeny who was seriously wounded, as were his New York regiment leaders, Charles Baxter and Ward B. Burnett. When the Mexicans defending the key bridge refused to be dislodged and the US advance stalled, Shield's brigade, in conjunction with Worth's command, were ordered to attempt a circling movement:

> After marching nearly three miles, over marshes and fields, we reached the enemy's right and rear at Los Portales. While our line was being forced to charge the breastworks and hacienda, the enemy endeavored to turn our left. We advanced under tremendous fire, from the effects of which Colonel Burnett was disabled by a musket ball in the left leg, and was compelled to turn over the command of the regiment to Lieutenant-Colonel Baxter. While leading my men into action, I was struck in the groin by a spent ball. It passed through three thicknesses of clothing and produced a painful, though not dangerous wound . . . Advancing farther, in a few minutes I was again wounded, receiving a ball from an escopette in my right arm above the elbow. The ball passed completely through the arm, but for a few minutes I did not know that I had again been wounded until I felt a stinging sensation in my

> arm . . . Looking down, I perceived a hole in my sleeve, slightly tinged with blood; the next instant my arm dropped powerless to my side, a sickening sensation came over me . . .[39]

Francis Pinto, a fellow New York lieutenant, caught Sweeny as he fell and helped him toward the rear and medical aid, braving the withering Mexican fire that was raining upon Shield's command. Captain Robert E. Lee of the Engineer Corps, sent to assess the dire situation, reported back to General Scott on the gravity of the situation, and Scott released a mounted rifle unit, all he had in reserve, to buttress Shields's command. When the firing had waned enough to permit it, Sweeny was evacuated to a temporary hospital in the village of San Augustin where he underwent a trauma all too commonly experienced by the wounded in the Mexican and Civil wars – immediate amputation. His description of the event in his 'Narrative of Army Service' is understandably short on details:

> The doctor pronounced my wound a serious one, and found that amputation would be necessary in order to save my life. Lieut. Francis E. Pinto . . . supported my shoulders during the operation . . . no anesthetics being then in use in our army.[40]

General Shields, present at the amputation, was reportedly brought to tears by the horror of the procedure and by Sweeny's steadfastness.[41] The now one-armed Lieutenant lay in a room shared with the wounded Colonel Burnett, a room adjoining the one where Lieutenant Colonel Baxter, in whose volunteer unit, years earlier in New York, Sweeny had been trained in the rudiments of military culture, lay dying. Sweeny was too weak to leave his cot and visit his dying mentor, after whom, as earlier mentioned, he later in life named one of his sons.

Twenty-five days' convalescence followed, and on 14 September, when American troops entered the Mexican capital, Sweeny did so prostrate: 'I entered the City of Mexico in an ambulance, and was conveyed to a hospital'. From the capital he and many other wounded were evacuated in a convoy of various wagons and ambulances back across the country to Vera Cruz through still less than pacified country; there was the danger of hit-and-run assaults the whole way. The convoy was escorted by dragoons commanded by Brigadier General William S. Harney, and, Sweeny later noted, 'even the wounded in the ambulances slept with revolvers under pillows'.[42]

His right sleeve now empty, Lieutenant Sweeny, along with the other wounded, was transported from Vera Cruz to New Orleans by ship. After a storm-tossed voyage across the Gulf, they disembarked amid joyous greetings from the New Orleans inhabitants. 'Balls, receptions and entertainments were gotten up for our amusement', Sweeny recalled, 'and had not our wounds prevented us from participating, we should have been loath to depart'. A contingent of wounded officers were then taken by rail to Washington and from there to Jersey City, New Jersey, where they arrived on 16 December 1847. Another warm reception greeted the soldiers when they arrived back in New York City. The way in which, as earlier noted, the trades were integrated into the war effort, and the way in which they took pride in the heroism of their representative volunteers, is indicated by the fact that Sweeny was designated guest of honour at the annual Printers' Ball at Castle Garden on 17 January. The affair, at which he was presented a medal by the Corporation of New York, ran well into the early hours of the next day, concluding with a speech by Sweeny honouring the printers' profession.[43] It was in the midst of this kind of post-war celebration and enthusiasm that Sweeny, his amputation nothwithstanding, was awarded a second lieutenant's commission in the regular army. General Winfield Scott petitioned Washington on Sweeny's behalf regarding the commission, citing the New York Irishman's 'gallant conduct during the war with Mexico'.[44]

This regular army commission in the newly revamped 2nd Infantry was fortuitous for a young man whose future might otherwise have looked bleak; resumption of work as a printer would have been all but impossible given his handicap. The commission also permitted him to become engaged to a girl with whom he had recently fallen in love, Ellen Swan Clark, the daughter of a prominent Brooklyn family. Sweeny was stationed at Fort Columbus, Governors Island, New York, from March to July 1848, during which time the couple were married in a ceremony in Brooklyn.[45] In July 1848 he received orders to report to his regiment now gathered at Jefferson Barracks, a post just south of St Louis on the Missouri banks of the Mississippi and the army's depot for departures west. Jefferson Barracks would figure significantly in Sweeny's later career, but for now the 2nd Infantry was bound for California and frontier duty, so he was destined for years of service in the arid stretches of the American southwest, years he would describe in his *Journal of Lt. Thomas W. Sweeny 1849–1853*.

In early July the 2nd US Infantry, under the command of General Bennet Riley, had been ordered to prepare for a journey overland from Missouri to California – until lately Mexican territory.

> The news made many a stout heart ache, for our officers had not had an opportunity since their return from 'the halls of the Montezumas' of even beholding their families and friends . . . and now their fevered and heart-sickening hope must live on itself for another five or six years more. In a few days, however, we reported ourselves ready for the field, but it was rumored that the Quartermaster's Department could not make the necessary arrangements and procure transportation for so long a march until the latter part of September . . . which was deemed too late in the season to begin a march of two thousand miles through an inhospitable country of which so little was known at the time.[46]

The only alternative to a long wait was a sea voyage from the east coast, which Washington ordered. The regiment departed Missouri for Fort Hamilton, New York, and a contingent including Sweeny's company set sail from there on 8

November 1848, on the SS *Rome*, part of a four-ship convoy. They would be five months at sea before arriving at their destination on 16 April 1849. The return to New York had the advantage that, as an officer, he could take his wife, to whom he was, and would remain, deeply devoted, with him on the trip around the horn. How pleasant her trip would be is open to conjecture, however, as her husband, off celebrating with the men in a Chilean Port, returned to the ship drunk and disorderly and was confined to their quarters by his superior officer, Major Samuel Heintzelman, a man he later came to despise.[47]

When the convoy cast anchors in Rio de Janeiro, Sweeny's journal gives some indication of how taken he was by the city's beauty – he quotes Shelley at length to suggest the charms of the tropical sunsets and, his devotion to his own pretty wife notwithstanding, waxes eloquent about the stunning Brazilian women:

> The black eyes of the women, large, full and sparkling, impart much brilliancy to their olive complexions, but the expression on their faces is more spirited than sensitive. Their eyebrows are beautifully arched; their eyelashes are long and silken, and their hair long, jetty and luxuriant; this they wear loose and flowing, or in extensive braids falling down their back.[48]

The officers were graciously entertained by officials of the American Legation in Rio; Sweeny noted 'their increasing efforts to render our sojourn in this magnificent port as delightful as possible'. The hospitality included a ball aboard the US steamship *Brandywine* and a meeting on Christmas Day with the Emperor and Empress of Brazil, a couple whose modesty and simplicity the lieutenant found striking: 'The Emperor wore a plain blue suit, with the order of St Benito on his breast. . . . The Empress was dressed as plainly as a Connecticut girl, and looked sweet, modest, and simple'.[49]

There was clearly more to Sweeny than the military officer and tactician. The 'touch of the poet' evident in his journal made him a keen, sardonic observer of people and places and his infatuation with the ladies of Rio was not soon forgotten – stationed in the Arizona wilds two years later, he would remember dancing with one of those 'nut-brown beauties' who gave him an orange blossom out of her hair: 'Withered as it is, it still retains its fragrance, even in this infernal desert . . .'.[50]

However, this taste of Rio's graces and of the amenities afforded the officer-gentleman there would be Sweeny's last for a long time. The years ahead would offer a meaner, rougher version of army life. Ahead lay a parched landscape where dwelt the Apache and Yuma – a landscape of mesquite and chaparral, rattlesnakes and scorpions.

NOTES

1. Thomas W. Sweeny, *Journal of Lt. Thomas W. Sweeny, 1849–1853*, (ed.) Arthur Woodward (Los Angeles, CA, 1956), p.57. Hereafter cited as *TWS, Journal*.

2. *New York Times*, 12 April 1892, p.2.
3. That is, a significant portion of General Sweeny's Fenian-related correspondence was appended to Joseph Denieffe's, *A Personal Narrative of the Irish Revolutionary Brotherhood*, (ed.) Stephen J. Richardson, then editor of *The Gael*, when the Denieffe book appeared in 1906. Those items are retained in the Irish University Press edition (Shannon, 1969).
4. Quoted by William M. Sweeny, General Sweeny's son, in 'Brigadier-General Thomas W. Sweeny, United States Army – A Biographical Sketch', *Journal of the American Irish Historical Society*, 2 (1899), pp.193–201. Hereafter cited as William Sweeny, 'Sketch', *JAIHS* (1899). William Sweeny wrote two biographical pieces on his father for this journal. The later version, published in *JAIHS*, 27 (1928), pp.257–72, is essentially a reprint of the 1899 article, with some additional text. It will be cited as William Sweeny, 'Brigadier-General TWS', *JAIHS* (1928). Complicating matters a bit further, William wrote a still longer biographical piece on General Sweeny, privately published *c.*1907, of which perhaps two or three copies exist. I have used the one in the holdings of the National Library of Ireland. This long pamphlet will be cited as William Sweeny, *Memoir*.
5. William Barnaby Faherty, *The St Louis Irish: An Unmatched Celtic Community* (St Louis, 2001), p.242 note.
6. Interest in American Fenianism and in the Canadian Raids has only very recently increased. Fenianism went entirely unmentioned, for example, in William Shannon's 1963 study, *The American Irish* (New York, 1963).
7. *Civil War: The Magazine of the Civil War Society*, 9, 2 (March–April 1991).
8. Narrated by Aidan Quinn. Available at www.historychannel.com
9. Woodward, 'Introduction', *TWS, Journal*, p.21. Hereafter cited as: *TWS, Journal*.
10. William Sweeny, 'Sketch', *JAIHS* (1899), p.196. Geronimo worked briefly as a guide and interpreter for Sweeny in 1850–51. See *TWS, Journal*, p.177.
11. The description is from Lieutenant Colonel Wilcox, 52nd Illinois Regiment, in 1862. General Sweeny Museum website. www.civilwar museum.com/gensweeny.html
12. Robert G. Cleland, 'An Exile on the Colorado', *Westerners Brand Book*, 6 (1956), p.17.
13. Roy Morris Jr., *Sheridan: The Life and Wars of General Philip Sheridan* (New York, 1992), p.1.
14. Captain C.W. Fish of the 52nd Illinois Regiment describing Sweeny. Quoted in William Sweeny,'Sketch', *JAIHS* (1899) p.198.
15. To the extent Sweeny was written about at the time, his perceived Irishness was often foregrounded. And even such a recent historical work as Albert Castel's 1992 book on the Atlanta campaign, *Decision in the West: The Atlanta Campaign of 1864* (Lawrence, KS, 1992), continues to draw Sweeny in terms of Irish clichés such as: 'His beard is fiery red; so is his temper'. The beard colour, at least, is incorrect.
16. *TWS, Journal*, p.11.
17. O'Mahony quoted by William Sweeny,'Sketch', *JAIHS* (1899), p.14.
18. The *Irish-American*, 1897. Thomas William Sweeny Papers, Huntington Library, San Marino, California.
19. Quoted in William Sweeny, *Memoir*, pp.3–4.
20. Thomas W. Sweeny, 'Narrative of Army Service in the Mexican War and on the Plains, 1846–53', *Journal of the Military Service Institution of the United States*, 42, 151 (January–February 1908), p.127. Hereafter TWS, 'Narrative of Army Service'.
21. *TWS, Journal*, p.122.
22. Hereward Senior, *The Last Invasion of Canada: The Fenian Raids, 1866–1870* (Toronto, 1991), p.23.

23. Woodward, 'Introduction', *TWS, Journal*, p.13.
24. See Walt Whitman's narrative of the Goliad massacre, part 34 of *Song of Myself*. Among the vocal opponents to the war with Mexico were Henry David Thoreau, James Russell Lowell, John Greenleaf Whittier and then congressman Abraham Lincoln.
25. See Bernard DeVoto, *The Year of Decision, 1846* (Boston, MA, 1943), p.4.
26. Brian McGinn, 'The San Patricios: Mexico's Fighting Irish', www.connemara.net/history/sanpatricios1.php
27. *TWS, Journal*, pp.56–7.
28. Scott's influence was greatest in the south, of course. In *Life on the Mississippi* (New York, 2001), pp.249–50, Mark Twain wrote of Scott's pernicious influence on Southern ante-bellum culture, his romantic enchantments and 'sham chivalries'. 'Sir Walter Scott had so large a hand in making Southern culture before the war, that he is in great measure responsible for the war'.
29. Robert W. Johannsen, *To the Halls of the Montezumas: The Mexican War in the American Imagination* (New York, 1985), pp.25–30.
30. Reported in the *New York Daily Globe,* 27 December 1846. Quoted in Woodward, 'Introduction', *TWS, Journal*, p.13.
31. TWS, 'Narrative of Army Service', pp.127–8.
32. Ibid.
33. Ibid.
34. Shields is best remembered in anecdotal terms for once having challenged Abraham Lincoln to a duel, though the two later became friends. In 1910 the Federal government erected a monument to him in St Mary's cemetery, Carrollton, MO, where he is buried. In 1914 the Kerry-born Irish-American sculpture, Jerome O'Connor, was commissioned to complete a statue of Shields for the Carrollton courthouse. O'Connor would later sculpt, for example, the Robert Emmett statue that now stands on St Stephen's Green in Dublin, the Éire Memorial in Merrion Square Park in Dublin, and the *Lusitania* memorial at Cobh.
35. General Winfield Scott, 'Official Report of the Battle of Cerro Gordo'. www.dmwv.org/mexwar/documents/cgordo.htm
36. *TWS, Journal*, pp.123–4.
37. 'Convento' in Spanish can refer to a monastery as well as a convent. This was apparently a monastery in fact. See Michael Hogan, *The Irish Soldiers of Mexico* (Guadalajara, 1999), p.74. I have retained, however, the English term, convent, because that is what is used in the American historical records.
38. The Irish-born soldiers involved had deserted the US Army, purportedly in disgust with their maltreatment at the hands of a largely Protestant and frequently bigoted officer corps and with the disproportionate number of Irish being thrown into battle by the United States (a resentment presaging the one that would trigger the New York Civil War draft riots of 1863). They felt more akin to the Catholic Mexicans. While imprisoned for his role in the San Patricio desertion Riley told his friend, Charles O'Malley, to 'be not deceived by the prejudice of a nation which is at war with Mexico, for a more hospitable and friendly people than the Mexicans . . . there exists not on the face of the earth', (quoted in Hogan, *Irish Soldiers,* p.244).

    Eighty-three San Patricios were captured at Churubusco; sixteen of whom were hanged on 12 September, and thirty on 13 September. Those not executed were flogged and branded on the cheek with a 'D'. The San Patricios who were hanged were spared no possible indignity. Directing the gruesome exercise, prolonging it, and wringing it for all the humiliation it was worth, was William S. Harney under whom Sweeny would later twice serve during his career. Harney later married into a prominent Irish Catholic family in St Louis and eventually converted to Catholicism. In 1850, in Louisiana he met Father Pierre-Jean DeSmet, the famous Jesuit missionary to the Plains Indians, and the two became lifelong friends. While commanding troops in Indian country on the upper Missouri in the late 1850s, he would appoint DeSmet as his unit's chaplain. See Hogans, *Irish Soldiers;* George Rollie Adams, *General William S. Harney: Prince of Dragoons* (Lincoln, NB, 2001); and Robert Ryall Miller, *Shamrock and Sword: The St Patrick's Battalion in the US–Mexican War* (Norman, OK, 1989). The 1997 Hollywood film, *One Man's Hero,* starring Tom Berenger was about John Riley and the battalion.

39. TWS, 'Narrative of Army Service', pp.130–1.
40. Ibid., p.132. Surgeons began to use anaesthesia in the 1840s, but it had not begun to be used in military field hospitals as yet.
41. William Sweeny, 'Sketch', *JAIHS* (1899), p.195.
42. TWS,'Narrative of Army Service', p.133.
43. Ibid., pp.134–5. *New York Herald*, 18 January 1848, p.1.
44. TWS, 'Narrative of Army Service', p.135.
45. William Sweeny, *Memoir*, pp.6–7; Richard J. Coyer, '"Hero of the Armless Sleeve": The Military Career of Thomas W. Sweeny', (Master's Thesis, University of San Diego, CA, 1978), p.26.
46. *TWS, Journal*, p.32.
47. Coyer, '*Hero*', p.33.
48. *TWS Journal*, p.37.
49. Ibid., p.39.
50. Ibid., p.38.

2

The Infernal Desert, 1849–53

> It was burning hot all day long, and the men and mules suffered terribly; had it not been for some water the men got from a cleft in a rock by digging eight feet with a tin cup, one half of the command would have perished with thirst.
>
> *TWS, Journal*[1]

> I may eventually become a salamander.
>
> *TWS, Journal*[2]

Of all Sweeny's varied adventures, one particularly worthy of note is the time he spent from 1849 to 1853 in the treacherous barrens south of where the Gila River enters the Colorado – in what Arthur Woodward describes as 'the hot, isolated, and unbearable hell hole of Fort Yuma'.[3] Sweeny's *Journal* and letters offer students of southwestern history a valuable first-hand account of this place and period, of a West emphatically 'wild'. This was not Jeffersonian America but rather a helter-skelter time and territory when government and rule of law were but a thin patina, and massacres were not infrequent. This was the weirdly liminal territory Stephen Crane would later visit and portray in some of his best Western stories – the border region into which Ambrose Bierce would venture in 1913, never to be seen again. It has been represented in all its 1850s nightmarishness in Cormac McCarthy's 1985 novel *Blood Meridian or the Evening Redness in the West*. Under a deadly, relentless sun, various parties of murderers, outlaws and sinister drifters crossed paths with religious visionaries and zealots, Mexican sheep drovers, hapless and vulnerable migrant families, prospectors using the southern Overland Trail, dangerous Apache, Yuma and Mojave raiders, and 'filibusterers' with their cobbled-together cavalries and manifest destiny dreams of founding their own private, slavery-based empires in Mexico. Added to which would be an historic event that would radically destabilize the military ranks tasked with policing this cruel, anomalous region.

Thomas O. Larkin, a businessman who operated as a confidential agent of the American government after settling in Spanish California in 1832, wrote a letter of historic import to Secretary of State Buchanan from San Francisco on 1 June 1848:

> Sir:
> I have to report to the State Department one of the most astonishing excitements and state of affairs now existing in the country, that perhaps has ever been brought to the attention of the government. On the American fork of

> the Sacramento and Feather River . . . and the adjoining lands, there has been within the present year discovered . . . a vast tract of land containing gold [4]

It was on New Year's Day 1849, when the regimental ships with Sweeny aboard were about to put out to sea from Rio, that first word of the gold discovery arrived.[5] The find would prove an inauspicious event for him and the other officers headed for California, and a destabilizing influence upon the US Army in the West. Gold fever would sorely tempt the California troops, causing great tension in the ranks and a generally excited atmosphere encouraging widespread disorder, insubordination and desertion. The US Army of the 1840s was already a crude, less than well-regimented – though often brutalized – assemblage by today's standards, regimentation as we know it having developed only later during the Civil War.[6] In light of the gold discovery, the army life to which soldiers had committed now seemed an intolerable hindrance; they were missing out, they felt, on an unprecedented opportunity for previously undreamed of fortunes. For troops stationed in California the precious metal lay near at hand, close by where they were fortunate enough to find themselves. The realization that, were it not for their Army obligations, they could be among the first into the promising hills, was maddening to many. When the regiment to which Sweeny was attached docked at Valparaiso, the soldiers saw their first specimens of the splendid stuff said to be plentiful in the mountains:

> Several massive ingots of this precious metal were shown to us, and gratifying as the spectacle might have been otherwise to our feelings, gave rise in our minds to uneasy apprehension of desertion on the part of our men when we should arrive in this modern El Dorado. The soldiers became much excited on the subject, and our fears became ultimately too well founded.[7]

After months at sea, Lieutenant Sweeny's unit arrived in Monterey on 6 April 1849 and then proceeded to San Diego, of which US troops took military control from the reluctant but resigned Mexican authorities around 23 April 1849. Tom and Ellen Sweeny, regaining their land legs, entered the rough-and-ready San Diego of this time with its pervasive drunkenness and gambling, the public square boarded in for bullfights, sulky ne'er-do-wells occupying the area in front of a few shabby, dusty, stores. The couple, Ellen now pregnant, ventured abroad in search of lodgings, eventually – after having to live in a tent temporarily – finding a small house where, as things would turn out, Ellen would have to spend a good deal of time alone. The culture shock must have been considerable, but the young Mrs Sweeny, for all her fairly privileged upbringing, appears to have been an exceptional 'trooper' – complaining in a letter to her parents only regarding the lack of an Episcopalian church for her to attend. Her husband would still be around when the couple's first child, Sarah, was born. Sarah Sweeny was baptized by a local Spanish priest, Father Juan, on 25 December 1849.[8]

During the mid- to late 1880s, California was changing demographically as this proto-state's population began to soar due to the gold discovery. At the same time, some of the male part of the Irish Famine influx was immigrating to California – the Irish male to female ratio in California was ten to one. Historian Timothy Sarbaugh has written that the state's Irish community was formed 'virtually overnight because of the Gold Rush'.[9] From 1850 to 1880, the Irish, ranging from wealthy businessmen to impoverished diggers in the gold-fields, formed the largest segment of the state's foreign-born population, and this did not include the sizable Irish representation in the US Army stationed there. Terence McManus, a leading figure in the 1848 uprising, who subsequently became part of the large Irish community in San Francisco, was of course one of those drawn to California for its opportunities, although ultimately he did not fare well.

One more Irishman new to California, Lieutenant Sweeny now found himself directly under the command of brevet Major Samuel P. Heintzelman, the West-Pointer with whom he had clashed aboard ship on the journey to California. While the regiment was at sea, it was Heintzelman who had confined Sweeny to quarters for inebriation.[10] Meanwhile, the contagion of gold fever, fed by reports of fabulous strikes, spread deeper still into the military ranks, occasioning the tide of desertion, dissatisfaction and resistance to discipline that Army authorities had feared would occur. On 21 May 1849, Major General Persifor Smith wrote to Washington from California reporting that the 2nd Infantry had for the most part arrived, but that, 'many men have deserted and some have been retaken. Nearly all the dragoons, it is said, have deserted from the southern posts'.[11] The Army tried stationing its troops as far as possible from the gold-fields, but to no avail. General Riley wrote to William Tecumseh Sherman in San Francisco in mid-April of 1849 that: 'The gold mania is greater at a distance from the mines than in their immediate neighborhood. The experiment of placing troops at a distance from the mines has . . . failed'.[12]

In a letter of 9 April to Sarah Barnard, his married sister in New York, Sweeny described San Diego as the crisis caused by the gold strike began to take hold on the command:

> When we reached the town we were not a little disappointed in finding it to consist of a collection of dilapidated adobe buildings, affording scanty shelter to a population of three or four hundred Spaniards and Indians. Habitations are not so indispensable here, for the climate is one of the finest in the world. We found tent life pleasant enough until better quarters were procured for us, but before this could be done, we needed less accommodation than ever; the gold fever had raged in our camp, and our command was thinned by desertion in the most alarming manner. Report, like the touch of Midas, had turned all the barren regions of Northern discipline into gold mines . . . and the imaginations of men were inflamed with the wildest rumors, till visions of discovered treasures and hidden wealth filled every mind.[13]

In this 'inflamed' situation there occurred an incident that threatened to terminate Sweeny's military career at this point. As desertions continued and increased – 'in their mad stampede to the gold fields the deserters took with them their arms, horses and equipment' – discipline among the remaining troops began to break down and the Army brass began encouraging forceful measures to bring rebellious elements in the ranks to account.[14] It was in this context that Sweeny, in charge of 'D' Company during Heintzelman's temporary absence, attempted to make an example of one recalcitrant private, Lawrence Kearney, bringing to bear punishment so harsh that the private died. Kearney had apparently been assigned to guard the stables but was reported gone all night, having taken two saddled and bridled horses with him. A guard found him drunk the next morning on the post grounds. Called before Lieutenant Sweeny, the private was still drunk and belligerent. On the morning of 23 June 1850, after waiting for him to sober up, Sweeny ordered him to report himself under arrest to the sergeant of the guard, which Kearney did not do. What is more, the private was heard out on the grounds loudly opining that it was a pity that that 'one armed son-of-a-bitch' [Sweeny] had not lost the other arm as well.[15] Sweeny's response was severe; he had Kearney 'bucked', trussed up in a backward arch, his wrists and ankles joined and tied. It was a standard punishment, but Kearney was a hard case. Still defiant, he was bucked until sundown that day, and the procedure resumed the next morning, 24 June. After the discipline, Kearney was not seen by a doctor until 25 June, by which time his limbs were gangrenous. He died on 29 June and, on the basis of the doctor's report, an investigation was launched.

The investigation was still on-going in October when Heintzelman's command received orders for Companies 'D' and 'H' to prepare for deployment on the Rio Colorado, at the sensitive Yuma Crossing. Earlier in the year John C. Morehead, a California lawyer, had raided the Yuma Indians with his 125-man 'state militia', destroyed a significant amount of the tribe's crop, and made blustering treaty demands he could not enforce. When the Yuma would not be intimidated, he had to retreat ingloriously back to San Diego. 'If what the ferry company told us be true', Sweeny wrote, 'the alleged victor [Morehead] was very glad to get back with a whole scalp to the settlements again'. The impression left with the Yuma was that US troops lacked perseverance and were, in the end, more bark than bite.[16] The need to counter this impression may explain orders being issued from Washington for the regular army to make a stern showing in the area.

Sweeny's civil court hearing meanwhile turned out well for him, Judge Oliver S. Witherby declaring that: 'After a careful investigation of all the testimony in the case it is ordered that . . . Thomas W. Sweeny be discharged, there being nothing in its testimony to warrant his detention'.[17] The decision to dismiss the charges the same day they were read in court perhaps reflected a political–judicial reaction to the turmoil in the area and a growing tolerance for authoritarian solutions. This Civil verdict no doubt took some of the drive out of the military investigation, and, luckily for Sweeny, no court martial action followed.

What was to be a long and acrimonious assignment for him thus began in late 1850 when, as Sweeny put it,

> we received orders to take up our line of march for the Rio Gila and establish a military post at the mouth of that river for the protection of our immigrants, who came pouring in by this route, and whose sufferings were, from the nature of the country and the hostility of the Indians, such as might have appalled and intimidated any but those infected by the invincible lust for gold.[18]

Companies 'D' and 'H' set out eastward according to orders on 25 October 1850, camping at Warner's Ranch in the desert along the way. They began to set up 'Camp Yuma' on the west bank of the Colorado, roughly a mile south of where the Gila flowed in, and near some derelict wooden structures owned by the Colorado Ferry Company. After his acquittal, Sweeny spent a few weeks with Ellen and Sarah while awaiting a supply train he could join in order to reunite with his unit. He arrived at the Yuma post on 22 January 1851 and was assigned quartermaster duties by Heintzelman. Six months of clearing brush and building brush sheds to serve as quarters followed, as well as, for Sweeny in his new assignment, the additional duty of arranging some sort of supply of food and animal forage through a contractor. It was not long before, in the trying desert conditions, the animosity between the lieutenant and the major worsened. Heintzelman's resentment toward Sweeny, his perception of him as arrogant and intractable, is evident in the journal the major kept during the period, in entries such as: 'Sweeny has been quite indignant because I would not let him do as he pleases . . . He pretends to discuss customs of service. He will have to be in the army some time longer before he will know much about them'. And in an entry for 18 March, Heintzelman writes: 'I gave Sweeny directions about some work I wished the carpenters to do; but either through his or their stupidity very little was done'.[19]

Sweeny had tried unsuccessfully to get a transfer out of the unit, and his letters written at the time accuse Heintzelman of laxity and intrigue. He refers to the Major's private business speculations driving things rather than 'Uncle Sam's requirements'.[20] Heintzelman's speculations concerned mines in the area and designs on the lucrative ferry operations that provided virtually the only way by which pioneering parties could cross the wide, dangerous waters of the Colorado. Of course, jealousies and disputes among Army officers are far from uncommon, especially where remote outpost duty is concerned, and often verge on the ludicrous. At one point in their association, for example, the Major had Sweeny confined to quarters on the suspicion he had appropriated some magazines from the post mails.[21] Arthur Woodward notes that which officer, if either, was in the right cannot be established, but he points to the major's interests in mining ventures as perhaps suspicious. 'After all, Sweeny, young and hot-headed as he may have been, was no fool'.[22]

It is also noteworthy as well that Heintzelman brought various charges against another officer in the command, Captain John W. Davidson, charges which were almost entirely dismissed when Davidson, a friend of Sweeny's, asked for a Court of Inquiry to investigate.[23] Woodward notes as well the fact that others besides Sweeny raised questions concerning the major's independent financial activities: 'Alonzo Johnson, veteran ferryman and steamboat owner, hinted that Heintzelman may have exceeded his military duty in his attempts to gain a lion's share of the passage fees [across the Colorado River] paid by immigrants'.[24] Historian Robert G. Cleland similarly concludes: 'evidence leads me to believe that Sweeny's judgment [regarding Heintzelman] was not greatly out of line'.[25] Entrepreneurial military officers besides Heintzelman took jealous note of the fact that ferries across the Rio Colorado were proving profitable as more and more migrant wagons began to appear. When some serving under the major considered starting their own ferry, however, he prevented their doing so. 'Heintzelman was opposed . . . because he had his own plans. He began causing problems for the ferrymen by creating a military reservation taking in their ferry landing'.[26]

This goes to the context, the historical theatre in which Sweeny's desert duties took place: the ford of the Colorado, long the cherished property of the Yuma Tribe, who oversaw it from high granite bluffs on the eastern side, a vantage point all but lost to them by the mid-nineteenth century through white incursions:

> [The Colorado River] . . . challenged any land crossing . . . and with a width of sometimes a mile or more, demanded that travelers take unrealistic chances. So everyone trying to get to California was looking for the same thing – a place they could cross . . . In the northern part of Arizona Territory, there were a few places to cross, but to get there meant passing through mountain ranges and possible freezing temperatures. Down in the flatter and more temperate south, there was a natural crossing where the ornery river briefly passed between two rocky mounds [which] calmed the river for a few miles south to the confluence of the Gila . . . The Quechan [Yuma] and Cocopah Indians knew the value of their land, but [after] the 1500s . . . this site suddenly became more competitive. Word about the crossing would soon spread around the world. Soldiers, natives, and even priests would literally kill to possess it.[27]

Of a particularly serious nature were Sweeny's charges in his letters regarding the major's indifference toward his duty to protect pioneer wagons in the wilderness – notably his indifference to the fate of a distressed scientific expedition and his failure to save the Oatman family, whose massacre on the Yuma trail created national headlines. The Yuma and Mojaves had been attacking white travellers since the first trappers had appeared in the 1820s; the Yuma could strike especially effectively at the natural river ford near which they lived. Camp Yuma, where Sweeny's unit was bivouacked, was located along this strategic part of the river near the place where, seventy years earlier, the Mission Puerto de la Purisima Concepcion had been overwhelmed by the Yuma and all its Spanish occupants killed.[28] The troops had moved there from their first camp: 'We . . . subsequently moved to a hill about a mile farther up, opposite the mouth of the Gila River'.[29]

The scientific expedition whose safety Sweeny felt had been neglected was one under the direction of the noted naturalist, Dr John Le Conte, then of the University of Georgia. In 1850–51 he and his brother, Joseph, travelled through Sonora and the Pima and Apache country while undertaking a study of the region's natural history.

> In February Sweeny wrote that the Indians had stolen [Le Conte's] horses and left him half-dead from thirst, starvation, and exhaustion some seventy miles from Yuma. A rescue party composed of members of the garrison saved the unfortunate scientists from certain death.[30]

The rescue, however, in Sweeny's opinion, succeeded no thanks to Heintzelman.

More awful than Le Conte's plight was that of Royce Oatman and his emigrant family who had ventured west from Illinois, joining a group of fifty-two followers of the apostate Mormon leader, Jim Brewster, toward a Canaan Brewster foresaw in California territory at the mouth of the Colorado. They were, as Sweeny described them,

> Mormons, who intend settling on the banks of the Colorado, as they say it is the Promised Land according to their prophets; the river Bashan in the Scriptures . . . being the Colorado according to *their* interpretation . . . they have separated from the Mormons of the Salt Lake: who, they contend, fell from Grace.[31]

The Brewster party split along the trail, most going with their leader on the northern route, but Oatman proceeded into the desert, toward the southern river crossing. The family's wagon was less than a day east of the army post at Camp Yuma – near what is presently Oatman Flats Arizona – when the wagon was set upon by Indians and the father and mother and four of seven children slaughtered. Lorenzo, a son who had been left for dead, made it to the army post, and the daughters, Olive and Mary, were carried off by the attackers. Emigrants who arrived in the army camp on 27 March 1851, Sweeny recounted, confirmed what the Oatman boy had earlier reported to the soldiers – 'melancholy intelligence in relation to the poor Oatman family . . . It appears that the . . . family were butchered in cold blood'.[32] Whether the original raiders were Apache, Yuma or Mojave, the two girls ended up in Mojave hands. Mary died in captivity, but Olive, seventeen at the time, survived for two years and was then rescued. She later toured and lectured on her experience and became the subject of one of the most famous American Indian Captivity narratives, Royal

B. Stratton's *Life Among the Indians: Narrative of the Captivity of the Oatman Girls* (1857).[33]

Major Heintzelman had received a desperate plea for help in a letter from Mr Oatman written on 15 February 1851. Carried to the Major by a Mexican guide, the letter described the family's desperation – their animals having been stolen and their lack of provisions. It began: 'To the honourable commandant of Fort Yuma Brevett Major S.P. Heintzelman Honourable Sir I am under the necessity of calling upon you for assistance. There is myself, Wife and seven children and without help Sir I am confidant we must perish'.[34] Four days after receipt of the letter the major sent out two soldiers with some provisions, a response Sweeny and others later criticized as belated and inadequate. The two soldiers returned to report having found an empty wagon and two dead bodies. Nor in Sweeny's opinion did Heintzelman at this point vigorously pursue the girls' captors in an effort to rescue them. The girls' 13-year-old brother, who miraculously survived the attack, having arrived at the army post, was put in charge of the mess hall for a time, probably with a view to taking his mind off the horror he had witnessed.

In a letter to his wife Sweeny reproached the major's lethargic response to the Oatmans' distress:

> Yes! There was a whole family murdered almost under his very nose; two girls taken into captivity by the Indians, and there was nothing done to avenge the murder or rescue the captives from worse than death; and what was the gallant major's excuse . . . why, that he had not sufficient force at his disposal to accomplish anything. At last, however, he did screw his courage up to send out a detachment to recover some Government animals that were stolen by a neighboring tribe from our grazing camp . . .[35]

Sweeny and Heintzelman were at loggerheads when the major received an order in May 1851 from the Secretary of War, calling for the abandonment of the desert post. Supplies, recruits – everything the garrison stood in need of – had had to be trekked in across the brutal, thirsty terrain from San Diego, 150 miles away, along what hardly deserved the name 'trail', and Washington was now, after six months, abandoning as unfeasible any idea of maintaining a major Gila River outpost. Sweeny describes the arrival of a wagon from San Diego, for instance, the trip having taken twenty days and the drivers having had to kill one of the oxen in order to drink its blood – not a drop of water being available for a stretch of ninety miles. In summer, he notes, the desert can be travelled only at night, the heat of the day being beyond human or animal endurance. 'I have christened it "bone desert" because the route is marked out by the line of bones and skeletons of oxen, mules, sheep, and other animals who have perished while traversing it'.[36] The government order to abandon the post allowed, however, that if all the camp equipment could not be carried out, Heintzelman had the discretion to leave a small unit behind – a greatly diminished military presence. The option was no doubt a happy one for the major to exercise since the small party could keep an eye on his ferry interests, and, at the same time, a problem officer whom he could hardly abide could be disposed of – temporarily or permanently. Which officer would stay behind was thus an obvious choice. The official orders instructed Heintzelman that, if he were to leave a party behind, he should construct a strong picketing for the protection of the detached party before quitting them, and should leave them five months' provisions. The command fell back, Sweeny noted, 'but neither constructed the picketing nor left the provisions'.[37] From June to December 1851, Lieutenant Sweeny and his small detachment were left isolated and vulnerable in the desolate, otherwise abandoned camp. They fortunately retained one big gun, a howitzer that boomed periodically in the hope of impressing and dissuading the surrounding Indians.

Convinced Heintzelman's plans were duplicitous, Sweeny was less than enthralled with his assignment:

> The Command left Camp Yuma on the 6th . . . The Major . . . ordered me to remain here with a non-commissioned officer and nine men in order to protect the lives and property of American citizens, and to keep several tribes of hostile Indians in check and prevent our Indians from making excursions into the Mexican territory: – in short to accomplish with a corporal and nine men, what himself was incapable of accomplishing with three companies of infantry and 5 commissioned officers . . . He heard no doubt of those charges I intend to prefer against him, and [saw] that by leaving me here, the Indians might rid him both of me and the charges . . . we were left here with some flour and pork, which is almost sure to kill those who have to live on it in a climate where the thermometer averages 108 degrees in the shade and 130 degrees in the sun.[38]

While no doubt puzzled at the army's reduction of forces at the Yuma outpost, the Indians were better pleased with the situation than was Lieutenant Sweeny as they were the beneficiaries of the departed garrison's cast-off equipment. They put the appropriated materials, Sweeny notes, 'to the most ludicrous uses'. He describes braves walking around adorned in their tribal loincloths but sporting US Army officers' caps and plumes. And the Indian females, the 'daughters of the desert' availed themselves of discarded army gear as well: 'It was irresistibly laughable occasionally observing one endeavoring to maintain her naturally graceful and dignified carriage, under the disadvantage of having her feet in an old pair of soldier's shoes'.[39]

Heintzelman and his command – less Sweeny and his unfortunate ten men – having now departed for duty at Santa Isabel, fifty miles from San Diego, there began a bleak period in Sweeny's life. The young, one-armed, Irish lieutenant had effectively been abandoned with his men in a scraggly, sweltering grove on the Mexican border of the 1850s, beset by Indians and desperados of every description, and:

> surrounded by at least two hundred and fifty miles of sandy desert in every direction, upon which no living thing (except an occasional lizard) is to be seen . . . and where wood, water, and grass, the three great essentials of military operations in the field, are as scarce as snow-storms in the tropics [40]

Added to these miseries, Sweeny also had to endure the loneliness of separation from his wife and daughter and the bitterness of his resentment against the commanding officer whose treachery, he believed, had put him in this place. He had been unhappy enough with the 'barren hardships' of desert duty as it was, but now, with his few enlisted men, a few tents set in a circle of desert brush he named 'Camp Independence', and only the most tenuous of connections to the outside world, things were grim indeed. This state of affairs, which involved no projected date of conclusion to which he or his men could look forward, prevailed for six scorching months:

> To be stationed here with ten men on this desolate spot, surrounded by hostile tribes, who neither want the will nor the power to annihilate us at any time . . . this is what I did not conceive of even in a dream. Nothing but fear restrains them, and nothing but ceaseless vigilance on our part can keep them in check and prevent them from trampling me and my small command into non-entity. At some unguarded moment, for nature cannot watch forever, I shall be surprised I suppose, cut off, massacred . . . To such end most probably will my aspirations after glory come.[41]

Should a full-fledged Indian attack occur, the command now resident in San Diego would be too far away to be of any assistance even if Heintzelman were inclined to be of help. Nor was it only the Yuma the little desert garrison had to fear. Threatening bands of whites would sometimes emerge from the scorching wastes with the same designs the Indians had on the small company's provisions. In order to survive, Sweeny was required to cultivate theatrical skills, abilities at bluff and bluster. He records a tense encounter, for instance, with forty malicious gold-field drifters, 'well-mounted and armed to the teeth', who rode up one afternoon. Surveying the meager army encampment, they demanded provisions. Sweeny explained he had nothing to offer them, barely enough supplies for his own men, in fact. The group's spokesman replied they would see for themselves and that they intended to take what they needed.

> I told the scoundrel that he forgot he was speaking to an American officer upon whom threats were wasted; that I was not stationed at my post to learn logic off him or to yield an inch to anyone; that he might sell the lives of his followers for provisions if he chose, but I should promise him they should find more powder than salt, and more bullets than bread in store for them.[42]

He had to live daily with this kind of danger, surviving by his wits and boldness. Marauders of this sort were more likely to come down the trail than were the wholesome *Little House on the Prairie* variety of emigrant families.

Indeed, since this was not the prairie at all, but the arid, antebellum southwest, which tended to draw more than its share of the reckless and crazy. Even the more domestic emigrant wagons often carried a lower order of the emigrant population, the people Francis Parkman observed leaving St Louis for the West in 1846:

> Among them were some of the vilest outcasts in the country. I have often perplexed myself to divine the various motives that give impulse to this strange migration: but whatever they may be, whether an insane hope for a better condition in life, or a desire of shaking off the restraints of law and society, or mere restlessness, certain it is, that multitudes bitterly repent the journey.[43]

Such travellers often thought the US Army Gila post would be a place of resupply and reliable protection from the native Indians, and were distressed to discover that it could offer little of either – especially after Washington had closed the camp save for the present tiny garrison. In fact, since the military's supply line of ox-drawn wagons from San Diego required a journey of 150 miles across the ungodly desert, the arrival of such wagons was a rare event. Sweeny had to expend his camp's already stretched food stores in order to feed emigrants who had set out insufficiently prepared along what the Mexicans called *Camino del Diablo*, the Road of the Devil, and who reached his camp desperate and starved. Sweeny's diary entry of 11 June 1851 suggests the burden these travellers could prove to be: 'The sick immigrant much better. Annoyed to death by the family, who seem to think I was left here to attend to their wants'.[44] The military, as Arthur Woodward observes, were thus often less than fondly disposed towards the wagon people who sought their protection.

> When one reads the various accounts of the emigrants who pressed doggedly across the deserts via the southern route and landed at the first settlements, such as Fort Yuma . . . one wonders at the stupidity and improvidence of those people. Scarcely an army officer who saw these emigrants come and go had anything favorable to report about them. Apparently there were worthy ones in the horde . . . but there were others such as those encountered by Lt. Sweeny . . . who were insufferable and became down right belligerent when the red carpet was not unrolled for them. In some of his letters home Lt. Sweeny was . . . vehement in his denunciations of the 'noble pioneers'.[45]

One of the most dramatic stories embedded in Sweeny's journal account of this period involves the very worst sort of riders who traversed the desert trail. He records the well-deserved slaughter of the infamous Glanton Gang by the Yuma in 1850 – an example of the militant disposition and formidable warpath capabilities of the indigenous Indians in proximity to whom Sweeny and company had to survive. John Joel Glanton, leader of a motley company of murderers and degenerates, contracted with the governor of Chihuahua in 1849 to attack raiding Indian tribes in that area of Mexico. His was the worst of the drifting gangs that roamed along the border during the late 1840s and early 1850s; indeed the Glanton Gang figures significantly in Cormac McCarthy's earlier-mentioned novel *Blood Meridian*, a book that chronicles the group's murderous orgies. Glanton made a good living turning in 'Apache' scalps for bounty until it was learned that, as Sweeny puts it, 'many scalps were presented that never grew on Apache heads'.[46] The scalps were, in fact, frequently those of Mexican peons, discovering which fact, the Chihuahua governor now sought Glanton's arrest, and the gang retreated northward. 'They struck the Colorado River near its junction with the Gila (about seven miles above this post)', Sweeny writes, 'where, perceiving the tide of immigration to California to be very considerable . . . they established a ferry'.[47] In doing so they knew what they were about – the invaluable piece of real estate that was the Crossing, and the money to be made there. The gang commenced to terrorize, rob and kill Mexican and American passengers at the ford. McCarthy's fictional representation of the situation accords with historical accounts, including Sweeny's.

> Glanton took charge of the operation of the ferry. People who had been waiting three days to cross at a dollar a head were now told that the fare was four dollars. And even this tariff was in effect for no more than a few days. Soon they were operating a sort of procrustean ferry where the fares were tailored to accommodate the purses of the travellers. Ultimately all pretence was dropped and the immigrants were robbed outright. Travelers were beaten and their arms and goods appropriated and they were sent destitute and beggared into the desert . . . Horses were taken and women violated and bodies began to drift past the Yuma camp down river.[48]

As noted earlier, there had been a famous massacre at the Yuma Crossing in 1781 when the Indians revolted against the Spanish. Another massacre, which would cost Glanton and his thugs their lives, was now in the offing.

Santiago, a Yuma chief with whom Sweeny was friendly, gave him an account of 'some striking incidents connected with the fate of Glanton and his party'. Santiago revealed the details after Sweeny had assured him that he himself considered the Yuma attack on the rogue party justified. Sweeny noted that the Indian's account jibed with the one he had received from one of the three white survivors of the attack who eventually made it back to San Diego. Having appropriated the ferry, Santiago told Sweeny, Glanton and his cohorts, besides preying upon travellers, 'made themselves very obnoxious to the Indians'. After having amassed a great profit from his river business, Glanton left for San Diego with half his group, leaving the remaining men instructions to be on constant guard against the Indians. However, on his return he discovered that there had not been the slightest signs of Yuma aggression; on the contrary, the tribe had been entirely friendly to the remaining personnel, even to the extent of asking the ferrymen to hold onto some valuable tribal articles for safe keeping:

> Glanton, shrewd and penetrating as he had always been esteemed, was thrown completely off his guard – the subtle scheme had succeeded admirably – the whiskey brought out from San Diego was produced, and the whole party, including their leader, proceeded to celebrate the success which had crowned their enterprise with a revel befitting the occasion.
>
> In the midst of their excesses, when they were stuffed with drink, a signal was given by a Mexican woman (who had been forcibly taken from a party of immigrants and detained by these outlaws against her will) to a body of Indians concealed in the chaparral. The signal was obeyed, and before the victims could rouse themselves from their stupor, they were each surrounded . . . The battle, or rather butchery, commenced . . . and while the massacre was proceeding the uproar was fearful. The yells and shouts were borne to the Colorado, where at a short distance from the ferry, the only three of Glanton's party not engaged in the orgy, happened to be occupied in cutting poles.[49]

These three leaped into a boat and got away, reaching San Diego overland only to meet, Sweeny notes, their own violent deaths there before long.

> The mercury continues to rise steadily – 108 in the shade today. The nights bring no relief now – the heat is too excessive to admit of sleep, and one rises in the morning feverish and unrefreshed. My appetite begins to fail and I am tormented with an unquenchable thirst. I really begin to despair of getting out of this horrible place.[50]

But while his diary contains such bleak material aplenty, Sweeny's account is at the same time, despite his plight, laced with an ironic good spirit, a keen sense of observation and a dauntless Irish wit. He describes at length a fight between his dog and a coyote, and another fight between two Mexican drovers on their way to the San Francisco markets when their multitudes of sheep become one confused bedlam crossing the river and ownership of some sheep becomes debatable. The rich detail of his writing is evident in another passage, this one regarding his horse:

> He is one of the best Indian ponies – gentle, indefatigable, and sustains himself on almost nothing. If he were not able to do so, he would have starved to death long ago, for besides a little careless weed (which, by the way, for want of better, we use as . . . table greens) the sprouts of young willows that come after the annual rise of the Colorado, and the mesquite beans which are soon harvested by the Indians, constituting as they do their 'main staff of life' for several months of the year – besides this fodder, and a meager supply of it, he can get nothing.[51]

Of his pet goat he writes: 'I paid ten dollars for it – all the money I had in the world. I never made a purchase with which I am better pleased. I would not part with "Nanny" for ten times the amount'.[52] His darker journal entries are thus balanced by ones in which his curiosity about the region, his interest in its flora and fauna, as well as in the culture of its indigenous people, are evident. He observes of the Yuma, for example, that 'it is impossible to convince them with respect to anything but what they see, hear, feel, taste or smell. They are at once as inquisitive as Yankees and as stubbornly incredulous as Hollanders'.[53]

An Indian boy possessed of uncanny trapping skills catches quail with snares made of horse hair that entangles the birds' feet. A Yuma girl gives Sweeny a few of these quail, which one would imagine, roasted, would have provided him a delicious respite from the unvaried and unappetizing camp cuisine. As the girl had done, however, Sweeny, a lifelong bird fancier anyway, becomes attached to the creatures:

> I domesticated them very easily, and fed them from my own hand, on bread chewed fine, and on the young, tender, leaves of the mesquite tree of which they are very fond. I let two of them go the other day, by way of experiment, just to see what use they would make of their liberty. During the first three or four days they returned regularly for their meals *alone*, but since then they have brought their friends . . . now it takes a whole biscuit for their daily rations . . . It affords me so much pleasure to watch their pranks and little quarrels, as they are called by the birds in the cage to their regular meals . . . and they seem so tame and confiding, even recognizing my voice and responding to my call when I am out of sight, that I cannot find the heart to kill them.[54]

Woodward remarks that Sweeny was 'an intelligent observer [who] recorded his thoughts and observations with more than the usual accuracy of diary keepers', and who revealed 'his appreciation of the beauties of the desolation surrounding him'.[55] The river is a great, insistent presence in the Sweeny diary – the Colorado that comes from the snows in the Rockies, bearing the greatest water supply to be found west of the continental divide:

> Spent a restless and uncomfortable night. Went out under the dark and spangled sky, and never beheld a sight more glorious . . . moon like the home of purity and peace. But there is the never ceasing hum of millions of insects, and the Colorado murmurs like an uneasy Titan, and shines, and whirls its red flood along.[56]

He sets down many other careful details and images of outpost life among the Indians. On 3 July 1851, for example:

> The Yumas are much disappointed because the river has not risen sufficiently this year to overflow its banks at this locality, so as to enable them to raise their usual crop, pumpkins and melons. But they say that a little below the mouth of the New River the banks are flooded, and thither they are all going as soon as the mesquite beans in the neighborhood are consumed.[57]

His invaluable profiles of the contemporary Yuma chiefs whom he was uniquely positioned to observe, are equally detailed and informative:

> My neighbors, the Yumas, have two chiefs, elected by the tribe for life, and acknowledged and obeyed implicitly . . . One is the war-chief, Caballo . . . whose duty it is to lead the warriors, and who has to maintain the reputation of the most puissant brave of his tribe . . . The other is Santiago, the peace-chief, whose province is to preside over the national councils, and in great emergencies, to call the nation together for the transaction of public business of importance. The captains, or sub-chiefs, are held responsible for any breach of discipline or violation of law . . .
>
> The two head chiefs . . . are as unlike each other personally as two men can well be. Caballo . . . is small, slight, active as a wildcat and capable of enduring the greatest fatigue with apparent ease . . . Santiago, is a perfect Hercules in stature . . . his eyes, which are small, dark, bright and penetrating . . . are as restless as thought; glancing from object to object . . . Over his features he has the most perfect control, and can assume the most friendly expression of countenance, blandness and suavity of manner, even while he grasps the hilt of his long hunting knife . . . which he is ever ready to plunge into your heart.[58]

The Yuma constantly poke about, testing Sweeny's installation. It appears that their failure to attack owed in part to Sweeny's blarney charm and in part to their puzzlement as to what this scanty bivouac with its one-armed chief could possibly be doing in their midst. On 7 June a 'deputation consisting of the principle chiefs of the Cocopas and Yuma, with about forty of their best braves' appear wishing to know why he has been left behind by the army and what his intentions are. When Sweeny recounts explaining the purpose of his mission to them, his sense of the humour in his situation is evident. He explains,

> It was the will of their great father at Washington that I should remain here to protect his children – the red man as well as the pale face . . . I would prevent the paleface from injuring them and afford them all the protection and assistance in my power; but the moment they disobeyed his commands, I would punish them with the utmost severity . . . and drive them beyond the Colorado towards the rising sun! Big talk, this, from an officer in command of a detachment consisting of a non-commissioned officer and nine men.[59]

'Removed 250 miles from the nearest settlement, in either direction', he writes in another entry, 'I expect some travelers will find my bones, and those of my company, bleaching in the wilderness.'[60] And the parched wastes would stir memories of what he termed 'certain comforts and elegancies'. He craves pleasant quarters and good food, laments the absence of women's company, and acknowledges: 'I suppose I may as well confess the truth – a kind of curiosity to ascertain whether sherry-cobblers, brandy smashes, gin cocktails . . . are really so palatable as we were wont to think them'.[61]

Immigrants arriving in San Diego reported the grievous state of affairs at Sweeny's camp as they had seen it on the trail west, but Heintzelman remained unmoved; arguing in his journal that the lack of water 'precluded sending a relief party'. Sweeny suspects the major of going so far as to try to deplete his ammunition – 'What a pleasant predicament I should be in if Caballo . . . should get it into his aboriginal head to pay me a warlike visit'.[62] The Indians have a few firearms but are basically dependant on clubs and bow and arrow, so they do a lot of feeling out with an apparent view to overcoming the camp eventually. The hellish heat in June and July is devastating ('I may eventually become a salamander', he observes). The arrival of mail is an infrequent occurrence. In one of the rare really personal entries in his diary, at least in its published form, on 12 July he writes: 'I would give more than I can say for a few lines from E. [Ellen]'.[63] His company, their diet consisting of hard tack and salt pork, meanwhile suffer from the effects of nutritional deficiency:

> The men . . . complain of violent pains in the head just above the eyes, and of soreness of the bones – the sure precursors of that dreadful scourge to crews and garrisons, the scurvy . . . I require the men to collect a quantity of mesquite beans daily, to pound them up, steep them in water long enough to extract the acid they contain, and drink the liquor as an antiscorbutic for want of a better.[64]

And the insects continue to provide one more contribution to the misery of sleepless nights:

> Oppressively warm. Myriads of insects swarm on every hand. They were somewhat amusing at first, but have now become excessively annoying. Enormous bats . . . fly into my tent and cling to the canvas, upon which I have caught some very remarkable specimens. Scorpions also are so numerous that I dare not put on my shoes in the morning without ascertaining whether they contain any of these fearful insects.[65]

He remarks a few days later that the Indians have begun to steal, something they have not done previously, and 'a sure omen of their hostility'. Fortunately, however, by 24 July the Yuma force around Camp Independence had thinned considerably due to the need for them to tend to planting crops elsewhere; the failure of the Colorado to flood sufficiently may thus have bought Sweeny and company some time. The regiment's own efforts at agriculture had been unsuccessful even when the river overflowed nicely and there had been some rain: 'We tried very hard to raise vegetables, but it proved a complete failure'. Only through the Indian practice of hovering over the crops and constantly protecting them from the insects and animals that swarm around the young plants, can anything be grown, he notes, 'except for careless weed – the principle food of our mules and beeves'.[66]

A letter of 29 September 1851, however, from Mrs E.P. Russ, a friend of the Sweenys at the Benicia army post north of San Francisco where Ellen was now living, brought happy news when it finally reached him at Camp Yuma:

> I have the pleasure of congratulating you on being the father of *another fine daughter*, the image of her Papa. Your sweet Ellen was taken with labor at five minutes of four o'clock this morning, and at half past, was safely delivered of a little Sweeny, with no one in the room but her servant woman and myself – and almost frightened to death at that (myself I mean). However, we did the best we could until help arrived in the shape of the doctor and a neighbor for whom Mrs. Park had run (*in her night clothes*). Mr. Gale and your friend, my husband, had left the house to embark aboard the *Oregon* for San Francisco only a short time before, so there was not a 'he-male' in the house to go for the doctor . . . Mrs. Sweeny says she feels perfectly well and would be quite content could she have the pleasure of showing to her dear Tom, this second 'specimen' of 'pure gold'.[67]

By late November 1851 the Indians were back in full force, resuming their oblique assertions against Sweeny's camp, and now making distressing advances – proposing generous trades that Sweeny found suspicious – good horses for poor blankets, for example. (The chief Santiago, it will be recalled, recounted the Yuma using this device preparatory to attacking the Glanton party.) Luckily for the camp, on 26 October 1851, Heintzelman had finally ordered a party led by Lieutenant Murray of his command to the Colorado to relieve Sweeny. Murray, aware of the miserable position Sweeny had been holding down for six months, was loath to inherit the camp and protested vigorously to the major before being forced to set out. Having arrived at Sweeny's camp, Murray found it as exposed and vulnerable as he had expected and was distressed by the evident warlike mood among the Indians. He wrote to Heintzelman that four men of a six-man party of Americans had been killed nearby by the Indians the previous day, and that he did not intend to stay there with a small party as Sweeny had done – indeed he refused to send Sweeny and company back to Heintzelman.[68]

At least, however, the Murray party increased the size of the outpost by ten. Then, on 30 November, a US government survey expedition of fifty men, much the worse for wear, appeared out of the desert to the east, out of food and supplies. Sweeny learned from Captain Lorenzo Sitgreaves that he and his twenty men, including a mix of engineers and scientists escorted by thirty soldiers under the command of Major Henry Kendrick, had been assigned to explore the Zuni River to its junction with the Colorado, and that they had run into trouble, having to kill their mules for food and fight off Indian attacks.[69] These men taken in, Camp Independence suddenly had a population of around seventy – a more impressive cohort to face the Yuma, but one for whom the camp's food stores were completely insufficient.

Having received Murray's appalled report regarding the state of affairs at Camp Yuma, Heintzelman, perhaps fearing a scandal, now sent a further relief party of sixteen men under the command of Captain Davidson. When this party arrived at Sweeny's installation on 3 December 1851 it was Davidson's decision that the place, now inhabited by nearly 100 men, should be abandoned and that everyone should return to San Diego. On 6 December the trek commenced, the men hauling the camp's one big gun in fear of Indian attack – '[we] took up our line of march for San Diego', Sweeny writes, 'carrying the . . . howitzer with us, with bullet in mouth and match lighted until we got beyond Cooke's Wells'.[70] Though he had by no means seen the end of desert duty, nor the last of Camp Yuma, relatively speaking, Sweeny was back in the world, part of the larger, normal military picture. The worst of his desert duty, his five torrid months of exile, were over.

As the troop journeyed west from the Colorado narrows on 6 December 1851 bound for an interlude of comparative civilization in San Diego, Sweeny noted that 'the mountains were covered with [Indian] signal fires from Carissa Creek to Santa Isabel'.[71] While he was away, white–Indian relations around San Diego and in the general California region had deteriorated badly, and he would once again be a participant in a significant historical event of the period, in this case a major uprising among the California Indians. When Sweeny and company arrived at Santa Isabel, where Heintzelman was then quartered, the major ordered Sweeny to take the thirty men who had been under Major Kendrick's command and proceed to San Diego. There he and his party were greeted with enthusiasm by a population worried about the growing Indian threat.

The immediate cause of the Indian revolt was the attempt by the San Diego sheriff, whose job included tax collection, to tax Indian livestock in the area. The chief of the Cupenos tribe, Antonio Garra, viewed this as the culmination of a long chain of abuses and recognized that if white incursion into Indian lands was to be halted, an alliance of all Indian tribes in California would be necessary. If that could be accomplished, the Indians would outnumber the whites by a considerable margin – there were then less than 300 whites in San Diego County.[72] Four of them had been killed by Indians at a remote ranch, and when Heintzelman's soldiery, for example, were in the field in pursuit of Indians, the number of armed men left in San Diego, now under martial law, dwindled to a precious few. Hence the town's relief at Sweeny's arrival with additional soldiery. It had been Antonio Garra's intention, unaccomplished in the end, to intercept Sweeny's troop before it got to San Diego and then strike the town.[73]

Besides guarding against Indian attack, Sweeny was almost immediately confronted by another problem when vigilante bullies arrived in town and contributed to the troubles. San Diego citizens had sent out appeals for help when the Indian threat arose, and a gang calling themselves The Hounds of San Francisco, after a gang that had once terrorized that city, came down on a steamer. By the time they arrived, San Diego had been pretty much secured, and the superfluous Hounds now became a drunk and disorderly nuisance. Things came to a head when Philip Crosthwaite, a local Irish-born civic leader and businessman, had two Hounds incarcerated for horse theft and other mischief. The Hounds 'captain' tried to persuade Crosthwaite to release the prisoners in his recognizance, and when Crosthwaite would not do so, threatened to take over the San Diego settlement. One day in early January 1852, Crosthwaite rode out to nearby La Playa where Sweeny's company was encamped and asked Sweeny for help with the worsening situation.

> When they arrived in town, Sweeny and his men found Crosthwaite in the Plaza with Judge Robinson making arrangements for the court martial of the two prisoners. Sweeny placed his men in a building at the edge of the square and walked into the Plaza alone. At this moment . . . Watkins of the Hounds approached Crosthwaite . . . Watkins called him a liar and struck at Crosthwaite, but he dodged the blow. Watkins then drew a pistol, leveled it at Crosthwaite, and squeezed the trigger. The cap failed to explode. Crosthwaite grabbed a pistol from under his coat and shot Watkins in the thigh. At this, the rest of the Hounds opened fire on Crosthwaite from various points in the Plaza. One of the shots struck him in the pelvis . . . When this happened, Dr. Ogden ran into the Plaza, picked up Crosthwaite, and carried him into a store. As the hounds made a rush for the building, Sweeny signaled his men. They charged into the Plaza, and the Hounds slunk away.[74]

The Indian emergency meanwhile subsided. Antonio Garra's dream of a united Indian insurrection in southern California was never realized. He was captured, tried, and sentenced to death by firing squad. Sweeny had been asked to sit on the jury but declined because the Garra trial was a local territorial matter, not a federal one. Garra was in his custody, however, before the trial, and Sweeny had the opportunity to discuss with him how things had looked from the Indian standpoint in the months when he and his ten men had been at Fort Yuma, what the designs of the surrounding Indians had been toward the camp.

> I visited him in his prison one night, alone, when he acknowledged that he knew me well – that he had first seen me at Aguas Calientes, and afterward at the Rio Colorado; that he was mainly instrumental in getting the Yuma, Cocopas, and Cuchanos to join in the hostility against the Americans; that he was present when the sheep party was killed within three or four miles of my camp, in November last, and that he was one of those who urged the necessity of sending up that party of four hundred, who surrounded my camp the same afternoon for the purpose of cutting me off . . .
>
> They were then to join the mountain tribes and make a general descent upon the settlements. He said the two skirmishes my command had with the Yuma were occasioned by his advising them to exterminate all white men, and that the only thing that saved me was my constant vigilance and my 12 pounder howitzer.

He writes of Garra's execution: 'I lent General Bean my musketoons and ammunition to carry the sentence into effect. [Garra] died like a man'.[75]

The remainder of Sweeny's three years of California duty would be taken up with what was now a sporadic but determined campaign to pacify the native

Indian population and with peace treaty negotiations. He would still have to return to Fort Yuma and its gruelling demands, but now at least it would be as part of more conventional military operations. Given the time he would have to continue to spend on desert duty, Sweeny was by now determined that Ellen should return to the east, something he had urged on her in a letter before the birth of their second daughter.[76] It was clear how little opportunity to see his family he would have, and the hardships and even dangers Ellen would be faced with in taking care of two small children in a California army installation made her staying on imprudent. She booked passage back around the horn to New York and was settled with relatives in Waterford, Saratoga County, by March of 1852 – moving between there and Brooklyn where she would stay with Sweeny's sister, Sarah Barnard, and Sarah's husband, who had their own small son. Sweeny wrote Ellen from San Diego on 1 February uncertain as to whether she had yet arrived in New York. 'I am very anxious to hear that you and our little darlings have arrived safe at home . . . Capt. Watkins of the steamship Panama . . . informed me that you must have arrived in New York about the latter part of December certainly'.[77]

Around this time, the wife and family of Sweeny's friend and fellow officer, Captain Davidson, also left California for the east coast. Sweeny wrote his sister urging that her husband, Daniel Barnard, not fail to meet the Davidsons at the boat. Daniel Barnard found in this concern of Sweeny's – the imperative of being at the dock to meet arrivals off the boat – a comical Hibernian note, as Sarah informed her brother:

> Even if we had received your letter in time, it would have been quite impossible for DRB [her husband] to have given your friends the attention that you wished, for the steamers do no arrive regularly; sometimes they are 24 hours in advance, and often that length of time over . . . and the favorite period of their arrival seems to be *midnight*. Nothing would have given us greater pleasure than to have seen Mrs. Davidson in Brooklyn had the thing been practicable – DRB has tickled himself almost to death with the fancy that you were guilty of the *Irishism* of saying that you hoped he would be on the dock to receive the bearer of the letter, &c.!! But I take your part and tell him it was no such thing . . .
>
> Don't you wish you could be translated for a few minutes and look in upon your dear wife and little ones? Ell is looking very well and much handsomer than before her marriage – she is a very fine looking woman . . . You don't know what a dear little pet Sarah is. She is an uncommonly intelligent child for her age, and possesses uncommon energy for a girl . . . She is very affectionate; we often accuse her of having kissed the Blarney stone. She says '*Mamma* kissed the Blarney stone, but Papa didn't', [Fanny] is very dear to me; she has been on my bosom – I have so much more 'titty' than Ell that Fanny will nurse me when she refuses her mother – she is a sweet, pensive-looking babe . . . Plenty of babies! I am just in my element entirely![78]

Ellen soon wrote him from New York likewise delighted at their daughter Sarah's intelligence and with how fond of the child, Sarah Ann Barnard, had become. Sweeny's letter in reply set forth his distinct educational views:

> I am glad little Sarah is so intelligent for her years . . . although, as a general thing, I dislike 'Prodigies' and never knew one to come to any good yet . . . Nor should children, in my opinion, be compelled to devote much of their time to study at that early age, particularly when they look on it as a task: let them study as long as they are *amused*, or take an interest in their lessons, but the moment they get tired or indifferent, take the book away immediately, and send them to play or amuse themselves so that they may recover their natural cheerfulness again. It is, I think, much more important that a solid foundation for a good constitution be laid, than a reputation of being an 'infant prodigy' at the expense of health and everything else.[79]

Though less intense than the period of his Rio Colorado isolation, the months of desert duty during 1852–53 were not without their own tensions, crises and dramas. Indian attacks occurred on occasion, relative to which, in May 1852, Sweeny managed an impressive feat for which even Heintzelman had to give him credit. Conducting raids against the Cocopa tribe in lower California, he was met with a white flag – 150 warriors and their leaders surrendered to Sweeny's twenty-five-man unit. He insisted they be willing to undertake a two-day march to Camp Yuma where Heintzelman could officially accept the surrender. The camp was amazed when Sweeny marched in rather pleased with his coup. 'My arrival created a great excitement as nobody could account for my bringing in 150 savage warriors armed with their bows and arrows, clubs and spears'.[80]

From the camp in July 1852 Sweeny wrote Ellen regarding that day being his daughter Sarah's birthday. He had been trying to devise a way to celebrate, he wrote, but

> I have been puzzling my brains all morning to devise some means to celebrate it in some way, but without arriving at any satisfactory conclusion. I've just sent an order to the Commissary Sergeant for a bottle of rye whiskey, who has sent back word that there is not a gill left. I'll have to drink her health in Colorado water. I'm afraid![81]

Meanwhile, though warfare with the Indians had reduced in intensity, there was no let up in army desertions. A grievous case of the latter, involving murder, had occurred in June 1852 when Sweeny was back in command of a unit at the Rio Colorado fort. Two soldiers, William Hayes and John Condon, deserted Sweeny's detachment in the desert. Searching for them, he encountered Lieutenant Colonel Louis G. Craig escorting a US Boundary Commission party, and asked him to keep an eye out for the fugitives and to arrest them and bring them back to Fort Yuma if he ran across them. Craig, in the company of two sergeants, did later encounter the pair, to his mortal misfortune. Sweeny described what happened in a letter:

> The next morning when he saw [Hayes and Condon] he dismounted and spoke to them, saying that he would use his influence with Major Heintzelman in their favor, and if they did not like Camp Yuma, he would take them with him to El Paso. They told the Colonel they would not go back, and cautioned him not to follow them any farther. The Colonel and his men were some five miles from the train at this time . . . The Colonel's mule broke loose just then [and] he beckoned the other sergeant to go and catch him. Hayes then said to Condon: 'Now is our time, there are but two of them', and immediately fired his musket at Craig, who instantly fell . . . Condon fired at the same time at Sergt. Beales, wounding him in the leg and killing his mule . . . Sergeant Beales was found ten miles this side. It seems he dragged himself thus far . . . The last he saw of Hayes and Condon they were making their way . . . towards Lower California. This explains their having eluded the strict search I made for them.[82]

The murderers were finally captured in the mountains by Indians and turned over to the army by a tribal chief. The pair were executed at Mission San Diego on 31 January 1853.[83]

Sweeny notes in a letter to Ellen the increasing volume of traffic passing through Fort Yuma by the latter part of 1852, the third year of the gold rush:

> There were, I should think, five or six hundred immigrants passed through here this year on their way to the mines – with a pretty fair sprinkling of women and children among them; there are a good many still behind who will probably reach here in a week or two. There will probably have passed here this year altogether, one-thousand immigrants, two hundred wagons, 40,000 sheep for the California market, and a large number of horses, mules, and oxen. We had a birth, marriage, and death occur at this place among the immigrants, besides various and sundry other accidents . . . We received forty-six head of beef cattle the day before yesterday, which completes the number contracted for this year by our commissary. The cattle came off Pio Pico's Ranch, and are in very good condition . . . driven here by 'Cockney Bill' and some of his Indians. You recollect Bill Williams . . . whom Matsell was in partnership with and had a ranch some five or six miles from San Isabel.[84]

The recruits arriving in California at this time, perhaps because the recruitment pool had been diminished by the gold rush, tended to be even more raw and intractable than had been the case when Sweeny first arrived. He was sent to meet a new recruit detachment of 250 in San Diego, outfit them for the field, and march them to the Gila River as reinforcements. His description of their behaviour up to his taking charge of them again serves to portray the nature of military culture as it differed from that of the present day. 'I was told the most awful stories of the conduct of the recruits', he writes, 'from the time they left New York to the present'. When their ship docked in Jamaica they had rioted and attacked the police who attempted to restore order. On the Isthmus of Panama, the authorities had had to keep the National Guard under arms while the recruits were in that port. In San Diego, Sweeny was told, they had behaved no better – 'got drunk, kicked up a row and did just as they pleased'. He makes a point, however, of how their behaviour immediately changed when he had them brought before him for review – 'they were as silent and respectful as so many old soldiers'.[85]

There may be a subtext here beyond Sweeny's boasting a bit about his command prowess. The two deserters just discussed, William Hayes and John Condon, were both Irish-born.[86] Private Kearney, over whose death Sweeny was almost court-martialled, may well have been Irish-born too. In his *Journal*, which he seems to have written with publication in mind, Sweeny never mentions his own ethnicity or anyone else's though many Irishmen move through the narrative. He never played the professional Irishman in writing, though he is himself almost never referred to in print *without* his Irishness being remarked. This has nothing to do with his Fenianism, an arcane matter until recently, nor is it true of many other Irish officers – General Shields, the Confederate General Patrick Cleburne, or General Thomas Smyth, for instance, the last of whom was born in Ballyhooly, Ireland, and was the last Union General killed in the Civil War. It may be that Sweeny was personally more given to playing up his Irishness, or was more evidently Irish, than was his written persona in his *Journal*. And in describing these recruits falling in line for him he may be implying their Irishness and the inability of Yankee officers to understand or deal with them – an issue that would bear on the earlier San Patricio insurrection. This was, after all, in the decade of anti-Irish sentiments and movements, the years when the Famine influx to America was a new, and to nativists provocative, reality. The Irishmen who ended up in the ranks Sweeny commanded, in the pre-Civil War military of the frontier West, would have been drawn from the most desperate and roughest element of the male Famine exile population.[87]

Sweeny marched the new men, at any rate, on the long journey to the Gila without incident. This increasing military presence in Yuma territory, and concerted US Army actions against the Yuma, led to attempted peace talks through August and September of 1852, though dealing with Indian cultural behaviour as regards arranging the negotiations, as in most other matters, proved mystifying to the soldiery at times. It is clear in Sweeny's narrative that the local Indian culture was marked by a genuine gregariousness that made watching out for their also genuine ferocity difficult. They tended to visit army camps with a view to trading, for example, even in times of heightened hostility. Sweeny presents a striking picture over all, in fact, of Indian behaviour vis-à-vis the US enemy. It is evident from his journal that the Yuma hung around small army outposts, visiting often, and interacting generally with the enemy whites – far from the traditional European war model. Describing a first attempt at setting up a peace meeting with the Yuma, he writes of the night before: 'About half an hour after the moon went down I went to the part of the camp where the Indians were – I forgot to state that about half a dozen warriors slept in my camp that night – and found them sitting up, smoking'. Setting out for the site of the talks the next morning, the warriors, neighbourly enough, load up his stuff with their own – 'they brought my baggage along'.[88]

He never has anything negative or mean to say about the Indians other than that they are an obvious danger to him; there seems to be no personal animosity, quite otherwise. He remarks at one point during this peace powwow that 'they all seemed glad to see me'. There are no remarks of the 'only good Indian is a dead Indian' sort, nor does he describe with any evident relish the raids on Indian settlements to which he was inevitably a party; although on the occasion of an Indian strike in which Major E.H. Fitzgerald's men came under attack, some being killed or wounded, Sweeny does record: 'We burned a number of their villages, destroyed their planting-grounds, and did all the mischief that we could'. He recounts, however, how during that same expedition, entering a village the tribe had had to abandon in such haste they left an old man behind, that 'fortunately for the old fellow, I was in command of the advance guard and came up just in time to save his life, as one of the men had covered him with his rifle – another second would have been too late'.[89]

'I have learned a great deal concerning the tribes of this region', he writes at one point in his journal, a reflection of the intelligent curiosity with which he seems to have regarded the world in general.[90] It is this quality, it would seem, that produced the study, the now-valuable observations of Yuma tribal behaviour and material culture remarked earlier. That study characterizes his writing throughout his California assignment and his observations are often set down with an anthropological precision. Discussing Pasqual, a Yuma warrior and sub-chief, he notes the man's mild expression – 'and yet he is the most remarkable character in this country for his indomitable love of adventure'. Pasqual's body is covered with battle wounds, and his dexterity with Indian weaponry is 'almost miraculous'. There follows a brief exposition on the nature of this tribal weaponry:

> These consist of a bow made of willow, and about five or six feet in length. The arrow heads are made of flint or glass; the half of the shaft near the head of the arrow, wood, and the remainder of cane, feathered with eagle's or hawk's plumes.
>
> The Yumas carry a quiver at their back, and wear a thick leathern bracelet on the left arm to protect it from the bowstring. The war club is a favorite weapon with them; it is about two feet long, very large and thick at one end and small at the other, to which is attached a leathern thong to retain the implement in the hand . . .
>
> They are never without a knife, (about eighteen inches long) which they use for every purpose. They also have shields of undressed leather, which are arrow-proof, and spears from eight to twelve feet in length, with long, sharp, tapering heads. They decorate themselves most splendidly for war. Their sole garment, as I said, consists of a belt or manta, or apron. When journeying across the hot sands they wear a rude kind of leathern sandal to protect their feet.[91]

On 2 October 1852 the 'great council', in which the Yuma Chiefs and US Army officers assembled to negotiate a peace treaty, finally got underway. The Indian leaders sat in a semi-circle on the ground, Sweeny and the other officers seated likewise. 'There was a great deal said on both sides, to very little purpose', Sweeny writes. The military wanted restitution of stolen animals and other property including boats, but the Indians pleaded that the boats had been destroyed, the stolen animals eaten, and so forth. 'They begged us to forget the past; they were sorry for what had taken place . . . Some bread and tobacco was now distributed, and the council broke up'.[92]

The physical appearance of these Yuma he had recorded in an earlier diary entry:

> In battle they sometimes wear a headdress, formed of the plumes of the heron, hawk, or eagle. They indulge in ponderous ear-rings and nose-rings, made of shell, which drag and distort their features, and rejoice, also, in necklaces of shells, or beads when they can get them. Their bodies are tattooed variously, according to their ideas of beauty or terrific effect, and their shields are painted in the same style. Their faces they paint black, with a red streak down the center, which makes them look as though they had been cloven with an axe, and their hair also they color red for battle, weaving it into a sort of helmet or turban, which renders them fearful to behold.[93]

Quieter times followed the peace talks, but duty at Fort Yuma continued to be a cruel and sweltering matter; no expedition could be sent out under the desert sun but that 'more or less of the men had . . . to be sent back before the return of the party'. These conditions are reflected in a letter written to Ellen on 17 September 1852 in which Sweeny reviewed the previous summer:

> We lost several men by sun-stroke. You recollect Fitzgerald of 'D' Company? Poor fellow, he died after two hours illness – came off guard complaining of a slight headache, and was dead before I knew he was sick. Leahey, 'D' Co. clerk, was lost in the mountains and never heard of since – he accompanied me on an expedition into the mountains in May last, against the Indians, when we all came very near perishing for want of water. I . . . had to abandon three of my men who broke down before we could reach water, one of the three made his way to my camp, another was found four days after by a mounted party sent in search of them, his haversack full of weeds. But poor Leahey was never found – in another month he would have been discharged. Another man, by the name of Brown, went out with Lt. Curtis on scout, and was brought back next day a corpse.[94]

And as if the desert had not already offered a full component of dangers, a horrendous earthquake commenced on 29 November 1852 and on 1 December was still in progress: 'It shakes so now that I can hardly write'. On 12 December there were still aftershocks, and 'the earth has been opened in every direction, and large quantities of water and scoria forced through the apertures'.[95]

Following the treaty, however, the Indians began paying frequent and peaceful visits to the army camp. 'They come down the river in their balsas with pumpkins, melons, etc., which they trade off for blankets, shirts . . . bread or tobacco, or anything else that may be useful to them'.[96] In January 1853, a party of journeying Yavapai Indians from further north and inland Arizona stop by Camp Yuma for a few days: 'They were very large men. They seemed much pleased with their visit. They all knew me and extended their hand, greeting me with the old salutation: "How do you do, Tabac?" They dress in buckskin as they inhabit the mountains . . . which are very cold'.[97] This was the kind of peaceful interlude that Sweeny saw little of during the desert years, though at Christmas 1852, he had recorded a pleasant holiday moment:

> In the afternoon we sat down to a *sumptuous* dinner, consisting of beef soup, roast venison . . . potatoes, onions and squash. Dessert-apple and pumpkin pies, cheese, ginger-bread, and one glass of egg-nog apiece, with which we drank . . . toasts . . . We then adjourned to my quarters to smoke some cigars that my wife had sent me, a few of which I had reserved for the occasion.[98]

Not that the combat with Heintzelman had diminished. On 27 September 1853 Sweeny wrote his wife regarding the major's continuing manipulation of matters related to the ferry:

> There is a large immigration passing through here this year; the Major has had considerable difficulty with some of them [who] requested to be crossed in the govt. boat as they had no money to cross at the Ferry, which is about a mile below. The Maj. would neither cross them, nor allow them to swim with their animals . . . He is secretly interested in the Ferry and therefore interested in making everyone cross below and pay . . . he has given the beef contract for this post to the Ferry company at $50. a head, while a gentleman from Sonora offered to supply the post for $22. a head.[99]

He would not have to worry about these matters much longer, however. The mail that arrived at Fort Yuma on 10 November 1853, stunned Lieutenant Sweeny in the happiest sense of the word. It brought news of General Orders No. 2, whereby his unit, the 2nd Infantry, would be redeployed, replaced in California by the 3rd Artillery sailing from New York. Two days later he wrote – in a '*happy* state of mind' – the following to his wife now in New York with their two daughters:

> The mail got here the day before yesterday, and I believe I've been half crazy ever since! . . . As the 3rd [Artillery] will come by way of Cape Horn, it will probably be six months yet before we can all get away; however as the order recommended that as many officers & non-commissioned officers as can be spared be sent *immediately* to New York on recruiting service, Gen. Hitchcock will no doubt break up some companies and send the officers . . . home . . . I have commenced packing up, and will be ready for any arrangement that may

> be made . . . Oh, Ell, how happy we will be after this long separation. Tell Prill to brush up, as I'm going home to dance at her wedding, and hear her sing 'Bad Luck to This Marching', as I shall be pretty well tired of it by that time . . . Believe me, my fondest wish is to be once more in the arms of my own darling wife.[100]

This would be his final letter home from the desert. The best-case scenario mentioned here, orders to immediately prepare for passage to New York, was what came about. Along with two other officers, Sweeny was able to leave the desert Fort on 11 December, and, on 31 December, the three were among those who sailed for New York City. His years in the 'Blood Meridian' were over. Sweeny concluded this last letter to Ellen with some plans:

> Captain Davidson and most of the officers who expect to go home the same time I do have made up their minds to spend about a week in New York before separating for their respective localities, in order to furnish themselves with such articles of wearing apparel as they may be in need of, besides indulging in a few luxuries we have almost forgotten the taste of, such as oysters, sherry-cobblers, Mint juleps, ice-cream.[101]

And his final glorious anticipation probably reflected his boyhood in Ireland: 'last, though not least in importance, potatoes, onions & butter'.

NOTES

1. *TWS, Journal*, p.157.
2. Ibid., p.132.
3. Ibid., p.18. Sweeny's diary covering his trip around the horn and his desert years was first published by the author in serial form as, 'Life on the American Desert', in the *New York Atlas* of 7 December 1856 to 29 March 1857. The *Journal of the American Military Institution* published a shorter version in 1909. Westernlore Press, Los Angeles, CA, published the diary, restored to the *Atlas* version, in 1956 as the *Journal of Lt. Thomas W. Sweeny, 1849–1853*. This edition was edited by Arthur Woodward and included a valuable introduction by the editor. Woodward, an eminent historian and archaeologist of the American southwest, wrote extensively on Western historical subjects, including the material culture of the fur trade, Navajo silversmithing and the California missions. His *Feud on the Colorado* (Los Angeles, CA, 1955) is a study of the early white exploration of the Colorado River. He was one of the authors – with Schofield DeLong and Leffler B. Miller – of *The Missions of Northern Sonora: A 1935 Field Documentation*, which was republished by the University of Arizona Press in 1993.
4. *Thomas O. Larkin's Letters to the Secretary of State about the Gold Discovery.* www.sfmuseum.org/hist6/larkin.html
5. *TWS, Journal*, p.40.
6. Looseness of military discipline continued up to and into the early Civil War. Accounts of Union troops on the march to First Bull Run, for instance, frequently note horseplay and generally undisciplined behaviour in the ranks. See, for example, Herman Melville's poem 'The March into Virginia', in Hennig Cohen, (ed.), *The Battle Pieces of Herman Melville* (New York, 1964), pp.42–4.

7. *TWS, Journal*, p.45.
8. Thomas William Sweeny Papers, Huntington Library, San Marino, California.
9. Timothy Sarbaugh, 'Post Civil War Fever and Adjustment: Fenianism in the Californian Context', *Irish Studies Program Working Papers*, 91, 2–3 (Boston, MA, 1992), p.4.
10. The details of Sweeny's extended feuding with Heintzelman are set forth by Woodward in his introduction to Sweeny's *Journal* (pp.24–7) and in Coyer, 'Hero of the Armless Sleeve', chapters 2 and 3.
11. Quoted in Woodward, 'Introduction', *TWS, Journal*, p.23.
12. Ibid., p.24.
13. Sweeny to his sister, Sarah Ann Barnard, 9 April 1849. Quoted in James Edward Moriarty, 'Fighting Tom Sweeny: The California Years', *Journal of San Diego History*, 26, 3 (1980), p.208.
14. Woodward, 'Introduction', *TWS, Journal*, p.24.
15. The military records of the incident are summarized in Coyer, 'Hero of the Armless Sleeve', pp.42–6.
16. Woodward, *TWS, Journal*, p.225, n.25. See also, 'Yuma Indians', *New Encyclopedia of the American West*, (ed.) Howard R. Lamar (New Haven, CT, 1998), p.1251. Sweeny refers ironically to Morehead and his army which he (Sweeny) saw proceeding on their 'triumphal return' to San Diego.
17. Court transcript quoted in Moriarty, 'Fighting Tom', p.212.
18. *TWS, Journal*, pp.48–9. Warner Ranch, set up by Jonathan Trumbull Warner while on a trapping expedition in 1831, was six days' journey into the desert and the only outpost and water source on the trek to the Yuma Crossing.
19. Heintzelman Journal, Library of Congress. Entries 1 March and 18 March 1851.
20. *TWS, Journal*, p.117.
21. Coyer, 'Hero of the Armless Sleeve', p.132.
22. Woodward, 'Introduction', *TWS, Journal*, pp.26–7. Sweeny in his letters more than once accuses Heintzelman of excessive caution, hesitation and neglect in terms of his military obligations. The major is similarly characterized by Stewart Sifakis in his *Who Was Who in the Union: A Biographical Encyclopedia of more than 1500 Union Participants* (New York, 1989) p.191. Sifakis cites Heintzelman's having had a negative effect on the already irresolute McClellan early in the Civil War. Sifakis also remarks that Washington authorities insisted that McClellan employ officers according to seniority even when there was no evidence of their battlefield competence, and that Heintzelman, so appointed, represented a failure of this practice.
23. Heintzelman journal entry, 24 December 1852. Captain Lorenzo Sitgreaves, whose survey party barely survived their desert expedition, arriving at Sweeny's camp just in time on 30 November 1851, is another who, like Davidson, and contrary to Heintzelman, considered Sweeny a competent and friendly officer. Sitgreaves visited Sweeny's sister in New York on his return there, and as she wrote to her brother: 'He says that there is not an officer in your regiment who can command more respect than you, and if you have any enemies, he never saw any'. (Letter to Lieutenant Sweeny, 7 March 1852, Thomas William Sweeny Papers, Huntington Library, San Marino, California.)
24. Woodward, 'Introduction', *TWS, Journal*, pp.26–7.
25. Cleland, 'An Exile on the Colorado', p.18.
26. Frank Love, 'Louis Jaeger Saw Opportunity in Yuma Ferry', YumaSun.com. (7 September, 2003). www.yumasun.com/artman/publish/articles/story_7065.shtml Heintzelman served, while in the army, as President of the Sonora Exploring and Mining Company in 1858–59. See Diane M.T. North, *Samuel Peter Heintzelman and the Sonora Exploring and Mining Company* (Tucson, AZ, 1980).

27. Gregory T. Jones, 'The Yuma Crossing'. www.desertusa.com/mag99/jan/stories/crossing.html It should be noted that the Crossing was apparently an area rather than, as the name would suggest, an exact spot. The ferry companies operated along miles of the river where it narrowed. See Woodward, 'Introduction', *TWS, Journal*, p.122, n.26.
28. Alan Axelrod, *Chronicle of the Indian Wars: From Colonial Times to Wounded Knee* (New York, 1993), p.171.
29. *TWS, Journal*, p.51.
30. Quoted in Cleland, 'Exile on the Colorado', p.18.
31. Quoted in ibid., p.19.
32. Quoted in ibid., p.19.
33. 'Royce Oatman' rootsweb.com/~indian/olive oatman.htm Regarding the material Olive Oatman used on her lecture tours, *see* 'Olive Oatman's Lecture Notes', (ed.) Edward S.J. Pettis, *San Bernadino County Museum Publications*, 16, 2, (1969).
34. 'Royce Oatman', Bancroft.berkeley.edu/Exhibits/nativeamericans/39.html
35. Letter of 28 June 1851, Thomas William Sweeny Papers, Huntington Library, San Marino, California.
36. *TWS, Journal*, p.114.
37. Ibid., pp.51–2.
38. Quoted by Woodward, 'Introduction', *TWS, Journal*, p.26.
39. *TWS, Journal*, pp.53–4.
40. Ibid, p.31. The camp's artillery piece as noted remained, helping the situation somewhat. The bronze mountain howitzer, a popular army frontier weapon at the time, was fairly compact, had a 220-pound barrel, and could fire a shell an impressive 1,005 yards (Woodward, *TWS, Journal*, p.232 n31).
41. Ibid., p.58.
42. Ibid., pp.58–60.
43. Francis Parkman, *The Oregon Trail* (New York, 1996), p.11.
44. *TWS, Journal*, p.62. Even before reaching the river outpost, at the less remote oasis of Camp Vallecito, near the end of the trail to California, Sweeny noted in November of 1850: 'Our provisions are getting scarce, having to issue daily to starving immigrants', p.50.
45. Woodward, 'Introduction', *TWS, Journal*, p.220, n18.
46. *TWS, Journal*, p.134.
47. Ibid.
48. Cormac McCarthy, *Blood Meridian or the Evening Redness in the West* (New York, 1992), p.262.
49. *TWS, Journal*, pp.135–6.
50. Ibid, p.74.
51. Ibid., p.79.
52. Ibid., p.82.
53. Ibid., p.112.
54. Ibid., p.80.
55. Woodward, 'Introduction', *TWS, Journal*, p.24.
56. *TWS, Journal*, p.61.
57. Ibid, p.121. 'The New River crosses . . . the outskirts of [present day] Seeley and meanders on . . . into Lower California'. Woodward, *TWS, Journal*, p.224, n.25. Sweeny reports at one point a Mr Ankrim, headed for the California market with 22,000 sheep (p.213).
58. *TWS, Journal*, pp.62–4.
59. Ibid., p.56.
60. Ibid., p.61.
61. Ibid., pp.52–3.

62. Ibid., p.117.
63. Ibid, p.130.
64. Ibid., pp.119–20.
65. Ibid., pp.118–19.
66. Ibid., pp.175–6.
67. Thomas William Sweeny Papers, Huntington Library, San Marino, California. The baby's christening was postponed, at Sweeny's request in a letter to his wife of 30 August 1851, until he could be there. It occurred on 25 April 1852 at the Church of the Holy Trinity.
68. *TWS, Journal*, pp.137–9.
69. Woodward, *TWS, Journal*, p.233 n33.
70. *TWS, Journal*, p.137.
71. Ibid, p.140. The Indian warpath signalled by these fires was the historic Garra Revolt of 1851. See George Harwood Phillips, *Chiefs and Challengers: Indian Resistance and Cooperation in Southern California* (Berkeley, CA, 1975). The southwest Indians at this time, notably the Yuma, did use horses to some extent, but were not the formidable cavalrymen Sweeny would later encounter in the Sioux of the northern plains. The Yuma in these years usually raided on foot.
72. *San Diego Biographies, San Diego Historical Society*. www.Sandiegohistory.org/bio/garra.htm (17 January 2004).
73. *TWS, Journal*, p.142.
74. Pamela Tamplain, 'Philip Crosthwaite: San Diego Pioneer and Public Servant', *Journal of San Diego History,* 21, 3 (1975), p.45.
75. *TWS, Journal*, pp.146–7.
76. Letter of 30 August 1851, Thomas William Sweeny Papers, Huntington Library, San Marino, California.
77. Thomas William Sweeny Papers, Huntington Library, San Marino, California.
78. 7 March 1852, ibid.
79. Sweeny to his wife, Ellen, 9 November 1852, ibid. The educational viewpoint expressed here was a fairly common one in the nineteenth century when there was a vogue, as there is presently, encouraging intensive early education. The counterview Sweeny expresses tended to gain some more credence with the publication of John Stuart Mills' *Autobiography* in 1873 in which Mills, the quintessential prodigy, expressed some misgivings about his early training in a narrowly analytical direction. See especially chapter 5. *Autobiography,* (ed.) Jack Stillinger (Boston, MA, 1969).
80. *TWS, Journal*, p.156.
81. Sweeny to his wife, 24 July 1852. Thomas William Sweeny Papers, Huntington Library, San Marino, California.
82. Sweeny to Sarah Ann Barnard, 14 June 1852. Quoted in Moriarty, 'Fighting Tom', pp.214–5.
83. Moriarty, 'Fighting Tom', p.216.
84. 17 September 1852, Thomas William Sweeny Papers, Huntington Library, San Marino, California.
85. *TWS, Journal*, pp.148–9.
86. Moriarty, 'Fighting Tom', p.216.
87. A US Army officer's distaste for the Irish element making its way into the ranks and even the officer corps in the frontier army is portrayed in John Ford's classic western *Fort Apache* – in the figure of the Fort Apache commandant, Colonel Owen Thursday. See Jack Morgan, 'The Irish in John Ford's Seventh Cavalry Trilogy', *Melus*, 22, 2 (1997), pp.33–44.
88. *TWS, Journal*, p.174.

89. Ibid., pp.152–3.
90. Ibid., p.201.
91. Ibid., pp.71–2.
92. Ibid., p.181.
93. Ibid., pp.71–2.
94. Thomas William Sweeny Papers, Huntington Library, San Marino, California.
95. *TWS, Journal*, pp.186–7.
96. Ibid., p.182. 'Balsas' were crude boats made mostly of rushes (Woodward, *TWS, Journal*, p.259, n105.
97. Ibid., p.193.
98. Ibid., p.191.
99. Thomas William Sweeny Papers, Huntington Library, San Marino, California.
100. Letter of 12 November 1853 to his wife, Ellen. Thomas William Sweeny Papers, Huntington Library, San Marino, California. The Irish song, 'Bad Luck to this Marching', expresses disillusionment with military life. The lyric was written by Charles Lever and put to the tune 'Paddy O'Carroll'. The song has been recorded fairly recently by, for one, Sean Tyrrell.
101. Ibid.

3

The Sioux Expedition and St Louis Towards War, 1854–61

> The property in this place will never fall into your hands. I'll blow it to hell first.
>
> Sweeny at the St Louis Arsenal, 1861[1]

On State Highway ZZ, a rural road in Republic, Missouri, just across from the entrance to the Wilson's Creek National Battlefield, there is a small Civil War museum named in honour of General Sweeny, something that would surely please him if he knew. Along with an outstanding collection of Civil War artifacts, the General Sweeny Museum has on display some of its namesake's military items, now memorabilia, such as his field glasses and a Tiffany presentation sword given him in September of 1863 by the officers of a former command, the 52nd Illinois. The gift was accompanied by a letter from La Grange, Tennessee, declaring:

> If the severity of your discipline was at first unpleasant, experience has convinced us both of its importance and necessity; thereby serving to increase our respect for you as an honest, faithful and impartial commander . . . By your promotion we sustain a loss. Yet we regard you as eminently deserving . . . to fill your [new] position.[2]

The museum is located where it is because, very early in the Civil War, as Brigadier General of Volunteers commanding the southwest expedition in General Nathaniel Lyon's Missouri campaign, Sweeny was significantly engaged in the critical efforts to keep Missouri out of Confederate hands.

There were six years between this period in 1861, however, and the conclusion of his desert assignment in January, 1854, when he had shipped out from California aboard the SS *Ohio*, arriving in New York to be reunited with his wife Ellen and his daughter Sarah, and to see his daughter Frances Ellen for the first time. He would later be summoned for duty in the action against the Sioux, but for now he had eight months of work as a recruitment officer in the city to look forward to – a pleasant prospect since his family would be nearby. He would meet incoming Irishmen at the disembarkation centre to extol the virtues of American Army life and attempt to sign up recruits. As well, his return to New York from desert duty coincided with a gathering Irish revolutionary ferment in New York and fledgling Fenian mobilization.

Thomas Francis Meagher, Michael Doheny, John O'Mahony, Terrence MacManus and other 1848 exiles arrived in the States from 1849 through the 1850s. John Mitchel arrived toward the end of 1853 and his newspaper *The Citizen* began appearing in 1854. The Emmet Monument Association, precursor to the Fenian Brotherhood, was founded in 1855. Two years later, in the autumn of 1857 in New York City:

> the noisy jangling of horse drawn carts accompanied by the shouts of draymen cursing their charges through the tangled traffic seeped through the cracks around the old windowsill at number 6 Centre Street making it hard to hear what was being said . . . Inside the room a thick cloud of intermingled cigar and cigarette smoke laid heavy. Below the layer of smoke, John O'Mahony and Michael Doheny plotted the imminent defeat of England. The time for the rising had come and they were sure that this time, unlike all the earlier ones, Ireland would be victorious . . . They would enlist expatriate Irishmen to be recruited and trained as soldiers. With this liberation army they would sail to Ireland where their arrival would signal a general uprising.[3]

But the following year in nearby Brooklyn, in a meeting with James Stephens at Doheny's home, General Tom Sweeny expressed pessimism about the feasibility of such an uprising on Irish soil.[4] Hopes along that line had risen during the Crimean War when Britain appeared to be getting bogged down militarily in Turkey. During the war Mitchel, Doheny and O'Mahony, among others, sought alliance with Russia and Russian assistance in transporting men and arms to Ireland. But those plans, some of which had looked promising, fell by the way with the conclusion of the war in 1856.[5] The logistics of an invasion of Ireland from America appeared, and indeed were, especially prohibitive – the greater an uprising's success, the greater would be the probability of a Cromwellian military response from London. The *Irish Times* judgement that American Fenians were 'more likely . . . to find their way to Tennessee than to Tipperary', and the US government more likely to get men from Ireland than to send them there, was not inaccurate.[6] The alternative possibility of an American-Irish military initiative against the British North American provinces, as distinct from in Ireland, had long preoccupied Sweeny. His counter-plan to the one the Fenians had been following, Sweeny's idea involving the nearby British soil of Canada, would increasingly take hold in the American Fenian ranks in the years to come.

He might have remained at his convenient New York assignment had not an inflammatory incident occurred on the Western frontier, in Sioux territory, in August 1854. A family making its way along the Mormon trail, by the Platte River, in present Nebraska, lost a cow which some native people later came upon and butchered for meat. When the family reported this to the Army at Fort Laramie, the commanding officer, Lieutenant Hugh Fleming, sent out a party of some thirty men under Lieutenant John L. Grattan, a young officer fresh out of West Point. Grattan recklessly rode into a Sioux village of 200 people and demanded the surrender of High Forehead, a chief. The Indians would not comply and suggested letting things lie until the return of the local government agent who was away at the time. Grattan was impatient and confrontational, however, and eventually the troops fired into the Indian village. The Sioux, with numerical superiority, counter-attacked and killed the entire army party, Red Cloud's Oglalas running down those who attempted to flee. The 'Grattan Massacre' immediately captured newspaper headlines nationally and led to popular and official political calls for retaliation and for pacification of the Sioux country. The government responded with a plan for a major military expedition into the region in question, one to be led by William S. Harney, a veteran of the war against the Seminoles in the 1830s and 1840s, and of the Mexican War in which, as already noted, he directed the San Partricio executions.[7]

In Paris when he got the call, Harney sent a message to Washington asking that arrangements be made for the acquisition of a fort on the upper Missouri from which his projected expedition could operate. In response, the War Department purchased Fort Pierre, a ruin of an old French trading post, from the American Fur Company in St Louis. Thus the Grattan incident

> marked the beginning of more than three decades of determined Indian resistance to white westward movement across the Great Plains, and Harney's expedition became the first major campaign, and one of the most dramatic ever, against principle tribes.[8]

The campaign would be one more historic American event that Sweeny in his lifetime would be an immediate witness to and participant in. His outfit, the 2nd US Infantry, was now back in the east and stationed at Carlisle Barracks, Pennsylvania. Sweeny reported as ordered to Carlisle and joined in the preparations for the anti-Indian campaign. In mid-November, however, he received news of the birth of his third child, Charles Baxter Sweeny, soon to be known as 'Charlie' in the family, born on 17 November 1854. Sweeny requested and got leave to be with the family for two months more, from 19 December to 18 February 1855. He then returned to Carlisle Barracks from which, on 2 June, the 2nd Infantry boarded trains to Chicago and then south to Alton, Illinois, on the Mississippi. The regiment proceeded on steamboats from Alton to the Missouri confluence and up the Missouri River en route to Fort Pierre. They did not get to their destination without incident, however; a boat carrying Sweeny's company and others ran aground and finally had to stop at Fort Leavenworth during which delay many were struck by cholera, and a number died.[9]

By early August of 1855 the 2nd Infantry was finally congregated at Fort Pierre and engaged in an attempt at restoring that shambles of a camp. Sweeny was part of those labouring at this restoration task when Harney, with 600 troops, set out from Fort Leavenworth bent on vengeance for the Grattan massacre. On 2 September the command arrived at Ash Hollow on Blue Water Creek, a tributary of the North Platte, along which were Brule and Oglala Sioux villages. The Indians faced the sometimes charming Harney at his nastiest – the punitive, cold-blooded officer the San Patricio soldiers had faced at Churubusco. He encircled the villages, which included women and children, and on 3 September attacked. No quarter was offered; the 'Battle of Ash Hollow' was a matter of carnage. One of Harney's lieutenants, Warren Taylor, remembered the scene afterward – the wounded children particularly – as 'heart-rending'.[10]

The subjugation of the Platte River Sioux was now fully underway, and the chiefs had increasingly to yield to Washington's demands at various councils. Sweeny, who took part in a number of these talks as an aide to Harney, would years later, in a *Brooklyn Times* interview, recall a significant gathering in March of 1856 at which representatives of all the Sioux nations were in attendance:

> The great chiefs sat in a semi-circle, three rows deep around the little knot of [US] officers. The principle chiefs were in the front row, the next in rank in the second, and the minor chiefs in the rear. The affair was conducted with impressive dignity. A great chief would rise, stand like a statue in the little open space and speak, and upon concluding would say, 'I have spoken', and take his seat.

He was impressed with Chief Red Cloud, but not with Sitting Bull whom he described as a shaman, a medicine man, and an instigator rather than a warrior.

> He fomented all the trouble, and because of his implacable hatred for the white race . . . his voice was always for war, and by his devilish incantations, auguries and predictions, he was able at frequent intervals to get the fanatical Sioux into war. . . . Then he would stand aside and let his deluded tribe take the consequences.

Sweeny remembered General Harney as an imposing figure at the talks. 'He was in full uniform, and he stood up to his full height of six feet four inches as straight as a ramrod. A grunt of involuntary admiration went around among the chiefs'.[11]

Duty at Fort Pierre was harsh, but at the other extreme from what Sweeny had known for years in the desert. Cold was the scourge here. The fort's flimsy, worn-out buildings offered little protection from the north country winter winds and blizzards. A third of the army horses, like the men inadequately sheltered and fed, died. Augustus Myers, a member of Sweeny's unit, would later write: 'I look back upon the winter passed at Fort Pierre as one of great suffering and hardship, by far the worst that I went through during my service'.[12] Desertions were not uncommon, and those who ran off, if they did not find refuge at an

Indian village, often faced death on the trackless prairie. Most of Sweeny's service in the West during these years – some two decades before Little Big Horn – was gruelling, but for the most part militarily undramatic in comparison to his career overall. His duties were related to supply, commissary, quartermastering and so on, duties that fell to most officers at one time or another. That he was even now, however, looking forward to playing a role in an Irish war against Britain, is evident in a letter home to his wife while stationed at the frozen post on 26 February 1856. The letter bears quoting at length since it notes the Fenian spirit taking hold even among these troops of the Sioux Expedition out on the winter plains, as well as noting the impending council with the Indians, the brutal conditions provoking army desertions, and a consequent incident of *cannibalism* no less:

> I write to Daniel P. Barnard [Sweeny's sister's husband] by this mail enclosing him a draft for $200 of which he will send you $150, the rest having been given me by some of the men of this command for papers in N. York . . . I write also to John Daly with instructions to receive from D.P.B. the $50 for the newspapers, &c. I see they are making another movement for Irish Independence. I hope it will amount to something this time. Ell, how would you like me to embark on such an undertaking? It would not be worse than being kept on the frontier all my life; besides, we might accomplish great things – do deeds that our children could point at on the page of history with pride: perhaps help to pull a sinewy tyrant from his throne, and raise a prostrate people from chains to liberty. Let me know what you think of it, Ell. There's much excitement here on the subject . . .
>
> Strong symptoms of scurvy have already appeared among the troops. Harney picked up two deserters on his trip down the river; they were in rather bad condition; *four of their comrades were frozen to death, and they had been living on the bodies for several weeks* . . . [italics added]
>
> There are over one hundred Indians here waiting for the great council to convene. Some of the principle chiefs frequently come to see me; they think I have great influence with the Genl. and beg me to intercede, as they seem to have an awful fear of 'Mad Bear' as they call him. The council will meet about the 1st of March. Let me know what kind of *furs* you would prefer that can be procured here, and I will try to get you some. I am collecting presents for all the folks . . . I have a beautiful pair of moccasins for Sarah . . . and another pair for Fannie . . . and a bridle and saddle fit for a king for Charlie.[13]

On 6 June 1856 he received orders to head to New York for six months back at recruitment. During these months, besides enjoying a stint of family life, he adapted his diary from the desert years for serial publication in The *New York Atlas*. Toward the conclusion of his tour, he applied for a three-month extension of his New York assignment. His wife Ellen was pregnant, and he remained at home, technically AWOL, in fact, a month beyond the extension. Not until 21 May 1856 did he arrive at Fort Randall, an installation that had in the meantime replaced Fort Pierre as the Army's Sioux territory outpost. He remained on duty at Randall for five months, at the end of which he received extraordinarily welcome orders – for a full two years in New York as a recruiter.[14] This good news was received in a grim context however – a darkness that had been gathering for some time would soon envelop the light of his life.

Something seemed to be wrong with Ellen. When he was out on the plains, in May 1857, he had received news of the birth of a fourth child and second son, but the baby lived only a month. The couple's plans for Ellen and the children to move out West to be with him began to seem unrealistic due to her health problems. He had written her from Fort Pierre on 10 March 1856:

> You speak of making your arrangements to come out here in the spring and hope you will have an opportunity of seeing Davidson or Lowell before you start. Lt. McLean received a letter from Captain Lowell by the last mail in which he desires to know if you intend coming out . . . that he may meet you and the children at some convenient point on the route. I told Mr. L. to tell him you would not come on account of . . . your health and was greatly obliged to him for his kindness . . . It was my intention if you came to meet you, if possible, at St Louis. As soon, however, as I heard of your indisposition, I wrote by the next mail requesting that you abandon all idea of coming. I trust the letter has reached you long ere this. It would be madness dear Ell to attempt such a long, long, journey in your delicate state of health! But I love you if possible more than ever for your willingness to brave the dangers . . . I have sent in a written application for the Genl. Recruiting Service [New York].[15]

Ellen's letters became less frequent and less energetic. Her health had been a concern for some time as is evident in Sweeny's letters home going back to as early as January 1853:

> I regret, dear Ell, that your . . . health does not improve, and hope you will take more exercise in the future, and stir about more: you ought to go out walking often, and take the children along – riding occasionally too, I think, would be very beneficial – then you might go places of amusement occasionally, such as concerts, museums, and such like places.[16]

He had written to his sister from Carlisle barracks on 27 November 1854, referring to Ellen's condition when last he was in New York and to his continuing worry:

> Her being subject to those *nervous attacks* kept me and keeps me in a measure still, in constant fear . . . I implore you, dear Sarah . . . to be over with her as often as your own household affairs will permit, and tell mother to do so likewise . . . God send that my fears may be groundless, and that Ell . . . may continue to improve until I return home.[17]

But by 1856 Ellen's letters to Fort Pierre had become yet more rare and feeble. He wrote to her on 10 January of that year:

> My own dearest Ell,
> I received a letter from Mary and one from Sarah Barnard by the last mail . . . informing me of what I dreaded all along, that your not having written me since the middle of September, was owing to sickness . . . Oh, Ell, if you knew my feeling when I read those letters, particularly sister Mary's, for I knew they must contain something explanatory of your silence. Not having received any letters from you in so long a time, and seeing that none arrived even by this mail, I could scarcely hold the letter, my hand trembled so, and I could not read the lines for some time my sight got so dim . . . Certain I am that I never felt half so timid on marching into the battlefield as I did on opening and reading those letters.[18]

Further communications from his sister and from his daughter Sarah began to hint that something was now very wrong. Their letters revealed that Ellen's seizures and severe depression were worsening – she could hardly complete a letter now. Shocked, he could only write more of the standard platitudes encouraging her to rest and get outdoor air and so forth, and express his fear of losing 'the only anchor my hopes of happiness in this life rest upon'. He sent a poem in the one of his letters:

> I think of thee, when soft and wide
>   The evening spreads her robes of light,
> And like a young and timid bride,
>   Sits blushing in the arms of night,
> And when the moon's sweet crescent springs
>   In light o'er heaven's wide, wondrous sea,
> And stars are forth like blessed things,
>   I think of thee, Ell, I think of thee.[19]

A letter from Fort Pierre, 24 March 1856, reveals his continued fear and grasping at medical straws:

> Ell, I think I'll have to put a veto on your writing more than a certain quantity in the future, otherwise you'll bring on those attacks again, and won't be able to write at all, besides injuring your health, which nothing can compensate for. When I go home – which I hope will be soon – I intend to deprive you of pen and paper altogether, and do all the writing myself; those not acquainted with my hand can scarcely tell it from a lady's.
>
> Seriously, Ell . . . you must only write to me, when you do write at all . . . very short letters; these are my *orders* which I expect you to obey, Ell! Now remember! In S.A.B's [his sister's] last letter she mentions a physician living in *Tivoli*, 18 miles below Hudson, who has been very successful in the treatment of the disease with which you are afflicted . . . She speaks of a friend of hers, a Mrs. Place, being cured by him, after being subject to those

> attacks for several years. Sarah thinks it would do no harm to try him at all events. I think so too; no means should be left untried that offers a shadow of success. I must now close as the mail is waiting. Love and kisses to our darling children, and accept a thousand fond embraces from your loving, affectionate, and devoted, *Tom.*[20]

He left Fort Randall by boat on 4 June 1858. Back home, however, he found Ellen unimproved and, in fact, declining hopelessly from what would now probably be diagnosed as a brain tumour. Her condition worsened during the two years Sweeny was at home, and he could only watch and seek to comfort her until she died on 30 August 1860, leaving him with three children – Sarah, who was 11, Fannie who was 9, and Charley who was 6. He considered resigning from the military to care for them, but he was now 40 years old, and a civilian career that would pay enough did not seem to be on the horizon. A group of New York friends, including the mayor of the city, wrote letters to Washington petitioning the Secretary of War to give him hardship consideration and a permanent New York post whereby he could keep his family together. But with a national emergency brewing, North–South conflict seeming evermore inevitable, the appeal was rejected.[21] He was ultimately forced to entrust his children to the care of his own relatives in Brooklyn and with his deceased wife's family in Saratoga County, New York. His sister would provide general oversight and keep him informed.

Two months after his wife's death, now a single parent, the children living with their maternal grandparents, he wrote a concerned, cautionary letter from Brooklyn to his eldest daughter, Sarah Sweeny, expressing an arguably nineteenth-century Irish aversion to dampness:

> I am glad to hear that you are all well and that you and Charley have recovered from your afflictions. You must be very careful of yourself for the future, dear Sarah, and also of Fannie and Charley, and not expose yourself unnecessarily, and above all things you must avoid getting your feet wet if possible. I know you can't help it sometimes, but then you can prevent any bad results following by taking off your shoes and stockings as soon as possible, and rubbing your feet with a coarse towel. You must never stand still nor sit down a moment with your feet wet . . . As Fannie and Charley are too young yet to know the danger of getting their feet wet, you must act the part of a mother to them, Sarah, and talk to and advise them for their own good . . . Next to having the feet well protected, the most important thing is to wear flannel, so as to guard the chest and lungs from the cold and damp.[22]

Secessionist agitation on the increase, he was ordered to return once again to Jefferson Barracks in St Louis. He had been promoted to captain in the regular army in January 1861, and the St Louis assignment placed him in one of the most politically and militarily volatile areas of the country at the time. Nor was he in an un-Irish environment at his new post. While St Louis' ethnic majority was German, the second largest foreign-born group was the Irish. When

Anthony Trollope visited the city the following year, he observed that, based on the accents he heard in the streets, nearly everyone was either Irish or German.[23] The Irish had preceded the Germans; as early as 1663, the Franco-Irish Marquis de Tracy, based in St Louis, was governor-general of all French possessions in America. In 1751 another Franco-Irishman, Chevalier McCarthy, 'was Commondant of the French Settlement of the Illinois Territory, and in 1769 . . . Alexander O'Reilly had command under the Spanish'. Irish immigrants became major real-estate owners in St Louis early on. The city's first newspaper, the *Missouri Gazette*, was founded by Joseph Charless, a native of West Meath, in 1808, and another Irishman, John Mullanphy, who arrived in 1804, was the town's first millionaire. Jerimiah Conners, who arrived the year after Mullanphy, came to own a sizable section of the city centre and in 1820 donated some of that land to the Catholic Church for the founding of St Louis University.[24]

In his *St Louis: A Concise History* (1992), William Faherty notes that the Famine Irish settled on the city's near-north side, 'around St Patrick's church at Sixth and Biddle'. By the Civil War the immigrant Irish population had spread west of Twelfth Street, between Mullanphy and O'Fallon Streets, to an area that took on the name 'Kerry Patch'.[25] The city had a thriving Irish nationalist circle as well – Philip Coyne, Henry O'Clarence McCarthy and Bernard Doran Killian being among its most notable Fenian figures. Before the war, Killian was editor of the St Louis Catholic newspaper, the *Western Banner*, prior to becoming a prime mover in the Fenian Brotherhood. He would negotiate the release of John Mitchel from a Union prison in 1865.[26] When McCarthy's funeral was held in the city in 1865, a crowd estimated as high as 20,000 jammed Mozart Hall, despite the fact that Peter Kenrick, St Louis' powerful, Dublin-born Archbishop, had forbidden the Fenian McCarthy's interment in Calvary Cemetery.[27]

As early as April 1861, Colonel James Mulligan's 23rd Illinois, the Chicago 'Irish Brigade', was bivouacked and drilling in northern Missouri and would see bloody action in the battle of Lexington, Missouri, before the year was out. Mulligan and Sweeny were only two of the many Irish nationalists – Meagher, Corcoran and O'Mahony among them – drawn into American military service around this time, and Mulligan's regiment was but one of numerous such Irish units, the most famous of them being Colonel Corcoran's New York Legion, made up of the state's 155th, 164th, 170th and 182nd Infantry regiments. Some of the others were the 9th Massachusetts, 37th and 42nd New York, the 17th Wisconsin, the 17th Michigan and the 10th Ohio. In addition: 'There were seven distinct companies of Irish in the Confederate armies. The most famous of these were Company E of the 2nd Tennessee, a company in the 6th Alabama, and one recruited at Augusta Georgia'.[28]

Ultimately, 180,000 Irish-born young men would enter the fray, and this figure does not include first generation Irish-Americans, of which General

Sheridan and Colonel Mulligan, for example, were two. Members of Irish units such as 'The Phoenix Brigade' and 'The Emmet Guards' were filled with military enthusiasm as war became more certain; they met, paraded and drilled now 'in order to prepare for the day of reckoning with their ancient foe'.[29] At the outbreak of the Civil War they were lured by the opportunity of seeing action and gaining real military experience that later, they believed, would redound to the benefit of Ireland. This motivation would be evident, for instance, toward the end of the war in the iconography of the Fenian bonds issued by the American Brotherhood. William D'Arcy, who in the 1940s owned a number of these now 'collectible' bonds, describes them:

> A picture in the center depicts Erin pointing with her left hand to a sword lying on the ground. A [US] Union soldier is kneeling to take the sword and depart for Ireland, which is shown in the background. A harp and Irish wolfhound complete the picture, which is flanked by pictures of Emmet, Wolf Tone, and other Irish heros.[30]

At first, John O'Mahony had reservations about Fenian members rushing to enlist, arguing that the first enemies Union recruits were likely to encounter would be other Irishmen in the Southern ranks.

> Finding himself powerless to stop the rising Irish enlistment [however], he made an adroit about-face and discovered the silver lining. Forthcoming battles would serve as the training ground upon which Irish generals, captains, sergeants, corporals, and privates could learn the art of war in preparation for the fight for Irish freedom . . . With the echoes of Fort Sumter still reverberating . . . Irish soldiers of the 69th New York marched off along the narrow, tenement-lined streets of the city . . . The exultant crowds witnessed a sight not seen for centuries: an Irish Army going to war . . . If you were one of the paid informers posted along the route that afternoon, the notes you jotted down were scarcely comforting to your paymasters . . . in Canada or back in Britain.[31]

Like O'Mahony, Meagher was doubtful about the war at its outset. But, utilizing office space in the same New York building where the recently founded Fenian Brotherhood was housed, he remarked to his friend, Michael Cavanaugh, another former Young Irelander, the double service that American-Irish troops would be serving in the coming war: 'I hold that if only one in ten come back when this war is over, the military experience gained by that one will be of more service in the fight for Ireland's freedom than would be that of the entire ten as they are now'.[32]

Like just about everyone else in the United States at the time, Meagher failed to foresee the years of 'patriotic gore' – to use Edmund Wilson's phrase – that lay ahead. The smooth bore musket previously used in battle was less than highly accurate at 100 yards. The standard-issue 1861-model Springfield rifle and spiralling conical Minié bullet soldiers would employ in the coming Civil

War would be deadly accurate at 300 yards and very effective at three times that.[33] Thus, as Thomas Keneally notes, Meagher probably thought that, speaking of one in ten surviving, he was rhetorically positing an unrealistically morbid scenario. But the enormity of the looming war would come close to the most pessimistic pre-war projections regarding loss of life.[34] Tom Sweeny, for example, very early in the war in Missouri, would be a participant in arguably the first major battle to bring home to people the murderous reality implicit in a new paradigm of warfare, one closer to the total war model to emerge in World War I than to anything preceding. An horrendous battle in Missouri, and a grim national epiphany, were in the offing.

When Sweeny arrived in St Louis it was a 'Casablanca' on the Mississippi, a city of political intrigues, turbulent factionalism and clandestine cabals, where rumours circulated with an electric rapidity. This Union state had a significant, though less than majority, pro-Southern population as well as two Confederate states bordering it on the south. More importantly, Claiborne Jackson, Missouri's governor and a politician of strongly Southern sympathies, held the power to muster and command a state guard outside federal government control.[35] Missouri's quasi-Southern identity was due mainly to its instituted slavery going back to the Compromise of 1820, and to St Louis' Mississippi River location and commerce, oriented southward. In the latter respect the city was not all that unlike New York, however, which, early on, was home to a good deal of pro-Southern sentiment – 'New York was the great cotton-handling port of America, and its merchants had [an] affection for and tolerance of the South'.[36]

The Irish-German demographics and cultural mix typifying St Louis extended north as well to the towns, influenced by St Louis, on the Mississippi western shore north of Hannibal. Eugene Ware, who grew up in that area and who later wrote about the Missouri campaign in which he sometimes served under General Sweeny, provides valuable images of the German and Irish culture and political atmosphere in this area of Iowa 'up river' from St Louis – Keokuck, Burlington, Davenport – just before the Civil War. It was from here that a large portion of the Union army in Missouri would be drawn in the first two years of the national conflict:

> The style of the up-river architecture was derived from St Louis . . . My first recollection of political discussion was upon the right and wrong of the Mexican War . . . The sugar of the day was brown sugar that came up in steamboats from Louisiana in hogsheads . . . The boys who were always playing on the wharf . . . ate the refuse sugar scraped from the sides of these hogsheads and fought each other with the stalks of cane. I remember on one of these occasions getting into a fight and being called an 'Abolishionist' . . . I went to my father and asked him what an 'Abolishionist' was, and was duly informed . . .

> Two military companies existed in our town, one composed of Germans and the other of Irish. They were both fiercely pugnacious . . . [The Germans] had festivals and balls and literary exercises . . . They were, as a rule, a very high-grade class of citizens . . . The Irish, on the other hand, were coarser. They did not plant vineyards and have literary exercises. They were boisterous, and yet among them were some very notable people . . . The Germans had their Turner Halls and Turner exercises, and they were all athletes. They used to have gardens where they had their speaking . . . It was about all that a man's life was worth to disturb one of these occasions. I remember one time, in an ill-advised moment, that I joined as a boy a party of Irish yeomanry who thought it would be a good idea to go down and break up one of the exercises. After having been thrown over a high-board fence, I was never guilty again of that indiscretion.[37]

As war approached, a great deal hung immediately in the balance in Missouri. If it fell to the Confederacy, the industrially weak South would gain an invaluable industrial centre in St Louis, the Union's border on the Mississippi west bank would move north to Iowa, the South's left flank would be greatly buttressed, and control of much of the Mississippi River system would essentially be in Confederate hands. It was a critical circumstance in which Tom Sweeny would play a major role. Indeed the Missouri campaign for the most part of which he was Second in Command to Lyon, would be the context for some of his most impressive military achievements. What is more, his Missouri experience and his relationship with General Nathaniel Lyon may well have helped shape and reinforce the uncompromising, direct-action military/political thinking he brought to the Fenian cause five years later.

In late January 1861, having been promoted to the rank of captain, he was provided with some forty recruits and ordered to assume command of the military guard at the St Louis Arsenal, a fifty-six acre complex on the river just southeast of where the Anheuser-Busch home office and brewery stand today. The only arsenal west of the Alleghenies, it held an immense store of ordnance – 60,000 stands of arms, forty artillery pieces, 1,500,000 ball cartridges and 90,000 pounds of powder, as well as extensive gunsmithing machinery for the assembly, repair, alteration and rifling of firearms. Although it housed this formidable stock of weaponry and explosives, the installation's twenty-two buildings had in peacetime been manned by a skeleton crew – a handful of military personnel and a few civilian workers, a crew increased, but not very dramatically given the threat, by Sweeny's contingent.[38] Federal arsenals throughout the South had recently been seized by the Confederates, and they would obviously have designs on this key one at St Louis if they could see their way clear.

In fact, the local secessionist fifth column saw capture of this arsenal south of the city's centre as the first item on its agenda, while the local 'safety committee' of Union loyalists, organized and led by the determined and aggressive US congressman Frank Blair, were doing their best, in a charged political climate, to prevent such a contingency. Blair, whose father, Francis

Preston Blair, was a powerful Washington Republican, tirelessly worked the city's Union ward clubs, German-American community clubs, and so on, to create an opposition force to the 'Minute Men', the St Louis secessionist organization. On 8 January 1861, in the course of his vigilant activity, Blair acquired a copy of a communication from the secessionist militia leader, Daniel M. Frost, to his subordinates which ordered them to be on the alert for an event that would be signalled by the ringing of church bells in the city. On hearing this summons, the militia members were to gather at their headquarters and await further orders. Blair's investigation revealed that the bells to be rung were those in Catholic churches and that the alarm responsibility lay with the Irish cohort among the secessionist Minute Men. With a view to thwarting the plot, Blair sought out Catholic Archbishop Kenrick.[39] Though the arch-Confederate Father John Bannon, a prominent and influential St Louis priest, was probably the prime mover in the bell arrangement, there were plentiful rumours about town that Kenrick himself had secessionist sympathies. He was a strong-willed, micro-managing administrator, and it is unlikely that subordinate Catholic clergy would have countenanced the bell plot without his certain consent.

Regarding ethnic political profiles at the time, Eugene Ware, harkening back to 1856 and the regional attitudes toward slavery then prevailing, recalled:

> It seems to me upon the slavery question the Germans and the Irish took opposite sides, although afterwards, when the war broke out, it was not so. But in 1856, my recollection is that the Germans were against slavery and the Irish were adherents to the Democratic party, and it used to be said that the Democratic party in New Orleans was composed very largely of the Irish who had settled there. Afterward they formed a noted portion of the Confederate army.[40]

The Confederate element among St Louis Irish Catholics, most of whom were Democrats, was in fact fairly extensive. Bernard Killian, editor of the Catholic *Western Banner*, has already been mentioned; his concerted opposition as a Fenian to Sweeny in 1865–66 may well have stemmed from a residual resentment of Sweeny's role as an anti-secessionist federal enforcer in the city in 1861. Joseph Kelly, an Irish immigrant and St Louis grocer, headed one of the secessionist militia units in the city, 'Kelly's Irish Brigade', which sang a song to the tune of 'Hail Columbia' addressing Irish Union loyalists:

> You call us rebels and traitors, but yourselves have thrown off that name of late.
> You were called it by the English invaders at home in seventeen ninety-eight . . .
>
> You dare not call us invaders, 'tis but state rights and liberties we ask;
> And Missouri, we ever will defend her, no matter how hard be the task.[41]

When the war came about, Captain Patrick Conniff was a famous St Louis Irish Confederate, as was Captain Arthur McCoy – later of Shelby's cavalry –

who, as a member of the Minute Men, climbed the Federal courthouse in St Louis and took down the US flag, replacing it with the Missouri state flag. Father Bannon was a native of Roscommon and a Maynooth graduate who served as assistant pastor of the St Louis Cathedral under the pastor, Patrick J. Ryan, himself later a spiritual adviser to Confederate POWs in St Louis-area Union prisons. Bannon joined the rebel army and was sent to Ireland later in the war to try to stem the flow of Irish emigrants enlisting in the Union army. Father Abram J. Ryan was another St Louis secessionist and a writer during the war of poetry in praise of the Confederacy.[42]

Consequently, Blair's astute political strategizing, aided by his considerable influence in Washington may, in fact, have extended to considering Sweeny's being Irish-born as a plus for the arsenal command in the light of these secessionist activists in the city's Irish neighbourhoods and Catholic parishes. Indeed, William Riley Brooksher suggests that Sweeny was assigned to Jefferson Barracks in the first place 'in the hope that he could offset the influence the Minute Men had with his [Irish] countrymen'.[43] Certainly there was a concerted effort to recruit the St Louis and up-river-area Irish into the Union army and away from Democrat-Confederate identity. The highly regarded 8th Missouri US Infantry was recruited in St Louis while Sweeny was there. And between 12 June and 14 August 1861, 'over 600 Irish boatmen and deck hands left the St Louis riverfront to fight for the [Union] under the command of Captain Morgan L. Smith'.[44]

The US arsenal's defence largely devolved upon Sweeny during the brief, especially difficult, emergency period prior to the installation's being sufficiently manned. Major William H. Bell, officially in charge of the facility before Sweeny, was one of those wavering army officers in what was a wavering, contested city, and Sweeny found himself having to function as the conspicuous regular army, Federal representative there. A North-Carolinian by birth, Bell was politically conflicted, and, when Governor Jackson sent state militia General Daniel M. Frost to visit him, Frost was able to convince Bell that state sovereignty laws gave Missouri the right to claim the arsenal, and Bell agreed not to defend the place if state authorities should lay claim to it.

An encounter that occurred as Sweeny, newly arrived in town, was registering at a hotel, gave him an indication of the complexity of the mixed allegiances prevalent in the city and the complicated environment in which he had arrived. A local politician, Nathaniel C. McKay, greeted him enthusiastically in the hotel lobby and encouraged him to get to the arsenal as soon as possible the next morning in order to replace the present officer on duty there, McKay's own son-in-law, Lieutenant W.G. Robinson, of whom McKay was suspicious. Robinson was a southerner, and McKay did not trust him to protect the arsenal against rebel intrigues. When Sweeny did show up the next morning, he was surprised when the suspect Robinson rather agreeably filled out the required paperwork to turn the garrison over to him and then wrote out his own resignation from the Federal army in order to accept a commission in the army of the Confederacy.[45]

Major Bell remained in place, however, and Sweeny, holed up in the arsenal complex with his recruit contingent, was thus undermined in his authority and in his intention to defend the site. He could only drill his small unit, fortify and wait. On 3 March he wrote to his daughter Sarah from the arsenal:

> I would have answered your letter sooner, but I've met with an accident that prevented my using my pen for the last ten or twelve days without great pain. While superintending the firing of my men at target practice, a splinter from a rock behind the target struck me on the hand and hurt me severely, but it is now almost entirely well. Just as I was recovering from the effects of the injury . . . we had small pox break out among our men and we all had to get vaccinated. My arm is quite sore yet, but not sufficiently so to prevent me using my hand.[46]

A further indication of the many intrigues abroad in St Louis at the time is the fact that a federal spy had been inserted into the small unit of recruits provided for Captain Sweeny for the defence of the arsenal. He appeared on the recruit roster as 'Spenser Kellogg'. Only later that year in Springfield, Missouri, did Sweeny learn, from the young man himself, the recruit's real name and identity: his name was in fact Brown and he was a son of John Brown the abolitionist zealot. 'So well did he play his part', Sweeny later remarked, 'that I suspected him of being a *rebel* spy and watched him closely'.[47]

The secessionists finally began to make moves by way of testing Sweeny. He had put his men on full alert and ordered that no one be allowed to enter the facility, but his small squad would prove no match for the kind of state militia forces the governor could bring to bear against them if he chose to. The pro-secessionist group felt that they could therefore intimidate a mere captain and take the arsenal before Washington, frantically trying to reinforce arsenals and other key sites country-wide, could get around to significantly securing this one. Sweeny was at his best in such situations, however; he had become a past master at games of bravado, facing down superior force during his desert years. So when secessionist city leaders sent George Croghan, the son of 1812 hero Colonel George Croghan, to the federal arsenal to discuss matters with Sweeny, and, they hoped, to back him down, their scheme did not work. After some cordial small talk as the two officers walked on the grounds of the facility, Croghan suggested that Sweeny would, of course, have to surrender the facility forthwith in the face of overwhelming military superiority – 3,000 militia against the arsenal's paltry contingent. When he became aware that the visit was thus not the friendly one Croghan had pretended it to be, Sweeny's answer was that he had 90,000 pounds of powder in the magazine, and that rather than surrender the arsenal he would 'blow it to hell first'. He later wrote that the threat was so clear that he stayed up for several nights anticipating an attack

> . . . and I am satisfied that the only reason for not making the attack was the belief that it was my intention to blow up the place; which, indeed, I had determined to do, rather than permit it to fall into their hands.[48]

He, meanwhile, had to worry as well about fatherly obligations and attempt to keep his hand in regarding his children's upbringing. He wrote the following to his daughter Sarah from the arsenal on 22 March 1861. Not in this nor in any other extant letters, it might be noted, does he mention the children's late mother – probably evidence of his enduring grief.

> My Dear Child,
> I should have answered your kind and affectionate letter of the 10th sooner, but I have been kept busy on a General Court Martial for the last two weeks at Jefferson Barracks, which is about ten miles from here. We had to go down there every morning and come back in the evening, as long as the court remained in session, besides attending to the duties of my company at the post, so you may perceive I had very little leisure time to do anything . . . Cousin Mary Kilby says in her letter that Charley's cough was very bad, and that the doctor thought he must have had whooping cough. I hope the poor child has entirely recovered before this . . . I suppose you will be thinking of making a visit to Brooklyn, to see the folks there. I don't think it would be advisable to go before your summer clothes were prepared. I have written to cousin Mary to have your outfit ready before starting, and have promised to send her means to do so in my next letter . . . I enclose two gold dollars, which you must not spend foolishly, my daughter, as I may not have the opportunity of sending again for some time . . . The first thing you must purchase are writing materials, and endeavor to keep them in proper condition. If I find that you make much improvement in your writing and composition hereafter, it will be a strong inducement to me to be punctual in sending you funds from time to time. You must take more time to write your letters, as nothing can be done *well* in a hurry, and I would rather not receive a letter at all than get one all blotted, scratched, and carelessly written. Give my love to all, and kiss Fanny and Charley for me; and keep a dozen for yourself.
>
> Your Affectionate Father,
> T.W. Sweeny[49]

On 6 February, the previously mentioned reinforcements arrived to secure the arsenal and Jefferson Barracks – 350 members of the 2nd Infantry under the command of the aloof, martinet Captain Lyon, who would within the year come to be known in the North as 'the saviour of Missouri for the Union'. In short order 250 more US Army regulars arrived from Kentucky, bringing the arsenal's protective force up to par. Sweeny's assiduous defence of the arsenal prior to Lyon's arrival in the city set the tone for the Federal campaign in Missouri generally. He would fit in well given Lyon's and Blair's aggressive, straight-ahead tactics, and Lyon and Sweeny got along suprisingly nicely since, as a rule, Lyon was not noted for getting along especially well with anybody. In fact, as earlier mentioned, he and Sweeny had had a confrontation during the 2nd Infantry's sea journey to California years before, and Lyon had been a party to charges being brought against Sweeny. Matters were patched up in the mid-50s, however, when the two officers were in Nebraska Territory and Lyon was himself under a cloud due to charges brought against him by a superior officer. Sweeny wrote his wife from Nebraska at the time:

> Lyon who is in command of 'B' company, is out of arrest at present, but the charges still hang over him, and he is liable to be tried at any time on them. He now has an opportunity of tasting some of the bitter waters of persecution that he at one time helped to force down my throat. But thank God! I can return him a good for evil: and instead of exhulting in his misfortunes, I have done everything in my power to make him forget what has passed, and to prove my sincere friendship, for which he seems to be truly grateful.[50]

This burial of the hatchet accomplished up along the Platte would prove valuable to the Union cause in Missouri, permitting the two officers to coordinate their efforts effectively in a time of uncertainty. Their combined aggressiveness on the war's western frontier would stand in sharp contrast to the reluctant and disinclined behaviour of General McClellan and his army on the eastern front during the same early stage of the war, and locally with the irresolution and foot dragging of the Union commander, General Harney, under whom both Sweeny and Lyon had served during the Sioux Expedition. No longer the dauntless authoritarian he had been when things were uncomplicated and he could come down with a vengeance on Irish immigrants and Indians, Harney was now hesitant in every direction.

A native of Tennessee who had married into the wealthy, Irish-American Mullanphy family, Confederate sympathizers, Harney could not bring himself to lay down the law to his many aristocratic friends and relatives in the city who were now lined up on the Southern side. 'As Harney fussed and did nothing, the deteriorating situation in the city was causing Lyon great anxiety'.[51] Sweeny and the rest of the Union officer corps in St Louis, already in a confusing and threatening situation, now found themselves serving under a commander who seemed dangerously ineffectual as regards rebel advances in the city. Harney on board or not, the Federal officers began to circle the wagons. The month of March, Sweeny wrote, 'was devoted to fortifying our position, strengthening it in every possible way'.[52] When Fort Sumter came under Confederate barrage on 12 April 1861, General Frost in Missouri became yet more overt in his secessionist activities, and a number of his military subordinates resigned as a result.

> In St Louis the effects of Fort Sumter were cataclysmic. Secessionist and Union flags flew all over the city – in some cases directly across the street from one other . . . [On 12 April] Lyon prepared furiously for his, and the secessionists', next moves. At 11:00 p.m. he called together only his most trusted subordinates – Captain Thomas Sweeny, Rufus Saxton, and Albert Tracy – for a secret meeting at his quarters.[53]

Byzantine intrigues were in full swing, and Lyon ordered round-the-clock patrols at the arsenal as the situation became yet more edgy, and positions grew ever more rigid. When, on 15 April, Lincoln issued an order for 75,000 troops, each loyal state to provide a given quota for the federal force, the order was rebuffed by the governor's office in Jefferson City. Jackson's reply of 17 April 1861 left no doubt about where the sitting Missouri authority stood; he characterized Lincoln's request as 'illegal, unconstitutional, and revolutionary in its objects, inhuman and diabolical' and declared he would not obey it.[54]

Lincoln, the War Department and some of the Union officer corps on site began to set up what was in effect a shadow military structure in St Louis, one circumventing Harney, in which Lyon was emerging as the *de facto* commander. A directive of 30 April 1861 signed by Lincoln and addressed to Lyon, no copy to Harney, called upon Lyon to enroll 10,000 men in the military service on an emergency basis and mentioned their employment to enforce martial law if need be.[55] These troops were to be over and above the nationwide enlistment quota already called for, regarding which call Sweeny observed: 'Soon after the president's call for 75,000 men, we commenced raising and mustering Missouri volunteers, by authority of the War Department, the Governor (Jackson) having refused the quota asked for. These were drilled incessantly'.[56] A major share of the responsibility for securing St Louis and preventing the Confederacy from gaining a quick foothold in the rest of the state thus fell by default to a small group of determined Union officers, Sweeny among them playing no small part – powerfully backed by the rigorously Unionist Republican congressman Blair in Washington. Blair returned to St Louis on 17 April with War Department orders for the issuance of 5,000 stands of arms to prospective Union enlistees. Lyon, however, pointed out to him that Harney had refused more enlistees. The quasi-mutiny against Harney was gathering force as it looked as if Missouri Union volunteers would have to cross the river to Illinois in order to enlist. Furthermore, when Harney ordered the patrols outside the arsenal discontinued, Blair visited him and told him frankly that he intended to work toward Harney's removal from command of the Department of the West – no idle threat coming from a congressman with Blair's connections in the Lincoln administration.[57]

The Missouri state guard, under the command of General Frost, had congregated meanwhile at various St Louis headquarters and marched on 6 May 1861 to the edge of the city where they set up, as per the Governor's orders, 'Camp Jackson' in open pasture land at Lindell Grove. Frost maintained this was merely the militia's annual summer encampment, but to Lyon, Blair, Sweeny and the other vigilant Unionists, this summer's bivouac was to be part of a move toward staking claim to the city, and Lyon lost no time in confronting the forces of insurrection. At another top secret meeting held in Lyon's St Louis quarters, on the evening of 8 May, with Sweeny, Blair and some others in attendance, it was decided that Camp Jackson should be seized and that the coup should occur while General Harney was away from the city – in Washington, in fact, pleading his case to be retained in his command position. Lyon was determined to neutralize the threat represented by Camp Jackson before Harney returned from Washington by train, having been – in the 'fog of war' perhaps – mysteriously reinstated by War Department authorities. On the very night of the meeting at Lyon's quarters, the sternwheeler *J.C. Swon* arrived on the St Louis river landing in the darkness, having travelled from Baton Rouge with crates of disguised military hardware taken from the federal arsenal at Louisiana city and intended for the St Louis anti-Union forces at Camp Jackson, to whom the material was directly delivered.[58] With his new authority however, Lyon undertook a series of preemptive strokes that stole the advantage from the secessionist forces and soon had them on the defensive. Lyon and Sweeny marched on the militia's suburban camp, Sweeny leading a core battalion of regulars with orders to attack the militia's artillery on the high ground beyond the camp should it open up on the Federal command. These regulars were Lyon's most reliable forces in this crisis, as Civil War historians William Piston and Richard Hatcher note, 'two companies of the Second US Infantry . . . commanded by an old friend, Captain Thomas W. Sweeny, a native of Ireland . . . If Sweeny's soldiers matched the national pattern, two thirds of them were either German or Irish by birth'.[59]

As the atmosphere became increasingly highly charged, Sweeny ordered his troops, as they approached the militia encampment, to move their cartridge boxes around on their belts in case shooting began.[60] Lyon wrote Frost a note calling for the camp's immediate surrender, to which Frost sent an indignant reply remarking the effrontery of Lyon's order, a reply the latter refused to accept, demanding instead capitulation within ten minutes. Taken aback by the sudden siege of his camp, Frost was unprepared – the weapons brought by the *J.C. Swon* were still crated – and he was compelled to send Lyon a hastily written note concluding: 'I am wholly unprepared to defend my command from this unwarranted attack, and shall, therefore, be forced to comply with your demand'.[61]

When Lyon received this communication from Frost's messenger, he turned to Sweeny as soon as the courier had departed and, climbing down from his horse, said, 'Sweeny, they surrender'. However, no sooner had he dismounted, than a horse belonging to one of his officers acted up, one of its kicks catching Lyon in the abdomen.[62] The moment could not have been more awkward since there was no time to be spared in accomplishing the capitulation. It would be a tricky matter at best; military surrenders involve fine details, and this one would have to be carried out in an exceptionally difficult atmosphere – surrounded by crowds of citizens no small number of whom were Southern partisans. The Federal commander meanwhile lay unconscious on the ground, apparently seriously injured. But this was another one of those improvisational situations for which the one-armed Irish officer second in command had a flair:

> At this inopportune moment, Frost's adjutant, Lt. William Wood, rode up with another message from his commander. Thinking quickly, Sweeny headed off Wood before he could see the stricken federal commander. He directed that the message be placed with him and assured Wood that he would see that it got to Lyon, who was at the moment 'occupied'. Wood inquired

> about the government weapons, the mode of evacuation, and whether militia officers would be allowed to retain their sidearms. Sweeny replied that the officers could retain their sidearms, that the government property would be confiscated, and that his troops would collect and guard all other private property. Wood left without knowing that Lyon lay incapacitated only a few yards away.[63]

When sufficiently recovered, Lyon was pleased to learn of Sweeny's alert handling of matters. He ordered Sweeny and his regulars to take control of Camp Jackson while he himself took charge of marching the militia captives east through the city to the arsenal. 'Camp Jackson was taken possession of', Lyon wrote, 'by two regiments of volunteers and two companies of regulars, under the command of Captain Sweeny, who remained in possession all night, bringing the entire camp equipage and munitions of war into the arsenal this morning'.[64] The orders were fortunate for Sweeny – just as he had been fortunate not to have been present at the Ash Hollow Indian slaughter, he would not now be involved in another infamous and controversial incident, one witnessed by William Tecumsah Sherman, then a civilian and president of the 5th Street Railroad in St Louis, who made his way carefully along Locust Street toward the captured Camp Jackson:

> As he listened to the sound of musketry and cannon fire from the direction of Camp Jackson . . . his seven-year-old son Willie tagged along. Earlier, Sherman's boarders, Charles Ewing and John Hunter, had urged him to join them in going out to the camp to 'see the fun', But he had declined, noting that in case of conflict the by-standers were more likely to be killed than the men engaged. Still, he remained curious to know what was happening in the standoff . . . As Sherman and his son approached Olive St a man came running toward them yelling, 'They've surrendered! They've surrendered!' On hearing that, Sherman moved farther along and soon came abreast of Lindell's Grove. There he saw a regiment of Union volunteers guarding a group of Camp Jackson prisoners, while a crowd . . . milled about. A band played martial music, and on-lookers cheered and taunted the troops and prisoners. A few minutes later, as the military column began moving toward the center of the city, a shot rang out, and then more, and Sherman could hear the balls cutting through the trees above his head . . . When Sherman saw troops reloading their weapons, he grabbed the boy and dove with him into a gully. They remained there until the shooting stopped, then arose unhurt. Others did not. At least twenty-eight people, including women and children, lay dead or dying.[65]

What was immediately termed the 'Camp Jackson Massacre' had profound repercussions. Among other things, it strengthened sympathy for the Confederacy and increased Governor Jackson's influence as well as leading to the creation of an independent Missouri state guard, a major portion of the Southern forces that would fight at the ultimate Missouri battle at Wilson's Creek.[66] On 12 June,

Governor Jackson issued a proclamation at Jefferson City that drew the state's rights line emphatically and amounted to a declaration of war:

> A series of unprovoked and unparalleled outrages have been inflicted on the peace and dignity of this Commonwealth, and upon the rights and liberties of its people, by wicked and unprincipled men, professing to act under the authority of the United States Government; the solemn enactments of your legislature have been nullified, your volunteer soldiers have been taken prisoners, your commerce with your sister states has been suspended, your trade with your own fellow-citizens has been and is subjected to increasing control of an armed soldiery, peaceful citizens have been imprisoned without warrant of law . . .
>
> Fellow citizens, all our efforts toward conciliation have failed. We can hope for nothing from the justice or moderation of the agents of the Federal Government in this State . . . [I] issue this proclamation, calling the militia of this state, to the number of 50,000, into active service of the state . . . [I]t is . . . my duty to advise you that your first allegiance is due to your own state, and that you are under no obligation whatever to obey the unconstitutional edicts of the military despotism which has introduced itself at Washington.[67]

Lyon, with his new authority, had seized Camp Jackson independently of General Harney. Harney, on his return to St Louis resumed his command duties and passed on Frost's outraged protests to Washington without offering any personal supporting arguments for Lyon and Sweeny's seizure of the militia camp. Things had come to a head, and it is a reflection of the irregularity of matters at this point that Lyon, only a captain, wrote an exceptional report on 12 May 1861 to the adjutant general in Washington, essentially calling for the removal of his suspect commanding officer, a general:

> It is with great delicacy and hesitancy that I take the liberty to observe that the energetic and necessary measures of day before yesterday [Camp Jackson seizure], require persevering and consistent exertion to [anticipate] . . . measures of hostility against the General Government, and that the authority of General Harney under these circumstances embarrasses, in the most painful manner, the execution of the plans I had contemplated, and upon which the safety and welfare of the government . . . so much depend.[68]

After months of inaction on the part of the War Department, on 30 May a federal government representative went to General Harney's home in St Louis and delivered what was an official and conclusive dismissal from his position in command of the Department of the West.[69] This was not only in response to Lyon's appeal but no doubt even more to Frank Blair's concerted efforts – Lyon had been writing to him in Washington.

Lincoln promoted the red-haired, red-bearded Lyon to brigadier general of volunteers in command of Union troops in Missouri, and when the officers of the 1st Unionist regiment of St Louis, mustered in accord with Lyon's new orders from the War Department, were called upon to elect a leader, the unanimous choice was Sweeny. Like Lyon, he was elected brigadier general of volunteers for the ensuing Missouri campaign while retaining his rank of captain in the regular army. The rank was largely a sign of his popularity among the ordinary soldiers owing to his good cheer and gregariousness which contrasted with – and complemented – the stern, abstract, aloofness of General Lyon. In his enlisted man's memoir of service in Missouri, Eugene Ware describes Lyon as 'a small man, lean, active and sleepless. He had a look of incredulity . . . He looked like an eccentric man, like an educated "crank" . . . There was something about his eyes that made me think they did not match . . . He was not a man that had . . . poise'.[70] Piston and Hatcher write of Lyon that, given his personality and obsessions, 'anyone well acquainted with the new officer [in St Louis] . . . might have considered him particularly unsuited to cooperate in an emergency with imperfectly disciplined volunteers'.[71] Ware describes Sweeny, on the other hand, as, with his one arm, 'a picturesque sight on a horse . . . a typical Irishman, full of fun, strict in discipline, and with a kind word for everybody. We all liked him very much'.[72]

Similar comments regarding Sweeny's brave spirit and infectious good-naturedness were commonly forthcoming from enlisted men who served with him. He was able to calm and motivate volunteer troops and to work well with whatever material he had at hand, being rough-and-ready and adaptable in times and contexts that called for just that. William R. Brooksher describes him as 'irrepressible';[73] and Jay Monaghan in his *Civil War on the Western Border* (1995) remarks, as did Ware, on the contrast between Lyon, a West-Pointer, and Sweeny, noting at the same time a problem that plagued Sweeny's army career and no doubt played a part in some of Sweeny's personal skirmishes – Monaghan mentions the clashes with Heintzelman, for example:

> Although Sweeny was a regular army man, West Pointers looked on him with condescension, because he had risen from the ranks . . . Sweeny lacked the West Pointer's hauteur towards enlisted men. He even joked familiarly with them in his Irish brogue. Volunteers loved him for this and because he pinned his empty sleeve on his brass-buttoned breast in the Napoleonic fashion approved for military photographs, then, with his stub, twitched the sleeve comically.[74]

NOTES

1. James Peckham, *General Nathaniel Lyon and Missouri in 1861* (New York, 1866), p.54.
2. General Sweeny's: 'A Museum of Civil War History': www.civilwarmuseum.com /sweenyartifacts.html (12 September 2004). Founded forty years ago by Thomas Sweeney, M.D. of Springfield, the museum focuses on the Civil War west of the Mississippi.
3. Michael Ruddy, 'Here Comes that Damned Green Flag Again', *Civil War Times*, vol. 1 (2003), pp.32–40; freepages.geneology.rootsweb.com/~mruddy/GreenFlag1.htm (25 September 2004), p.6.

4. William M. Sweeny, letter to the *New York Sunday News*, 18 June 1893. Reprinted in Denieffe, *Personal Narrative*, pp.266–72.
5. D'Arcy, *The Fenian Movement*, pp.6–7.
6. Quoted in Joseph M. Hernon Jr., *Celts, Catholics and Copperheads: Ireland Views the American Civil War* (Columbus, OH, 1968), p.52.
7. Adams, *General William S. Harney*, pp.120–1.
8. Ibid.
9. Augustus Myers, *Ten Years in the Ranks of the US Army* (New York, 1914), pp.54–61. Myers describes Sweeny's regiment's journey west in some detail, and his account of the cholera epidemic at Leavenworth and the dismal army medical care in the face of it is a vivid one.
10. Quoted in Adams, *General William S. Harney*, p.132.
11. 'He Fought the Indians: a Sketch of the Career of General Sweeny', *Brooklyn Times*, 17 January 1891. Thomas William Sweeny Papers, Huntington Library, San Marino, California.
12. Myers, *Ten Years in the Ranks*, p.107.
13. Thomas William Sweeny Papers, Huntington Library, San Marino, California (emphasis added).
14. Coyer, 'Hero of the Armless Sleeve', p.169. Sweeny's recurrent assignments to New York recruitment in all probability reflected his value as an officer in recruiting arriving Irish immigrants in whom the Army recognized a promising pool of prospective enlistees.
15. Thomas William Sweeny Papers, Huntington Library, San Marino, California.
16. Ibid.
17. Ibid.
18. Ibid.
19. Fort Pierre, 1 December 1855. Thomas William Sweeny Papers, Huntington Library, San Marino, California. I have not been able to find this poem in searches; it may be original, but more likely Sweeny inserted his wife's name into the last line of an existing poem.
20. Thomas William Sweeny Papers, Huntington Library, San Marino, California.
21. Ibid.
22. Ibid.
23. *North America* [1862] (Baltimore, MD, 1968) p.192.
24. Francis J. Ward, 'Early Irish in St Louis, Missouri', *Journal of the American Irish Historical Society*, 6 (1906), pp.46–50.
25. William B. Faherty, *St Louis: A Concise History* (St Louis, MO, 1992), p.49. 'Parnell Street', near the central city area today, is one remnant of the former Irish presence there.
26. Coyne and Killian were active in the O'Mahony wing of the Brotherhood. Coyne was a Southern sympathizer during the war (D'Arcy, *The Fenian Movement*, p.44) and Bernard Killian, later a major figure in the movement nationally, was active in Irish circles in St Louis as early as 1860 (D'Arcy, *The Fenian Movement*, p.78n.).
27. See Jack Morgan, '"The Dust of Maynooth": Fenian Funeral as Political Theater – St Louis, 1865', *New Hibernia Review*, 2, 4 (1998), pp.24–37.
28. Mabel Gregory Walker, *The Fenian Movement* (Colorado Springs, CO, 1969), pp.18–19.
29. D'Arcy, *The Fenian Movement*, p.16.
30. Ibid. pp.112–13n.
31. Ruddy, 'An Irish Army in America', *Civil War Times*, 41 (2003) pp.32–40.
32. Thomas Keneally, *The Great Shame and the Triumph of Irish in the English-Speaking World* (New York, 1998), p.320.
33. Arthur C. Danto, 'Gettysburg', *Grand Street*, 6, 3 (1987), pp.99–101.
34. Keneally, *Great Shame*, p.320.

35. A chapter title in William Garrett Piston and Richard W. Hatcher, Wilson's Creek: *The Second Battle of the Civil War and the Men who Fought it* (Chapel Hill, NC, 2000), sums up well this situation: 'Nothing was clear-cut, it was simply Missouri'.
36. Keneally, *Great Shame*, p.317.
37. Eugene F. Ware, *The Lyon Campaign in Missouri and the History of the 1st Iowa Infantry,* (Topeka, KS, 1907), pp.2–4.
38. Peckham, *General Nathaniel Lyon*, pp.49–53; Christopher Phillips, *Damned Yankee: The Life of General Nathaniel Lyon* (Columbia, MO, 1990), pp.138–140; William Riley Brooksher, *Bloody Hill: The Civil War Battle of Wilson's Creek (Washington, DC, 1995)*, pp.32–37.
39. Brooksher, *Bloody Hill*, p.34.
40. Ware, *Lyon Campaign*, p.39.
41. 'Civil War Music on the Western Border'. www. bartonpara.com/civilwar/index.html> (18 August 2004).
42. 'Father John Bannon and St Louis Irish Confederates'. www.sterlingprice145.org/kelly.htm (8 July 2004). Regarding the participation of St Louis Irish on the Confederate side during the war *see* Phillip Thomas Tucker, *The South's Finest: The First Missouri Confederate Brigade from Pea Ridge to Vicksburg* (Washington, DC, 1993). Also by Tucker: *Westerners in Gray* (Jefferson, NC, 1995), pp.18–28. And see William Barnaby Faherty's biography of John Bannon, *Exile in Erin: A Confederate Chaplain's Story*: *The Life of Father John B. Bannon* (St Louis, MO, 2002).
43. Brooksher, *Bloody Hill,* p.34.
44. 'Brief History: 8th Missouri Volunteer Infantry'. members.aol.com/Infantry8thmo/htmhistory.html (10 July 2004).
45. Sweeny, interviewed by James Edward Kelly, 16 January 1886, J.E. Kelly Papers, New York Historical Society. (Hereafter citied as Kelly, TWS interview, January 1886.) This is not a formal interview but merely some notes handwritten by Kelly after an afternoon stroll and talk with Sweeny. An Irish-American sculptor, Kelly did sketches of remarkable incidents in the experience of famous Civil War figures, sketches based on his own interviews with the persons involved. He was apparently planning to sketch a scene portraying Sweeny at Shiloh. Kelly's poem, 'Sweeny at Shiloh', is included in the Shiloh pages of the present book.
46. Thomas William Sweeny Papers, Huntington Library, San Marino, California.
47. Letter to his daughter Sarah from Iuka, Mississippi, 3 November 1863, ibid. In this same letter Sweeny writes that Brown was soon discharged 'and entered the gunboat service as Master's Mate, I think, and held that position when he was captured. The last time I saw him was at St Louis in the summer of 1862 . . . His mother wrote me a note while I was at the St Louis Arsenal, requesting a short leave of absence for her son, which I granted. Of course I didn't know who he was at the time. I was quite surprised to see an account of his execution as a spy in the papers'.
48. Kelly, TWS interview, January 1886.
49. Thomas William Sweeny Papers, Huntington Library, San Marino, California.
50. Sweeny, to his wife from Fort Pierre, 7 August 1855, Thomas William Sweeny Papers, Huntington Library, San Marino, California. Some recent historians, it should be noted, reject the whole idea of Lyon as saviour of the state from the Confederacy. They view him as having unnecessarily inflamed the bitter factionalism in Missouri to the point where compromise was impossible. As mentioned, however, forceful prosecution of the war in Missouri anticipated what became the going Union policy in the Civil War – that of Lincoln, Grant, Sherman, et al.
51. Brooksher, *Bloody Hill*, p.45.

52. TWS, Report to Adjutant General, in W. Sweeny, *Memoir*, p.9. In 1873, the adjutant general's office in Washington requested of all former Civil War generals a narrative of their service from 1861 forward. Sweeny's response is included in the William Sweeny *Memoir*. (Hereafter citied as TWS Report to Adjutant, 1873, W. Sweeny, *Memoir*).
53. Phillips, *Damned Yankee*, pp.156–8.
54. Brooksher, *Bloody Hill*, pp.41–2.
55. US War Department, *The War of the Rebellion: A Compilation of the Official records of the Union and Confederate Armies*, 128 vols (Washington, DC, 1881), vol.1, p.675. (All citations are from series 1.) Hereafter, citation form using this example will refer to volume and page thus: *OR*, 1, p.675.
56. TWS Report to Adjutant, 1873, W. Sweeny, *Memoir*, p.9.
57. Phillips, *Damned Yankee*, p.159–60.
58. Ibid., p.181.
59. Piston and Hatcher, *Wilson's Creek*, p.35.
60. Phillips, *Damned Yankee*, p.188.
61. Ibid., p.189
62. Ibid., pp.151–2.
63. Ibid. pp.189–90.
64. *OR*, 3, p.5.
65. Adams, *General William S. Harney*, pp.215–16.
66. Piston and Hatcher, *Wilson's Creek*, pp.36–7.
67. Christopher Phillips, *Missouri's Confederate: Claiborne Fox Jackson and the Creation of Southern Identity in the Border West* (Columbia, MO, 2000), p.259.
68. *OR*, 3, p.9.
69. Phillips, *Damned Yankee*, p.208.
70. Ware, *Lyon Campaign*, p.339.
71. Piston and Hatcher, *Wilson's Creek*, p.29.
72. Ware, *Lyon Campaign*, p.231.
73. Brooksher, *Bloody Hill*, p.146.
74. Jay Monaghan, *Civil War on the Western Border, 1854–1865* (Lincoln, NB, 1955), p.149.

4

The Battle at Wilson's Creek, 1861

> Let us eat the last bit of mule flesh and fire the last cartridge before we think of retreating.
>
> Sweeny before the engagement[1]

St Louis provisionally secure, Lyon planned a two-pronged march to converge on the hostile forces at Springfield. Sweeny would lead one prong of the expedition, Lyon the other. General Lyon's campaign plan called for the sending of 'four regiments and two four-gun batteries, under the command of Brigadier General Sweeny, to the southwest . . . in order to hold that part of the State . . . and to intercept the retreat of Governor Jackson and General Price' – whom, along with their troops, Lyon planned to drive out of north-central Missouri southwest to Springfield.[2] Lyon would embark part of his command on steamboats headed up the Missouri River towards the state capital, bent on capturing that key site and securing the river in the process; that accomplished, he would commence the drive southwest toward where the major threat, out of the south, was anticipated to materialize. The rumours regarding a Confederate troop movement from Arkansas under Ben McCullough, Lyon reported,

> have assumed shape and consistency . . . To meet it . . . before leaving St Louis, [I] dispatched a large force consisting of the regiments of Colonel Sigel, Captain Salomon, and Colonel Brown, under command of Brigadier General Sweeny, commanding the Home Guard of St Louis.[3]

Sweeny was to take this force to Rolla and then to Springfield. That city's Union loyalists were under some duress, and refugees from areas under Confederate threat had gathered there. Sweeny's 2nd US Infantry regulars were reliable troops, but this core unit was supplemented by a motley assembly of amateur volunteers however willing. Sweeny would remember one of the untrained cohorts he had to work with initially.

> It was comprised principally of Germans, and I had to get rid of the officers as they had the beer-saloon men for those positions . . . They had no discipline, as they thought the war would be over soon, and they did not like to offend their customers, nor did they like putting them under fire for fear of losing them.[4]

The secessionist state guard, under the command of Major General Sterling Price, had fled Jefferson City by the time Lyon arrived there on 15 June. Lyon planned to loop north and drive the rebels south out of Boonville, hoping that Major Samuel D. Sturgis could march two Kansas regiments from Fort Leavenworth and attack the enemy retreat along its way. Another rebel group under General Parsons, it was thought, might be engaged by Sweeny's Springfield troops as the former approached the city from the northeast. The darkest possibility was that the Confederate forces under Price might reach Springfield intact and merge with the large Confederate force under McCulloch thought to be advancing north from Arkansas. Fearing that contingency, Lyon emphatically stressed to General McClellan, then commanding western theatre forces, that reinforcements would be essential.

> If these parties [Price and Parsons] should be able to unite with McCulloch and the troops from Arkansas, it will swell his numbers from 10,000 to 12,000; and as it will be necessary for me to leave detachments at various points to secure my communications with St Louis, it will be necessary to have an additional force to repel the invading force from Arkansas, and I therefore ask . . . that you will order three regiments from Illinois.[5]

These troops, as well as needed supplies, were to come via the Pacific Railroad's southwestern branch, along a track that by then would have been secured by Sweeny on his way southwest, so Lyon was confident that reinforcements could reach him rapidly. In accord with this plan, Sweeny's command arrived by train in Rolla, the western limit of the railway, on 14 June, where they encamped. He had sent Sigel's troops ahead toward Springfield. Rolla was the stepping-off point for Union action in the state's southwestern parts and the depot for military supplies going to Springfield. Eugene Ware describes Springfield at the time as 'a nice inland town, – not very large, but doing a great business. It had some large wholesale stores, principally grocery stores . . .'.

In July 1861 goods that came west by rail to Rolla and hauled to Springfield by wagon'.[6] Sweeny had orders to see to it that Rolla was properly established as a supply depot and then to march his column the remaining 110 miles to Springfield. He writes that upon his arrival in Rolla:

> I found that the arms and ammunition, camp and garrison equipage, which I had made requisition for before I started, had not been forwarded. Nevertheless, feeling the necessity of moving to the front, as I knew that the enemy, after his defeat at Boonville, would endeavor to escape southward, I took up the line of march the next morning with four companies, leaving Brown's regiment to follow as they could, and requesting the authorities in St Louis to forward the necessary supplies without delay.[7]

Arriving in Springfield on 1 July 1861, he took military command of the city and established his headquarters but learned that a portion of the rebel militia fleeing Lyon's troops had already by-passed Springfield and joined with McCulloch's army on the Missouri–Arkansas border.[8] Sweeny sent Colonel Franz Sigel and his regiment to reconnoitre the area west of Springfield around

Carthage in search of Governor Jackson's troops and on 4 July issued a proclamation to the citizens of the Springfield area. In it he was at pains to assure the residents that the presence of his troops in the area would not mark the freeing of the local slaves, of whom there were 1,668 at the time – that rather the army was there with regard to an imminent Confederate threat upon the city and the state. The proclamation, delivered to a population well aware of the violence rampant in 'Bloody Kansas' recently, reflects Sweeny's considerable rhetorical skills. Somewhat as Thomas Paine had had to do in his first 'Crisis Paper' of 1776, making Toryism untenable in the colonies, Sweeny had to make secessionism untenable, to characterize the terms of the crisis in Missouri in 1861 along Union lines, introduce the issue of treason and the implied consequences of that choice, and at the same time not sound like a tyrannical invader. He managed to speak in effect as at once 'good cop' and 'bad cop' while being sure the good cop persona was the one the people involved would perceive as the dominant one. As Paine had had to assuage colonist fears that the British might swamp American resistance and hang rebel supporters forthwith, Sweeny had to blunt local fears and rumours of Confederate troops descending upon the area to wreak vengeance on those who collaborated with the Federals. At the same time, he had to convey the assurance that Springfield area people who affirmed Unionist loyalties could rest assured they would not be left in the lurch later on – that their part of Missouri would not eventually be yielded to the rebels:

> To the Citizens of Southwest Missouri:
> Your Governor has striven to cause the State to withdraw from the Union. Failing to accomplish this purpose by legislative enactment, he has already committed treason by levying war against the United States. He has endeavored to have you commit the same crime. Hence he has called for troops to enter the military service of the State – not to aide but to oppose the Government of the United States.
>
> The troops under my command are stationed in your midst by the proper authority of our Government. They are amongst you not as enemies, but as friends and protectors of all loyal citizens.
>
> Should an insurrection of your slaves take place it would be my duty to suppress it, and I should use the force at my command for that purpose. It is my duty to protect all loyal citizens in the enjoyment of all their property – slaves included . . .
>
> I require all troops and armed men in this part of the state, now assembled, to immediately disperse and return to their homes. If this shall not be done without delay those hordes of armed men will be taken prisoners or dispersed.
>
> I request every citizen who acknowledges he owes allegiance to the United States, to aid me to prevent the shedding of blood, and to restore peace and quiet to this portion of the State.[9]

On 5 July Sigel's command encountered Jackson's near Carthage, engaged them, and, outnumbered, had to retreat. Sweeny's later reports would suggest that he wanted Sigel to occupy Carthage and scout outward from that firm base, but Sigel got caught overextending his force and then lacked a secure Carthage to fall back to: 'Had Sigel, according to my orders, occupied Carthage – which is a naturally strong position', Sweeny later wrote, 'I am satisfied that he could have held the place until I joined him . . .'. The situation was becoming tense. 'I had heard nothing from General Lyon from the time I left St Louis until the 11th of July, when one of my scouts, who had fallen in with him on Grand River, brought me a note from him'.[10] Lyon's note read in part: 'Sweeny, I have heard of Sigel's affair at Carthage and how his men behaved. They fired too high and did but little execution. I am marching at the rate of forty miles a day to get to you. I am afraid I will get out of provisions'.[11] In reply Sweeny 'sent him two wagons loaded with provisions, and told him to give himself no uneasiness about Springfield, that I felt confident that I could hold it . . . I had two thousand five hundred men and eight field pieces'.[12]

In Springfield rumours were rife that Confederate and rebel militia forces were even now gathering for a major assault on the city. Sweeny's written report to the Secretary of War from Springfield on 12 July repeated what he had asserted to Lyon – that he felt confident he could defend the city until Lyon arrived 'who I learn is within two or three days march of me'. He noted however:

> I am very deficient in ammunition for the eight field pieces attached to this command; also for .69 caliber rifle musket with which the principle part of my command is armed. I have repeatedly repeated my wants in these particulars, and pressed them upon the attention of the authorities at the St Louis Arsenal without effect.
>
> The inhabitants of this part of the country are generally loyal, and since my arrival here I have organized several regiments of Home Guards, but they are very deficient in arms and ammunition. Mounted troops are much needed.[13]

Sweeny's plan was to go out to meet the Confederate forces and prevent their effective coordination. After some skirmishes, however, it was decided to return to Springfield. 'The enemy followed us up as we fell back', he wrote, 'and [they] took up a strong position on Wilson's Creek ten miles south of Springfield, and commenced fortifying'.[14] Lyon reached Springfield on 13 July having been informed that the enemy was moving upon the city in three columns. He met immediately with Sweeny to discuss the situation, which was dire – the troops had not been paid, the three-month volunteers were nearing their release date, supplies were short, and not everyone, by any means, was possessed of Lyon's zeal. The command's quartermaster, for example, whom Lyon considered to be 'lacking in earnestness', and whom Sweeny had had to by-pass and requisition supplies directly from Washington, took umbrage at the slight and cancelled Sweeny's order. 'By the time it was discovered, it was far too late. In the meantime, Lyon's troops growled as loudly as their stomachs'.[15] Sweeny's troops now occupied the city itself and camps to the south 'while the men in the columns of Lyon and Sturgis who had arrived more recently camped to the west'.[16]

Little did Sweeny or anyone else know at this point that the pastures outside town would be the site for a battle of historic and terrible proportions; before long he would find himself in the midst of what the historian, Stanley Horn, described as 'the hardest four hours fighting that up to that time had ever taken place on the American continent'.[17]

General Lyon's devout Federalism verged on zealotry. Historians have compared him to John Brown. Christopher Phillips, in his 1990 Lyon biography, describes him as a 'queer little man with an uncontrollable temper who evoked either terror or anger from so many around him'.[18] Lyon had taken upon himself the burden of the Union cause in Missouri and, in his overbearing way, had done his job brilliantly on the whole, driving the secessionist forces into the state's far southwest corner. He had thus far been strikingly successful in his campaign. Given the shortages of horses, mules and wagons, Piston and Hatcher observe, no officer in the Union Army had accomplished more during the summer of 1861.

> In the initial movement of his own column and the one under Sweeny, [he] had made masterful use of rivers and railways . . . his operations were as swift as humanly possible. His subordinates Sturgis and Sweeny had performed creditably operating on their own.[19]

After taking Jefferson City and Boonville, Missouri, Lyon's command had set out in pursuit of the rebels. 'Everybody was excited on 3 July 1861 when the column started south after Claiborne Jackson. Would Sweeny be able to hold the refugees until the column arrived?'[20] Lyon had been operating at the highest intensity for months, however, and, lacking Sweeny's resilience and sense of humour, by the time he reached Springfield he was physically and emotionally exhausted and appeared dazed.[21] Meanwhile, a combined rebel army of over 10,000, at least twice the force Lyon had, was converging on Springfield, and the reinforcements he had fervently and repeatedly sought from the Army Department of the West were evidently not going to be forthcoming. Lyon felt far removed from central command, and as of 18 June matters had been made worse; Missouri was assigned to the Military Department of the Ohio under General McClellan in Cincinnati, even further away than St Louis.[22] Lyon's success had been based on his consistent audacity, but now he wavered, tending to lean more on his staff for support and advice since it appeared little or no support could be counted on from higher command. At this point it was Sweeny in particular who served, as best he could, to embolden and sustain Lyon in his crisis. Even Union Army headquarters in St Louis seemed oblivious to the situation to the west. General Fremont, in command there, was at that time almost obsessively focused upon the Mississippi and his own grandiose plan to split the Confederacy by taking Memphis, Vicksburg and New Orleans. Securing Cairo, Illinois, was thus more of a concern to him than was Lyon's situation at Springfield. William Brooksher notes Fremont's lack of understanding of the national significance of what was unfolding in western Missouri, in the theatre of the war for which he was responsible.[23] Worst of all, Lyon was unaware that most of his requests to St Louis Army headquarters, those sent before 25 July when Fremont arrived in the city, had not even reached Fremont but were 'lost in the great bureaucratic void of the War Department'.[24]

> Lyon [had] requested food, clothing, and 10,000 men as reinforcements. What he received was an order detaching . . . Sweeny and many of the regulars for service elsewhere. As Lyon was noted for his temper, his reply to this potentially devastating directive was remarkably calm. On July 17 he wrote another letter to the war department, patiently explaining his needs and his peril once again, concluding that he would 'delay' executing the order to detach Sweeny and the Regulars until the authorities in Washington had time to reconsider his requests. . . . Sweeny stayed put.[25]

Traces of Lyon's increasing uncertainty come across, however, in his report of 9 August sent to General Fremont from Springfield and noting the enemy's presence a mere ten miles off:

> He has taken a strong position and is recruiting his supply of horses, mules, and provisions by foraging into the surrounding country, his large force of mounted men enabling him to do this without much annoyance from me. I find my position extremely embarrassing, and am at present unable to determine whether I shall be able to maintain my ground or be forced to retire. I can resist any attack from the front, but if the enemy move to surround me, I must retire. I shall hold my ground as long as possible, though I may, without knowing how far, endanger the safety of my entire force, with its valuable material, being induced by the important considerations involved to take this step. The enemy yesterday made a show of force about five miles distant, and has doubtless a full purpose of making an attack on me.[26]

Even the rather passive phrasing of 'being induced by the important considerations involved to take this step', arguably suggests his fatigue and growing demoralization. Having stalled Washington regarding the release of Sweeny for duty elsewhere, Lyon, in near despair, wrote to Lieutenant Colonel Chester Harding, his St Louis liaison to Washington. 'It seems strange that so many troops must go [east] from the West and strip us of the means of defense. But, if it is the intention to give up the West, let it be so; it can only be the victim of imbecility or malice'. He concluded with an exasperated plea: 'Cannot you stir up this matter and secure us relief? . . . Everything seems to combine against me at this point'.[27] Though much the worse for wear, Lyon still retained some of his naturally aggressive spirit at this point, however, and was still thinking in terms of an offensive: since it appeared that things could only worsen, 'He would attack the enemy immediately, and Sweeny . . . would lead the attack'.[28]

In late July he ordered Sweeny to lead an expedition against the garrison and supply depot that, according to intelligence reports, the rebels had lately set up at Forsyth, Missouri. Rumours abounded in Springfield as to the depth of rebel strength gathering at Forsyth, and Lyon was determined not to let the enemy set themselves. Sweeny was to take some 1,200 men, a section of artillery and two companies of cavalry to capture the town and disperse the rebel force.[29] On 20 July he set off on an alternately hot and rain-soaked march into the hills toward the town in question at the head of the White River, but there was a happy diversion along the way when he and his troops came to the village of Ozark. A secessionist merchant there had panicked, stocked a wagon with goods, including a great supply of whisky, and set out to escape southward, only to get stuck in mud and captured by Sweeny's cavalry. The festive possibilities presented by the liberated whisky were not lost on Sweeny. He organized a distribution of the liquor to the men in the ranks, an event later recalled by Eugene Ware, who was with the 1st Iowa on this rainy march:

> [T]he bugle called, and we got into line and waited; the first sergeants were called to the front of the line; it was about a half-mile long. Soon [the sergeants] came to each company with something filled with whisky; some had buckets, some had crocks, and some had very inappropriate earthen jars . . . Each sergeant . . . began giving each man a half tin cup of whisky . . . General Sweeny was riding up and down the line . . . [T]he boys at the other end naturally got excited and wanted to see the fun . . . General Sweeny rode up in the rain and shouted 'Right dress! Get back there, get back!' The boys, taken somewhat by surprise, were a little slow, when the general shouted, 'Right dress there, right dress! I'm pretty drunk, but I would right dress if I were you'. Back into the line the boys went, and with the rain dripping down their noses laughed . . . Of course he was not drunk, nor partly drunk, but that was the way he got at it, and that was why the boys liked him. Finally we got all we wanted, and started off singing 'Happy Land of Canaan'.[30]

On the morning of 22 July Sweeny told his troops that they had a hard march ahead of them and to save their strength for there might be 'a little fight before night'. He sent a small cavalry force ahead to Forsyth, after which he learned from a captured Confederate that the town was heavily fortified and manned by 1,000 soldiers. This was untrue, but Sweeny now feared for the safety of the advanced guard he had sent out, and ordered his already fatigued troops forward marching double-time over the last four-mile dash, no small feat. 'For boys who had not been very well fed and hadn't had much sleep for some time', Ware writes, 'and had [already] marched twenty-six miles, an order for double-quick with our load came unwelcomed'.[31] They did it, however, and in good humor – a tribute to Sweeny's officership. Ware would later remember the experience when, as an old man in 1902, he wrote to Sweeny's son recalling the heavy downpour along the White River and how 'your father went along with us through the heavy rain, cheering up the boys and enlivening the march'.[32]

When they got to the town 'the artillery horses were crowded down hill, and the cavalry were pushed out to the flanks; we went in yelling . . . Everybody in town fled; we saw hundreds of horsemen take to the river and swim over with their horses'.[33] Sweeny's troops, he wrote in his official report, captured invaluable supplies –

> arms, munitions of war, flour, meal, sugar, syrup, salt, clothing, boots, shoes, hats, camp furniture, mule and horse shoes . . . The arms and munitions of war were distributed among the Home guards of the county, and the clothing and provisions among our troops, of which they stood in great need.[34]

Perhaps even more importantly, a significant part of the Union force had now had a taste of combat; the victory at Forsyth would serve to encourage and invigorate them in the forthcoming battle at Wilson's Creek where the performance of the Union soldiers was to prove surprisingly robust given their disadvantage.

The Sweeny expedition returned to Springfield where, on 7 August, with the enemy at the gates, Lyon called his officers to a council of war. Sweeny was unable to attend the meeting and was greatly distressed to learn afterward of the officers' recommendation – the majority had urged a fall-back to Rolla or Kansas City. 'Lyon would almost certainly have given in to the majority opinion, as he had at previous meetings', Piston and Hatcher observe, 'were it not for Thomas Sweeny'.[35] He headed immediately for Lyon's quarters at the Boren House. When Sweeny rode up, Lyon came out on the back porch, and the two began a critical discussion, Sweeny arguing 'in as forcible language as I could command', to convince Lyon to ignore the consensus arrived at earlier. It was Sweeny's conviction that, even if defeated, the Federal command would be in better position to retreat if it engaged the enemy than if it withdrew without striking a blow, and that more men might be lost in that 120-mile retreat march in the sweltering heat than would be lost in battle. He foresaw a roused, rejuvenated rebel army pursuing a withdrawing Union force which would be encumbered by an immense supply train and hundreds of refugees. He argued that the enemy's superior cavalry and their knowledge of the terrain could permit them to assault the retreat west of Rolla at the Gasconade River and possibly vanquish it there. He was convinced as well that a fall-back would be unfair to those people of southwest Missouri who had committed to the Union cause and who would now be left abandoned.

> I told [Lyon] that when I arrived in Springfield, I assured the people that I had not only the will, but also the power to protect them, and that if we abandoned them now, without striking a blow, the very worst consequences were, in my opinion, to be apprehended.

In a bit of rebuttal, Lyon stated that their stocks were short and that, furthermore, the possibility could not be ignored that the Confederates would surround them and prevent any effort to replenish supplies. Lyon was concerned that the Confederates might at any time come around his own force on the east rendering a retreat to Rolla impossible. It was possible that they could simply be starved out, Lyon worried, and what about water? 'I told him', Sweeny writes, 'that I could collect beef and corn within a radius of three miles around Springfield, sufficient to supply his command for three months'. As regards water, Sweeny was of course an old hand, a veteran of years in some of the most parched land to be found anywhere. 'This place is called "Springfield", General', he pointed out to Lyon, 'the very name indicates that it was built over springs. Even if we are driven from the Plaza, there is not a square foot of ground we stand on where we cannot find water by digging twenty feet'.[36] Lyon held Sweeny in high regard, Christopher Phillips notes, and 'Sweeny's pluck seemed to enliven the federal commander'.[37] Lyon promised to consider Sweeny's arguments to stay the course, and by the next morning had changed his mind and rejected the previously planned retreat. Later, however, as the battle approached, Sweeny found out that Lyon, depressed by the lack of support or counsel from General Fremont, had listened to the advice of a subordinate besides himself, and a most dubious one at that.

Franz Sigel was reputed to have had some military education in Germany and some battle experience in the German 'Peasant Revolution' of 1848. With a gift for self-promotion and public relations generally, he had managed to become, of all the Union officers in Missouri, the popular and newspaper favourite. Eugene Ware's recollections of him are not glowing:

> I care to say but little. We Americans never liked him . . . He was a little lean fellow with a most impertinent face. He wore spectacles and kept looking around like a weasel. The common expression was, 'Sigel is hell on the retreat'.[38]

As things turned out, even that sarcastic characterization, as we shall see, did him too much credit – he was not even good at retreat. Writing with regard to the battle at Carthage some years later, Sweeny too suggests less than the highest regard for Sigel's authenticity:

> When I met Sigel at Mount Vernon, in answer to a question of the force the enemy had at Carthage, he told me that they had two regiments of cavalry, about 400 men each, and 300 infantry, with seven pieces of artillery, mostly old. His official report, however, set the number down at 2500, which he afterward altered to 3500 before I sent it to Washington.[39]

Sigel's poor performance at Carthage notwithstanding, however, Lyon now bought into the persuasive, theatrical German's plan for the major clash in the offing – Lyon was unfortunately convinced to divide his already outnumbered command for a two-force attack, one led by Sigel, who would take two regiments and attempt to come around behind the Confederate encampment, while Lyon led the main force regiments.[40]

On hearing that a divided operation was in the works, Sweeny was appalled. As he had done previously with regard to the erstwhile retreat plan, he set off in search of Lyon, finding him this time at the general's Jefferson Street quarters. Sweeny took issue with the proposed battle strategy. He was not alone among the officers in recognizing that the anticipated plan of action, by dividing the command, violated the most elementary military rules for troop deployment in battle, especially in this case where 5,000 Union troops were poised to encounter 20,000 secessionist ones. Sigel's plan would split an already outnumbered force and create two smaller ones that would essentially be out of communication with one another in the critical hours. Furthermore, the Sigel force, even if it did surprise the enemy momentarily, was rather a light one. But Lyon was by now committed to the Sigel plan and chose to go ahead.

In mid-July, before Sweeny's sortie to Forsyth, Lyon's force had been diminished by what had been long feared: the departure of volunteers who had answered Lincoln's call for three-month enlistments and whose commitment had run out. This could be devastating – both Sweeny and Lyon, as Mexican War veterans, no doubt recalled that the US advance toward Mexico City had ground to a halt at Puebla in 1847 when great numbers of Winfield Scott's volunteers had likewise departed for home when their commitment was fulfilled. Sweeny's command was depleted when Colonel Brown's regiment and three companies of McNeil's regiment, all volunteers, exercised their right to return to St Louis and civilian life. This left Sweeny without his brigade, and Lyon appointed him inspector general on his staff. Sweeny was thus shorn of his soldiers for the Wilson's Creek battle. Despite the critical role he had played in the events defining it, as inspector general he would have no brigade officially under his command – something reflected in historic 'order of battle' lists, in some of which he is not mentioned at all. An official report from Adjutant General Schofield, written to headquarters, Army of the West, on 19 July, however, contained Lyon's orders that: 'The following troops . . . will report to Brigadier-General Sweeny, viz: Second Regiment Kansas Volunteers, under Colonel Mitchell; a battalion, about 500 strong, of First Regiment Iowa Volunteers . . . two companies of cavalry . . . and one section of Captain Totten's battery'.[41]

It would appear that the disruption and revision of command that followed the departure of so many volunteer troops was such that Sweeny's assignments were last-minute ones as the conflict approached. He eventually led a cavalry company and part of the 2nd Kansas mounted infantry in the fight. Eugene Ware remembered General Lyon's words to the Iowa company he was part of, words meant to be encouraging, but which rang hollow and fell short.

> Lyon might have spoken a few sentences that would have raised his men up . . . but that was not Lyon . . . On the other hand, dear old . . . General Sweeny . . . made a speech to his cavalry, of which I have no notes except that he said among other things, 'Stay together boys and we'll saber the hell out of them'. This had enthusiasm in it.

The 'Kansas' designation for this unit Sweeny led, it might be mentioned, is probably misleading; Piston and Hatcher note that more than 90 per cent of the

1st Kansas, and this would probably apply to the 2nd as well, can be identified as to place of birth, and only one member was born in what was then the Kansas territory. The majority of the unit was Irish.[42]

Springfield in the second week of August held its breath. Hurrying wagons threw up dust into the humid, oppressive, Ozark heat of high summer. The area's rocky earth radiated that heat – near 100 degrees daily, and the trees and brush were tick-ridden at this time of year. The depleted Union forces tried to digest the endless rumours and get ready to carry out whatever strategy the commanders had arrived at. In the evening of 9 March they were commanded to fall in; things were under way. The Union forces moved out from the city in the direction of the rebel encampments, through fields in silence, avoiding main roads. Not until near 1 a.m. on 10 March did they see the light of enemy fires in the distance. The main Union force rested briefly on the Norman farm before being ordered forward toward they knew not what. They were unaware of what a poor idea, despite Sweeny's efforts to have it dropped, the Union strategy would prove to be.

The degree to which Sigel was a loose cannon, even a charlatan, is not reflected in most Wilson's Creek histories; some of the misapprehensions common among journalists in 1861 – that he was a colourful, charismatic figure – seem to have survived and coloured accounts despite ample records and testimony indicating his incompetence. His presence before, during and after the battle was a crippling one, a burden on the Union force. He bungled his mission badly, mistaking the 3rd Louisiana Infantry for the friendly 1st Iowa, and ended up cut off and unable to carry out his mission. A Rebel counterattack scattered his force, which retreated in disarray. The terrible disconnections that Sweeny had anticipated came to pass and are evident in Sigel's own rather stunned official report to General Fremont on 18 August:

> Our troops expected the approach of our friends and were waving the flag . . . when at once two batteries opened their fire against us . . . [one from] the hill on which we had supposed Lyon's forces were in pursuit of the enemy . . . It is impossible for me to describe the consternation and frightful confusion which was occasioned by this unfortunate event. The cry 'They (Lyon's troops) are firing upon us' spread like wildfire through our ranks.[43]

'[Sigel's] men gave way in every direction, leaving his guns and everything in the hands of the enemy', Sweeny later wrote.[44] Eugene Ware's perspective from the enlisted ranks was similar: 'At Wilson Creek [Sigel] was no good . . . He apparently lost entire control of himself and then of his men'.[45] Sigel set out alone for Springfield while the battle was still in progress, in what William R. Brookshire describes as 'abject flight and abandonment of his leader [Lyon]'.[46]

Lyon now confronted a massive enemy force with woefully diminished ranks. Despite that, the Federals enjoyed an initial success – the secessionists were once again surprised by Lyon's audacity. But the rebels regrouped and struck back in a series of attacks that ultimately gained them the upper hand. Unaware that Sigel's troops were out of action, Lyon's troops fought on, anticipating a relief force that never came. Lyon abandoned any safety his rank might have offered: 'When Sweeny came up, Lyon directed him to take charge of the Iowans. He then pulled the second Kansas out of the line . . . and into the gap'.[47] In short order Lyon's horse was shot, and he was himself cut down by a bullet through his chest – the first Union general killed in the Civil War. Ironically, the previous day Fremont had finally released two regiments from Jefferson Barracks to buttress the army at Springfield – Lyon's long-sought reinforcements were on the way, too late.[48] Sweeny ordered Lieutenant Hines, Lyon's old first sergeant, to remain with the General's body until it could be placed in an ambulance, which Hines did, and Sweeny went on afoot into the fight. 'I subsequently learned that [Lyon's body] was afterward taken out [of the ambulance] to make room for a wounded man'.[49] The general's corpse was left on the ground, forgotten by Sturgis in his retreat. It was later come upon by a Confederate unit and taken to Springfield where Mrs Mary Phelps had it encased in zinc and stored in her ice house. Rogue Confederate troops harassed Mrs Phelps and threatened to 'drag [the body] behind a horse like Hector had been dragged at Troy'. The remains were finally retrieved by Union authorities, however, and borne by train across the country for burial near Ashford, Connecticut, Lyon's home ground.[50]

Attempting to keep things together on the battlefield after Lyon's death, Sweeny finally went down himself, severely wounded in the left leg. Although short-lived – six hours in all – the bloody engagement at Wilson's Creek resulted in 1,317 Union and 1,230 Confederate casualties – 23 per cent of all engaged, the highest percentage of overall losses sustained in any battle of the Civil War. 'Never before', Thomas L. Snead, an aide to Claibourne Jackson later observed, 'had so bloody a battle been fought on American soil; seldom has a bloodier one been fought on any modern field'.[51] While the Confederates won the day, their officers proved tactically inept in the battle, badly misusing their forces and never effectively bringing their numerical advantage to bear. 'The Confederates' Eugene Ware writes, 'had shown no tact or generalship. Their way of handling their men was brave but crude'.[52] Sweeny believed that Sturgis, who had assumed command after Lyon fell, retreated unnecessarily:

> The fight lasted two hours after Lyon's death, when the enemy entirely disappeared from the field. Major Sturgis, however . . . determined to retreat, and though sustained in my opinion by other officers, that the enemy had abandoned the field, still Sturgis persisted in falling back to Springfield . . . The enemy did not pursue us at all; in fact, it was several days before they entered Springfield in force, fearing a ruse, as they could not believe that we were retreating.[53]

Ware remarks Sturgis's 'bad luck and want of ability'[54] – and some contemporary historians confirm Sweeny's and Ware's perception here. 'Appalled,

1. Battle of Churubusco. The Mexican War battle of 20 August 1847 in which Lieutenant Sweeny was wounded and his arm amputated.

2. Lieutenant Sweeny and his wife Ellen, 1856.

3. Yuma warrior posed for photographer.

4. Sweeny daughters, Sarah and Fanny.

5. Chief Red Cloud.

6. Pittsburgh Landing, Shiloh.

7. Quarters at Corinth occupied by the 52nd Illinois Volunteers during the winter of 1862–63.

8. General Sweeny.

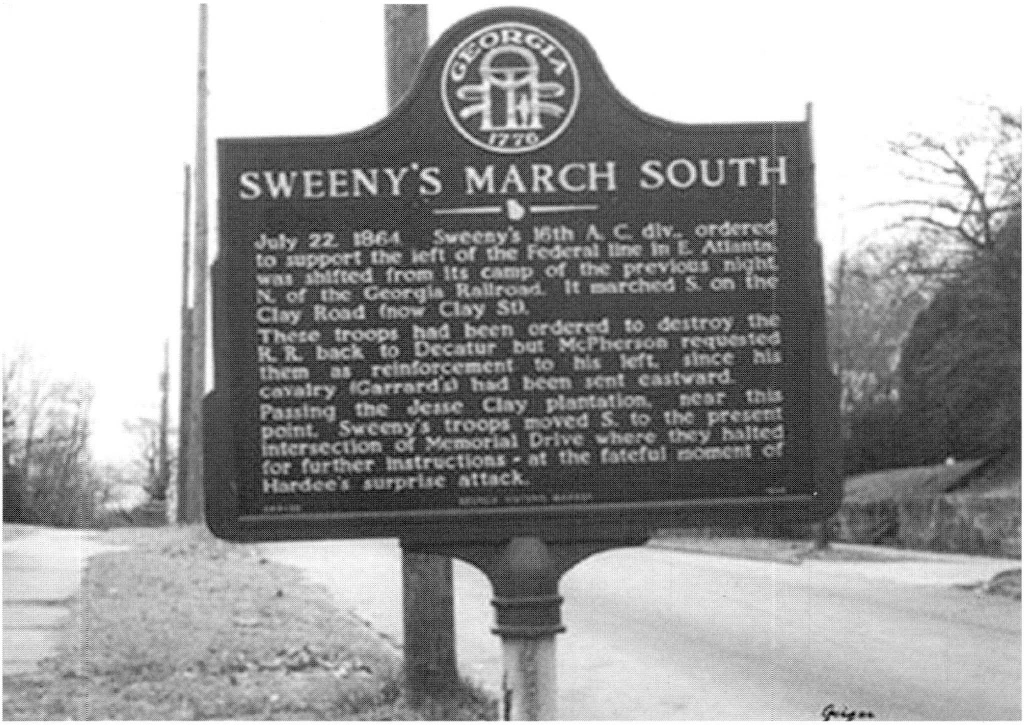

9. Sweeny historical marker, present-day Atlanta, Georgia.

10. Colonel John O'Neill.

11. General Samuel C. Spear.

12. General Michael C. Murphy.

13. Canada under Fenian siege. Troops deployed on James Street, Hamilton, Ontario.

14. The United States steamer, *Michigan*, with captured Fenians on a scow-boat.

15. General Spear, General Sweeny and Colonel Meehan.

16. Eugenia Reagan Sweeny.

17. T.W. Sweeny in retirement.

[Sturgis's] subordinates pleaded with him to stay', writes Brooksher, '. . . The Union troops were standing firm against the best the South could do . . . but upon hearing of Sigel's rout, [Sturgis] ordered his men back to Springfield'.[55]

When the smoke cleared, the carnage was evident. Among the seriously wounded was Captain Naughton of the Irish Dragoons. Dr Samuel Melcher, the Union Army surgeon who was instrumental in finally recovering Lyon's body, later wrote: 'I found Captain Naughton the next day in a house, half a mile or more west of the battle ground, with a bullet in his right lung, from the effects of which wound he never entirely recovered, and died under my charge in St Louis in 1873'.[56] Army surgeons were overwhelmed by casualties on an unprecedented scale. Union surgeons stayed behind when the army retreated and Union and Confederate casualties were treated as best the surgeons of both sides could do in various houses and makeshift infirmaries. A Confederate surgeon described Springfield on 17 August 1861 as 'a vast hospital'.[57]

With Lyon dead, Sweeny, had he not been wounded, would have been an invaluable asset at this point and might well have assumed command. Instead, an uncertain Sturgis repeated Lyon's mistake and yielded to Sigel's hollow reputation and ostentatious confidence. Sigel immediately proceeded to botch all efforts toward an orderly and disciplined retreat, however. In his official report of 20 August, Major J.M. Schofield describes riding into Siegel's camp when all other units were ready to undertake the march:

> At 1:30 o'clock, I went to Colonel Sigel's camp, and found his wagons not loaded, his men apparently making preparations to cook their breakfast, and no preparations to march. I could find no officer to execute my commands, nor anyone to pay the slightest heed to what I said. I rode at once to Colonel Siegel's quarters . . . and found him asleep in bed.[58]

If the rebels had been aware of the confusion of the retreat under Sigel's direction, they could have struck and decimated the Union army. 'On the morning of the third day', Schofield's report notes, 'the whole column was detained three hours for Colonel Sigel's Brigade to have beef killed and cooked for breakfast, the remainder of the command having made their breakfast on such as they had'. Things degenerated to the point that Sturgis had to take back the command he had yielded to Sigel. 'The clamor for relief [among the troops] became such that almost total anarchy reigned . . . Major Sturgis resumed command . . . giving as his reason that although Colonel Sigel had been acting as an officer . . . *he had no appointment from any competent authority*' [italics added].[59] Major Sturgis's report of 30 August on the battle at Wilson's Creek read in conclusion regarding General Sweeny: 'This gallant officer was especially distinguished by his zeal in rallying broken fragments of various regiments even after receiving a severe wound in the leg, and leading them into the hottest of the fight'.[60] Of Sigel's performance, on the other hand, Sturgis, after declaring that he would prefer not to have to go into the matter, wrote:

> Justice to the cause of truth compels me to give such account of the operations of that column as I have received from some of the officers and men who formed part of it. When Colonel Sigel opened his fire the enemy were completely surprised and fled from their camp, whereupon many of Colonel Sigel's men and officers, instead of standing to their guns and pursuing the enemy, turned their attention to plunder, and thus permitted the enemy to return, seize all his guns, drive the entire column from the field in every possible direction, and finally turn our own guns on the gallant men under Lyon, who were contending with such fearful odds already.[61]

The New Orleans *Picayune* of 17 August represented the battle with a Southern slant, describing the rebels as 'gloriously' victorious, Lyon killed, Sigel in flight and perhaps captured. They added erroneously: 'Sweeny is killed and southwestern Missouri cleared of the national scum of invaders'.[62] Perhaps seeking for some new hope after the disheartening humiliation at Bull Run a few weeks earlier, the Union press on the contrary portrayed the battle more or less in the terms Sweeny did. Northern newspapers hailed Wilson's Creek as a moral victory – at the very least the battle had demonstrated that the North could field credible and disciplined troops. Seizing on the fact that there were no immediate signs of further major offensives from the Confederacy into the state, and despite the fact that the federal army had fallen back to Rolla, the *New York Times* headlined the 'Great National Victory in Missouri'.[63]

Sweeny reached Rolla on crutches on 16 August and not until reaching St Louis did he received expert examination of his leg wound. Doctors determined that removal of the bullet would pose more dangers than leaving it in, so Sweeny continued his life with the lead in his leg as a complement to his missing right arm. He had dodged another bullet, as it were, in that his wound did not get infected, the common consequence of bullet wounds at the time; thus he escaped what would have been devastating – another amputation. There followed some months of office duty in St Louis to allow his leg to recover before any reassignment.

Emboldened by their quasi-victory at Springfield, the Missouri Confederates marched north to the Missouri River at Lexington, in Lafayette County, where the 23rd Illinois, Colonel James Mulligan's Irish Brigade out of Chicago, had taken up a defensive position. A few weeks after Lyon and Sweeny had fought General Price, Mulligan's garrison at Lexington – which General Fremont had failed to reinforce – defended by 3,500, came under assault by Price's Wilson's Creek army of around 12,000. The Irish regiment held out for a week, sustaining 1,700 casualties, before surrendering their garrison.[64] This was to be the extent of significant rebel successes in Missouri, however. The Union efforts in the state in 1861, in which Sweeny had played such a major role, had been effective: Price and Claiborne Jackson would have to recognize that a sustained military presence in the state was untenable, and return south; and the Confederacy would have to be satisfied with raids and limited assaults along Missouri's southern border for the rest of the war.

NOTES

1. Phillips, *Damned Yankee*, p.247.
2. This description of Sweeny's mission is from a Confederate source, the twelve-volume *Confederate Military History,* Vol. 9, ch. 5, *Missouri in the Civil War.* www.civilwarhome.com/missouri5.htm (1 October 2004).
3. Lyon to McClellan, *OR*, 3, pp.11–12
4. Kelly, TWS interview, 16 January 1886.
5. Lyon to McClellan, *OR,* 3, p.15
6. Ware, *Lyon Campaign*, pp.228–9.
7. TWS Report to Adjutant, 1873, W. Sweeny, *Memoir*, p.10.
8. Monaghan, *Civil War*, p.150.
9. TWS Report to Adjutant, 1873, W. Sweeny, *Memoir,* p.45.
10. Ibid., p.12.
11. Peckham, *General Nathaniel Lyon*, pp.297–8.
12. TWS Report to Adjutant, 1873, W. Sweeny, *Memoir*, pp.10–11.
13. *OR*, 3, pp.15–16.
14. TWS Report to Adjutant, 1873, W. Sweeny, *Memoir*, pp.12–13.
15. Phillips, *Damned Yankee*, pp.231–2.
16. Piston and Hatcher, *Wilson's Creek*, p.118.
17. Stanley F. Horn. *The Army of Tennessee* (New York, 1941), p.28.
18. Phillips, *Damned Yankee*, p.3.
19. Piston and Hatcher, *Wilson's Creek*, p.105
20. Monaghan, *Civil War*, p.144.
21. Phillips, *Damned Yankee*, p.2.
22. Ibid., p.224
23. Brooksher, *Bloody Hill*, pp.229–30.
24. Piston and Hatcher, *Wilson's Creek*, p.121
25. Ibid., p.121.
26. *OR,* 3, p.57.
27. Quoted in Brooksher, *Bloody Hill*, p.130.
28. Piston and Hatcher, *Wilson's Creek* p.121
29. TWS Report to Adjutant, 1873, W. Sweeny, *Memoir*, p.12.
30. Ware, *Lyon Campaign*, pp.232–3. 'The Happy Land of Canaan' was the 1st Iowa's favourite marching song.
31. Ibid.
32. Letter from Topeka, Kansas, 25 April 1902. W. Sweeny, *Memoir*, p.53.
33. Ware, *Lyon Campaign*, p.235.
34. Sweeny. *OR,* 3, pp.44–5. Ware, *Lyon Campaign*, pp.237–9.
35. Piston and Hatcher, *Wilson's Creek*, p.173.
36. Brooksher, *Bloody Hill*, pp.172–3. TWS Report to Adjutant, 1873, W. Sweeny, *Memoir,* p.13.
37. Phillips, *Damned Yankee*, p.247.
38. Ware, *Lyon Campaign*, pp.336–7. After muddling virtually everything he had anything to do with at the battle of Wilson's Creek, Sigel was again erroneously hailed as a hero at the later Arkansas battle of Pea Ridge. Regarding Pea Ridge, in his biography of Sigel, Stephen D. Engle writes of General Samuel R. Curtis, who deserved the real credit: 'Significantly, Curtis's major difficulty was forcing Sigel to bring his troops i the field. It was Curtis who displayed the characteristics of leadership in this camp Engle, *Yankee Dutchman: The Life of Franz Sigel* (Fayetteville, NC, 1993), p.11

career concluded with his retreat down the Shenandoah Valley upon being defeated at the battle of New Market, Virginia, after which he was replaced by General David Hunter.

39. TWS Report to Adjutant, 1873, W. Sweeny, *Memoir*, p.11.
40. Brooksher, *Bloody Hill*, p.175.
41. *OR,* 3, p.299.
42. Ware, *Lyon Campaign*, pp.310–11; Piston and Hatcher, *Wilson's Creek*, p.64.
43. Sigel Official Report on Wilson's Creek, 18 August 1861. www.civilwarhome.com/sigelwilsoncreek.htm
44. TWS Report to Adjutant, 1873, W. Sweeny, *Memoir,* p.14.
45. Ware, *Lyon Campaign*, pp.336–7
46. Brooksher, *Bloody Hill*, p.210
47. Piston and Hatcher, *Wilson's Creek*, p.268
48. Phillips, *Damned Yankee* p.259.
49. TWS, Report to Adjutant, 1873, W. Sweeny, *Memoir*, p.15.
50. Phillips, *Damned Yankee*, pp.258–61.
51. Brooksher, *Bloody Hill,* pp.228–29. The battle at Springfield and General Lyon's death there are the subject of a poem – doggerel really – by Herman Melville, part of the volume, *Battle Pieces,* previously cited.
52. Ware, *Lyon Campaign*, p.337.
53. TWS, Report to Adjutant, 1873, W. Sweeny, *Memoir*, p.15
54. Ware, *Lyon Campaign*, p.209.
55. Brooksher, *Bloody Hill*, p.114
56. 'Captain Patrick Naughton: Fifth Iowa Volunteer Cavalry'. scriptoum.org/c/p/naughton.html
57. '"Springfield is a Vast Hospital": Civil War Medicine at Wilson's Creek'. www.nps.gov/wicr/cwmedicine.html
58. *OR,* 3, p.64.
59. Ibid., emphasis added.
60. Sturgis, official report, *OR*, 3, p.70.
61. Ibid., pp.70–1.
62. Quoted in W. Sweeny, *Memoir*, p.47.
63. Phillips, *Damned Yankee*, p.257.
64. James A. Mulligan, 'The Siege of Lexington, Missouri', *Battles and Leaders of the Civil War: Based on the Century War Series, 1884–87* (Reprint, Secaucus, NJ, 1982), 4 Vols. Robert Underwood Johnson and Clarence Buel (eds), pp.307–13. On the 20th, the Confederates advanced behind a breastworks of dampened hemp bales they had found in the area and Mulligan had to surrender. The 23rd was re-mustered later in the war after its colonel's release from captivity and Mulligan eventually died in a battle near Washington, DC, in July 1864.

5

Shiloh to Atlanta, 1861–65

> Go, Mr Dodge of Iowa, you God-dammed political general. I shall expect a note from you, sir.
>
> Sweeny[1]

On 1 September 1861, Sweeny received a thirty-day leave owing to his leg wound from the Wilson's Creek battle, and when he returned to St Louis from New York he reported to General Fremont. Lyon, as earlier mentioned, had due to the emergency in Missouri refused to obey a War Department order that would have sent Sweeny to Virginia, so Sweeny now asked Fremont if he might be allowed to follow those original orders. 'He asked me if I preferred going to Virginia to serving in his department. I told him . . . I desired to be put on duty where I could be most useful . . . He wished me to remain, and said he would write to Washington and have my orders countermanded'.[2] Sweeny was given staff duty in the course of which he returned as adjutant in November 1861 to Springfield, a town still stunned from the recent battle there. He wrote to his daughter Sarah, now 12 years old, from his headquarters, appealing to her to do what she could to care for her younger sister and brother now that their mother was gone.

> My Dear Daughter,
> I received your affectionate letter . . . the day before yesterday, and would have answered . . . immediately, but I have been very busy since my arrival at this place . . . I am very glad to hear you were all well when you wrote, and that Charlie's eyes were so much better; I am in hopes they will be entirely well before this reaches you. Has Fanny been well since I left home? You know she is a delicate child, Sarah . . . You must be very indulgent to her, and not get out of patience with her little whims and oddities. Charlie must also come in for a share of your love and affection . . .
>
> By looking on your map you can find Springfield in Green County in the southwestern part of the state of Missouri. I have been to Wilson's Creek today to view the battle ground where I was wounded last August. Numerous evidences were still around the field of the terrible slaughter that took place on that eventful day. We buried . . . many of our brave soldiers whose remains were yet bleaching in the sun.[3]

Staff duty did not appeal to him for long, however, and in December he requested a return to active infantry duty. Offered a regular army rank of colonel in command of the 52nd Illinois Infantry, he accepted, and arrived at his base, Smithland, Kentucky, on 6 February 1862. Typical of the disarray prevailing this early in the war, when he arrived at Smithland he found his regiment largely without any arms at all and the installation woefully vulnerable. He had to commandeer what he needed from a wharf boat on the Ohio River at Paducah – arms and ammunition left there 'by some regiment that had received a new supply of a different caliber'.[4]

He was informed on 14 February that steamboats would be sent to ferry his regiment and others on the Cumberland River, from where it entered the Ohio near Paducah, to reinforce Grant's troops in the Cumberland valley near Fort Donelson, Tennessee. The rebel position at Fort Donelson fell to Grant's troops on 15 February, however, the day before the 52nd arrived, and Sweeny's regiment was put in charge of moving some 5,000 Confederate prisoners of war on six transports north to Cairo and Alton, Illinois, on the Mississippi. The 52nd then returned south from St Louis and down the Tennessee River to Fort Henry where Sweeny was to report to General Grant for further orders. Grant directed the regiment to Pittsburg Landing on the Tennessee where they arrived on St Patrick's day of 1862 – near where a small wooden church, the Shiloh Methodist Meetinghouse, stood peacefully in a clearing in the woods.[5]

Sweeny's command's next action would be at this river location and would be major indeed – the historic battle of April 1862. Beforehand he was given command of the 3rd Infantry Brigade, which took in six regiments made up of 5,500 men – the 8th Iowa, and the 7th, 50th, 52nd, 57th and 58th Illinois. Grant's troops, including those under Sweeny, encamped comfortably on the Confederate side of the river, awaiting the arrival of General Buell from Nashville with 30,000 more men. Grant was unconcerned, convinced the rebels were at Corinth and were not disposed to an imminent attack. There were no entrenchments, no defensively prepared and trained artillery batteries set up.[6] Though things were drowsy and peaceful, the air fragrant with spring flowers, soldiers did notice rabbits and deer running as though startled out of the woods. In fact, a hostile army of 40,000 was right in the neighbourhood, some two miles off in the forest, poised for a massive assault, and on Sunday morning, 6 April, they struck. Gathered on the wrong side of the Tennessee, the river itself at their backs precluding retreat, the outnumbered Federal army was caught. Sweeny's unit was at the landing three miles from the ignition point of the battle, at the point toward which the panicked Union troops would attempt to fall back when the assault upon them commenced. He had just completed an inspection when things exploded. The Union's centre came under the direct fire of sixty-two Confederate cannons and had no artillery prepared to answer. Sweeny directed his men into the fighting.

'Each man seemed to feel as if the fate of the day depended upon his conduct alone', he later recalled, 'knowing, as we did, that if we could keep the enemy at bay until Buell's troops crossed the river the army would be saved'.[7] He managed to keep his line for the most part intact despite severe losses. The troops he had had to bring up to par in a short time at Smithland performed well. One 52nd Illinois soldier, Captain C.H. Fish, later recalled in an article his own astonishment at Sweeny's seeming unconcern for himself in the field at Shiloh as he commanded from horseback; his cap had blown off and 'his black hair, streaked with gray, fell a twisted, tangled mass over his eyes'. Fish writes that it seemed to him – a corporal at the time – that Colonel Sweeny 'ought not to expose his life so needlessly, so I rose from my incumbent position, and taking his horse by the rein asked him if he would not dismount'. Sweeny replied 'Lie down corporal; lie down there . . . That's your place and this is mine; thank you'.[8] Amid the confusion Sweeny, doing his best to seal the breaches in the defences and rally the disoriented Union troops, rode up to an artillery battery whose identity he could not make out for the smoke and darkness. Only after riding to within a few yards of the battery did he realize this was a Confederate unit. They were too startled to react, however, and he was able to turn around and ride off unmolested. The battle was horrendous and disoriented throughout. Albert Richardson, the correspondent who described this near miss of Sweeny's, noted the chaos that reigned after night fell – 'companies were commanded by sergeants, regiments by lieutenants'.[9] And Ambrose Bierce, a platoon sergeant in the 9th Indiana there, described the same dreadful night in his narrative 'What I Saw at Shiloh'.

Bierce arrived as part of the Buell forces much awaited by Sweeny and the rest of the Union command that night. He arrived after the initial hours of the clash, to a scene of panic, the air 'full of thunder and the earth trembling'. The Federal army was on the verge of collapse; when the Rebel artillery unloaded: 'there was conflagration. The river shuddered in its banks, and hurried on, bloody, wounded, terrified!'[10] Soldiers – predominantly deserters – 'several thousands of men', tried desperately to get on one of the two steamers that could ferry them through the darkness to the safety of the eastern side of the river. 'But on the heights above the battle was burning brightly . . . a thousand lights kindled and expired in every second of time'.

> By the time my regiment had reached the plateau night had put an end to the struggle . . . foot by foot we moved through the dusky fields, we knew not whither. There were men all about us, but no campfires . . . The men were of strange regiments; they mentioned the names of unknown generals. They gathered in groups by the wayside, asking eagerly our numbers . . . The night was black-dark . . . it had begun to rain . . . Inch by inch we crept along, treading on one another's heels by way of keeping together. Commands were passed along the line in whispers; more commonly none were given . . . But where was the enemy? Where too, were the riddled regiments that we had come to save?[11]

Sweeny took a bullet in his only arm early in the day and had his horse shot out from under him, but he continued to command his troops until loss of blood would permit no more and he was taken to a medical tent. He lay there bitterly reviewing the day's events – the military confusion and the appalling loses in the battle. William H.L. Wallace, Sweeny's division commander, had been mortally wounded. Among the commanding officers in his own brigade, besides himself, Colonel Moses Bane had been wounded, as had Colonel James L. Geddes, and Geddes and Colonel William Lynch – years later part of Sweeny's Fenian campaign – had been captured. Here in the hospital Sweeny's outspokenness would lead to a military *faux pas* he would come to regret. General Grant sent his adjutant, J.A. Rawlins, to visit wounded officers in the packed hospital tents. The extent of the slaughter had yet to be recognized, but when the smoke cleared the count, taking in both sides, would be 23,000 men dead or missing, including two generals in the division of which Sweeny was a part. The arrival of reinforcements and arguably the Confederate leadership's failure to press their advantage enough, resulted in a battered Federal victory, but the fight had been ugly, and, as noted, grave military errors had been committed before the battle in terms of Northern deployment of forces. In talking to Rawlins, Sweeny angrily remarked that 'somebody should be punished for this!' The aide interpreted the remark as referring directly to General Grant whose manifest mistakes at Shiloh would become the subject of fierce criticism in the newspapers. Sweeny believed Rawlins later repeated his observation to Grant who hardly needed to hear such a thing in the aftermath of what had just occurred. Grant was sensitive; this was an early point in his Civil War career, before which he had never held more than a company command. In an interview years later, Sweeny observed that Grant was never friendly to him after that.[12]

Battle verse of a hagiographic, romantic tenor was still a strong tradition during the Civil War – Herman Melville's poem 'Lyon' reciting that General's fall at Wilson's Creek, is an example. Many pages in the eleven volume *Rebellion Record*, compiled during and after the war, were in fact devoted to preserving this kind of verse, most of which had appeared in newspapers. Another example of such battle verse is 'Sweeny at Shiloh – April 6th, 1862':

> The Sabbath dawns on Shiloh
>   From out the dark, gaunt pines,
> Bursts Sidney Johnston's vanguard,
>   On Grant's raw, startled lines.
>
> The dread ravine re-echos
>   With crash and batteries' roar,
> Their rebel yell high pealing
>   With Hardee at the fore.
> Back huddling on the river,
>   Swirls Sherman's crushed command,
> When cross the course of conquest,
>   'Tom' Sweeny takes his stand.
> Firm, cheerful, keen and valiant,
>   He curbs his chafing horse;

Amid his hard pressed soldiers,
He stands – an untold force.
His sword-arm sleeve hangs empty –
It tells them of his past;
This day, they feel, means victory,
Or it will be his last.
His lone left arm is wounded,
Down drops his bridle rein;
His horse is pierced by bullets,
He grimly mounts again.

The honor of the army,
Now rests with him today;
His men's true, steady volleys,
Repel the lines of gray.
Each mad assault grows stronger,
While his brave soldiers fall;
Re-echoing his order
The clear, crisp bugles call.
'Bring up, – bring up – the colors!'
'Tis answered mid a cheer –
His thin line rallies 'round him,
With colors in his rear.

He says: 'We're here to die men!'
While lit by sunset glow,
His flag pikes point to heaven,
His bayonets to the foe.
He saves Grant's waning glory,
And Sherman's laurels too,
While Buell's rescue column
Comes bristling into view.
Then swaying in the saddle,
He's slowly led away,
While cheers ring out for Sweeny, –
The 'savior of the day!'[13]

The hero of this poem spent some leave time back in Brooklyn to recuperate from his Shiloh wound and was presented an honorary sword by the city.[14] At the conclusion of his leave, he reported to northern Mississippi where his unit was placed under the command of Major General William S. Rosecrans. On 4 October 1862, at the crossroads town of Corinth not far south of Shiloh, Sweeny took part in yet another major Civil War engagement.

Corinth, described by Ambrose Bierce as 'a wretched place – the capital of a swamp',[15] was a railway hub that the Confederates were keen to recapture after having been driven out by the 'siege of Corinth'. General Sterling Price, who had come south after defeating General Mulligan's garrison at Carthage,

Missouri, was the Rebel commander in the battle. Sweeny, having fought Price's troops at Wilson's Creek, had that old score in mind, and the death of Nathaniel Lyon. From his headquarters on 15 October 1862 he described the battle that raged from 3–6 October as his command, the 52nd Illinois, 1st Brigade, saw it unfold:

> About 2 p.m. a sharp artillery duel commenced between our battery and the enemy, which was posted 600 yards in front of our line near the white house, which was subsequently converted into a temporary hospital . . . The enemy burst from the woods in front in magnificent style in columns by divisions, and moved swiftly across the open field until within point-blank range, when they deployed into line and opened a tremendous fire, moving steadily to the front all the time. Our men, who had been ordered to lie down, now rose and poured in their fire with such deadly effect that the foe, after a short, sanguinary struggle, reeled, broke, and fled in dismay. Again they advanced, but were forced back at the point of the bayonet with great slaughter, our men driving them across the open field and into the woods.
>
> Our loss in this fight was heavy, but that of the enemy must have been terrible. The fire was so hot and well sustained by the men that several officers of the Fifty-second . . . told me that the gun-barrels were so heated that the men could scarcely hold them, and the charges actually exploded while being loaded . . .
>
> From early dawn until 8 a.m. [the next day] a brisk fire was kept up between our batteries and those of the enemy until the latter were silenced or captured . . . An ominous silence took place for a few moments, when a sharp rattling of musketry was heard . . . and the enemy's columns burst from the woods in front and to the right . . . It was a terribly beautiful sight to see the enemy's columns advance, in despite of a perfect storm of grape and canister, shell and rifle ball; still on they marched and fired, though their ranks were perceptibly thinned at every step.

The Union troops on his flanks broke, and he lost artillery support, but his group rallied back. In the midst of the battle, when his unit captured some enemy artillery, he ordered one of the pieces, which he named 'General Lyon', turned on Price's troops – 'General Lyon did good execution on the flying enemy', he observed.[16] Union forces took brutal casualties: 'The division numbered between four and five thousand at the commencement of the action', he wrote to his daughters from Corinth on 13 October, 'and I don't think it will number much more than half that now . . . Thank God I have escaped without serious injury'.[17] The Confederates now resorted to hit-and-run strikes in the environs. In early December, commanding an anti-guerrilla reconnaissance group sent out from Corinth, Colonel Sweeny came upon a Confederate outpost, 300 strong, at Cherokee Station, Alabama. In his report of 13 December to Grant, General Grenville Dodge, now in command at Corinth, described the events that followed and which constituted a spectacular coup for Sweeny and his men:

> I have just received a dispatch from Colonel Sweeny, in command of the forces sent out. He struck the outpost of the enemy at Cherokee, 300 strong, under Colonel Warren, pursued them five miles, fighting all the way, when they met Colonel Roddey, with 1,400, who, after a sharp engagement, fell back to Little Bear Creek, four miles this side of Tuscumbia, from which they were driven after burning their stores, camp equipage, and bridges. Roddey had here four cannon and some infantry from Bragg's army. We captured 32 prisoners, a number of horses, arms, &c.

In his report to Grant on the following day, Dodge wrote: 'Colonel Sweeny used him [Roddey] up badly and brought in a large amount of his troops . . . Great praise is due Colonel Sweeny for the manner in which he carried out the orders and the valuable information he obtained'.[18]

A letter to his daughter Fanny from Corinth on 9 May 1863 reveals that his love affair with birds, evident in his Fort Yuma journal, continued undiminished in the midst of battles:

> My Dear Child,
> . . . I was glad to hear you were all well in Waterford, and that grandmother was getting better. Sarah ought to feel quite proud of carrying off the prize at school, and getting such a nice book as 'Hood's poems', for her pains. You must try and deserve a prize next year, Fannie . . . What a splendid time you must have had at the Public you attended! Sarah wrote a description of the whole thing, how you and she were dressed, &c. I wish I had been there to have seen you . . . I have four pet birds, Fanny, that I intend to take home with me if I can – three of them at all events, one for you, one for Sarah, and one for Charley! They were caught in a trap last winter, and have never been in a cage, but fly around the room I occupy and seem perfectly reconciled to their imprisonment. They are quite tame, and two of them sing beautifully. I shall endeavor to get a mocking bird, there are numbers of them around here, but they are difficult to capture . . . I send you my love and lots of kisses.[19]

Other family obligations had to be looked to as well, the war notwithstanding. He was having to deal with getting money to the appropriate people for his children to live and be educated, and was dependent on relatives to see that all such matters were taken care of, which they not always were. In January he writes to Sarah from Corinth that he has just received a letter from Brooklyn:

> I also received one from your teacher, Miss Vanderwerkin, with a bill enclosed for tuition for you and Fannie for the last two quarters. The tone of the letter is anything but pleasant, and I was very much mortified when I read it as I had no idea that the bill was unpaid.[20]

Meanwhile General Rosecrans, unhappy with the performance of his command at Corinth in many regards – there had been widespread panic in the lines – singled Sweeny out, as had Dodge, for enthusiastic praise. He wrote to Grant calling attention to Sweeny's exemplary service and nominating him for a brigadier generalship:

> Such a record should not remain unnoticed, and it is not only a duty but also a pleasure for me to testify to his worth and to urge his nomination to the rank of Brigadier General. Col. Sweeny has nearly always commanded a brigade and his many honorable wounds show with what zeal and faithfulness he has for so long a time served his country.[21]

Thomas Davies, Brigadier General commanding the 2nd Division, Army of West Tennessee, referencing Corinth, likewise urged that Sweeny be promoted: 'Colonel Sweeny, commanding first Brigade, behaved in the most gallant manner throughout, and should be immediately promoted'.[22] Grant endorsed the recommendations of these officers and on 30 October forwarded his own recommendation to Washington with the added accolade: 'A more gallant and meritorious officer than Col. Sweeny is not in the Service'.[23] A month later, on 29 November 1862, Sweeny was commissioned Brigadier General by President Lincoln.

There had been some tensions in the officer corps at Corinth, however. Sweeny was a stickler for the details of military protocol, especially on the commissioned officer level. This may have been due to his sensitivity to slights owing to his immigrant background – things being done strictly in accord with regulations would help prevent old-boy networks and political cliques within the army gaining too much of an advantage. It had been McClellan's idea that the Federal Army early in the war should bide its time until an extensive professional officer corps could be trained. The decision in Washington, however, was to the contrary – likely gentleman who held executive business positions in civilian life would be brought in to hold command positions in the Union forces. Inevitably, candidates were suggested and sponsored by local political figures. Such appointees were suspect among career officers such as Sweeny, already in the military, who had usually risen in rank through demonstrated battlefield performance.

Besides being a good deal younger than Sweeny, Grenville Dodge, the 16th Corps commander, was – not unlike Sweeny's prior adversary Heintzelman – an entrepreneurial sort; he had been successful in business and banking in Iowa before the war and Sweeny seems to have viewed him as a military amateur, not through-and-through army. He took offence, for instance, when a staff officer at Dodge's headquarters in Corinth issued a special order absent Dodge's signature – something in violation of the regulated procedures whereby staff men could not issue orders on their own authority. Sweeny fired off a memo to his staff ordering them to ignore any orders thus illegitimately issued. Angered, Dodge in turn informed General Sherman about the matter and wrote indignantly to Sweeny demanding an explanation. In January 1864 the two were at loggerheads again. The 16th Corps medical officer, Dr Norman Gay, issued an order from Dodge's headquarters, but without Dodge's signature. When it arrived at Sweeny's division, dictating medical procedures and operations, he returned it with the note 'no authority to issue Special Orders 14' and declaring that his 2nd Division medical officer 'will not therefore obey said orders'. A return communication from Dodge hotly declared 'As you peremptorily ordered an officer to disobey an order from these Headquarters, you will immediately forward an explanation'. Dodge also wrote a complaint once again to Sherman's headquarters.[24] Sherman had more to worry about, however, and the antagonism was let lie for the time being. It would revive, however, with great volatility, later in the Atlanta campaign.

Sweeny's nerves were perhaps becoming frayed; he was a field officer and had been under the guns throughout the war thus far – he was not by nature an executive officer functioning at some remove from the ferocity of battle. The fight at Corinth had been yet another awful bloodletting following upon the ones at Wilson's Creek and Shiloh. At Corinth a panicked artillery battery had galloped in wild confusion through Sweeny's troops, its horses and pieces killing some of his men; the Union general, Hackleman, was killed; gun-barrels, as mentioned, became so heated that rounds would explode while being loaded, and Sweeny had to order his men to continue firing until the guns burst if necessary. There were 7,197 casualties at Corinth right on the heels of the massive mortality at Shiloh, and Sweeny's brigade lost a third of its soldiers in the second encounter. The crisp officer's reports in the *Official Record*, unlike Ambrose Bierce's searing accounts, do not register the dreadful reality in the fields of the Civil War, and Sweeny's reports, like the rest, reflect the cool, unaffected style of military discourse. However, after five months more of this stress and carnage in the southern heat, his health began to falter – on 2 June 1863 a medical officer recommended that he be given a leave of absence based on his wounds as well as liver and stomach problems. He was given the leave, his command passing to Colonel E.W. Rice, and spent June and July with his children in New York. A physician he consulted there judged him to be in need of still further rest, but this recommendation the army rejected.[25] As mentioned earlier, Corporal C.W. Fish remarked on seeing Sweeny in the midst of the struggle at Shiloh, *his black hair streaked with grey* [author's italics]. At this point Sweeny was 42 years old.

Nor was the stress to ease in his new assignment. Returning from sick leave in September 1863, he was given command of the 2nd Division, 16th Army Corps, at La Grange, Tennessee, his unit's duties in the main involving anti-guerilla protection of the railway line along which Union reinforcements were dispatched from Vicksburg. Here he would again find himself fighting battles having to do with military administration as well as with the hostile forces of the Confederacy. In his new assignment he would also encounter another bane of the Civil War infantry officer – the aloof, self-involved cavalry officer mindful more than anything else of the dashing figure he aspired to cut in the war. Sweeny's reports during this period, and those of others, reflect painful frustration, much of it issuing from the arrival on 8 October of Colonel Edward Hatch with orders from General Hurlbut allowing him to operate pretty much independently of Sweeny and General Eugene Carr. He began to do so, freelancing around the countryside, no one knew whither, not bothering to coordinate with the local infantry. Sweeny's reports during this autumn note his receiving little word from Hatch sometimes for days at a time.[26] On 13 October 1862 Sweeny wrote to headquarters: 'I have heard nothing from the cavalry since yesterday morning, and have not the slightest idea of where they are or what they are doing'.[27] Lacking cavalry support and cooperation, Sweeny was stymied, unable to deploy his forces more effectively and mount offensives, and communications in this sector of the war appear to have been unsatisfactory at the time even aside from Hatch. Sweeny received a dispatch on 11 October 1863, for example, stating that 'Sherman, with his train, and Collierville are in the hands of the enemy'. He began to act on that shocking intelligence only to receive later word from General Carr that the report was inaccurate. On 14 October, Sweeny received a message from Hatch that he had engaged General James Chalmers' Confederate force near the Tallahatchie River. Sweeny wrote to Carr: 'Had he [Hatch] communicated with me before, I should have been able to checkmate the enemy, but I fear it is too late'. It was: Sweeny attempted a forced march to the river to prevent Chalmers' crossing and escaping, but he was not in time.

Hatch had the support of Hurlbut against Sweeny in the matter, but the other general in the area, Eugene Carr, a veteran of Wilson's Creek and later Congressional Medal of Honor recipient, was a victim of Hatch's cowboying as well, and when General Hurlbut wrote to Carr, and Sherman too, implying Chalmers' escape was Sweeny's fault, Carr came unequivocally to Sweeny's defence in a return letter of 15 October affirming that Hatch had left Sweeny 'working entirely in the dark':

> In reply to a telegram received last night . . . I feel it my duty to say I do not think General Sweeny was to blame for not placing the troops in better position to intercept Chalmers. Sweeny was not able to get control of the cavalry, and it does not seem to have acted under his instructions; he could get no news where it or the enemy was, and I do not see how he could have done better than he did . . .
>
> If the cavalry had been ready so that he could have started from here on Saturday morning, according to my orders, he would have intercepted the rebels on their way to Collierville . . . and would have thrashed them handsomely. I think the principle cause of the failure was the fact that the cavalry acted independently. I never received any report or information from them except what I got by accident; and after Sweeny was ordered to take command Hatch did not send him any report for two days, and neither Sweeny nor I knew where he was, east, west, north, or south . . . I consider Colonel Hatch solely responsible for the movements of the cavalry during this raid. He certainly did not act under my instructions nor, so far as I can learn, under those of General Sweeny.[28]

In November Sweeny's division was assigned to duties in Pulaski, Tennessee, along the Nashville and Decatur railway line, repairing and guarding it during the winter of 1863 into the early spring of 1864. The duties were largely of an engineering sort, the 16th Corps' commander, General Dodge, having had an engineering background in civilian life. A glimpse of things at this duty station is provided by a letter to Sarah Sweeny of 28 August 1864 sent from Pulaski:

> My Dear Daughter,
> Your last letter dated Jan 3rd was a long time coming, owing, no doubt, to its being wrongly directed. But that was my fault, not yours. When we left Iuka [Mississippi] last October, everybody supposed we would remain a permanent portion of Sherman's army in the field, and I have no doubt we would have if this R.R. hadn't to be repaired and guarded, and if Gen. Dodge was not so expert at that kind of business. So . . . we got 'switched off' here. This is an important position, to be sure, and of the most vital importance to the whole army; so much so that all our supplies have to be sent to the front by this channel, and in fact our movements would be entirely paralyzed without this line of communication. Still, it is not the kind of duty I fancy; and if I had my choice, would much rather be with Sherman at present, than here . . .
>
> It strikes me, Sarah, that you must have spent some of the money I sent you within the last five months very imprudently, as I can not see what you have to show for it. A hundred dollars, my child, ought to buy a good many things, and if you could but realize the privations and hardships I have to undergo while earning them, you would attach more value to them than you do. I do not say this in anger or reproof . . . but to guard you against acquiring a habit of extravagance that you might be unable to indulge in hereafter. You must not forget that my profession is fraught with danger . . . and if it should be God's will that I should fall in this coming campaign, or during this war, who then could you call upon to supply you with funds . . . I want you to let me know in your next what disposition you made of the money I have already sent you. Enclosed you will find $50 to purchase a watch . . .
>
> Your affectionate father,
> T.W. Sweeny[29]

In the spring of 1864 General Sherman was placed in charge of the military division of the Mississippi, a 100,000-man army of which General James McPherson's Army of the Tennessee was a primary part. On 27 April 1864, Sweeny's 2nd Division, part of Dodge's 16th Corps, received orders to proceed to Huntsville, Alabama, whence McPherson and his 6,000 troops set out for Villanow, Georgia, arriving on 1 May. Sherman was directing the Army of the Tennessee through strategic moves that he was confident would conclude in the fall of Atlanta, but the resistance would be formidable. On 8 May, Sherman instructed McPherson to move through Villanow and occupy Snake Creek Gap. Sweeny, under McPherson's orders, marched his division twenty miles to the south end of the Gap and occupied that point. From there they would proceed, along with other forces, to a crossroads within two miles of the occupied town.

Sweeny's command was then ordered to take part in the assault on Bald Hill, which was defended by a Confederate infantry numbering 1,400.

'In a combined frontal-flank assault', Albert Castle writes, 'Sweeny easily and quickly does so. In fact, the Confederates flee in panic. From the top of the hill Sweeny's soldiers look across a valley filled with dead pine trees and behold Resaca, less than a mile away'.[30] A confederate counterattack had looked promising:

> they showed great steadiness, and closed up the gaps and preserved their alignments; but the iron and leaden hail that was poured upon them was too much for flesh and blood to stand. Fuller's and Sweeny's divisions, with bayonets fixed, charged the enemy and drove them back to the woods.[31]

As Sherman's troops closed on Resaca on 14–15 May, they met with very strong resistance including stunning barrages. Sweeny received General Sherman's orders to move his division several miles south to Lay's Ferry where they were to cross the Oostanaula River and attack the Confederate route of communications with, and retreat from, Resaca. Sherman further ordered Sweeny to construct two pontoon bridges over which Union forces could pursue the enemy retreating from Resaca.

Sweeny and his command arrived at Lay's Ferry late on 13 May, brought their artillery to bear on the rebel side of the river, and then sent 200 men across in pontoons.[32] This effective strike was undone, however, when incorrect intelligence from the cavalry arrived claiming the rebels were constructing a bridge at a part of the river between Resaca and Lay's Ferry, and Sweeny had to order the troops that had crossed the river to return to the north bank. He then set out to reconnoitre the area identified in the erroneous reports.[33] Finding no such Confederate action as had been reported, he had to return to the river and plan to recapitulate his attack of the previous day. He regrouped his division on 15 May and ordered Colonel Elliot Rice, commander of his 1st Brigade, to set up the pontoon bridges under fire. General Corse, part of Sweeny's command, reported to Sherman:

> General Sweeny will make every effort to get a bridge over. An officer has just reported that we have got two boatloads over, and the rest of Colonel Rice's Brigade is crossing rapidly as possible in a place about one mile distant from where the pontoon boats were launched (and which is a dangerous place now, the enemy having discovered our object).

The division then battled its way across the Oostanaula in full force. Corse was able to report to Sherman later in the day: 'The bridge is finished, one brigade across and the balance of Sweeny's command crossing. The troops are entrenching themselves'.[34] Confederate General Walker's attempt to counter-attack and dislodge Sweeny's force was unsuccessful, and the Confederate force at Resaca was now flanked and had to abandon the town. Brigadier

General Corse's report from the field on 15 May 1864 to General Sherman began: 'General Sweeny crossed about 200 men in boats after dark last night, and pushed the pickets in their immediate front, capturing some 20 to 30 prisoners and a flag'.[35] In an account of the battle, Sherman later noted that the holding of the pontoon bridge at Lay's Ferry by Sweeny's division was 'well and handsomely done'.[36]

The foregoing suggests the intensity of these months for Sweeny, the almost ceaseless actions and challenges. There was further action brewing, however, and of a different kind – involving the enemy within as it were. That figure of speech would serve here to refer either to Grenville Dodge, Sweeny's immediate commander, or to Sweeny's own high sensitivity to slight and his short temper. Even through these days of what would appear to be extraordinary military performance on Sweeny's part, Dodge's reports frequently play him down and focus on Sweeny's subordinate officers such as Rice and Corse. It is possible that Dodge resented Sweeny's often spectacular command in the field with which he himself was having trouble keeping up. He may not have been happy having to write reports like the one of 15 May to McPherson: 'General Sweeny occupies the Rome Cross-Roads, two miles out from the river. Am closing up as fast as possible'.[37] The confidence that the highest brass was coming to have in Sweeny's generalship may also have begun to bother Dodge. In a report of 18 May he has to note, for example, that on 16 May, 'The Second division, General Sweeny, had received orders, direct from Major-General Sherman, to move out at once and secure the Rome and Calhan cross-roads'.[38] Dodge began to go around Sweeny, issuing orders directly to officers lower down the chain of command.

In July Dodge was promoted to major general, but, as Leslie Anders observes, 'rarely in the Union Army had so much rank commanded so little force . . . All Dodge could call his own in XVI corps was Sweeny's division and one brigade of Fuller's 4th Division'.[39] In effect, there were not enough troops to go around among the egos involved, and given Dodge's intrusive micro-management inclinations, things could only get worse. With the Federal army closing on Atlanta, Dodge's previously mentioned medical officer, Norman Gay, upon discovering that Sweeny was retaining an ambulance for his divisional use, reported the affront to Dodge who sent him to reclaim it from Sweeny's medical unit as corps property. Sweeny, whom one of his soldiers described as speaking three languages – 'English, Irish-American, and Profane',[40] descended upon Dodge's agent with a vengeance:

> 'I was most grossly insulted by Brig. General T.W. Sweeny', Gay reported to Dodge. Not only had the irascible division commander given the corps surgeon a strong reprimand, but he had climaxed his tirade by challenging the shocked medico to a duel. Gay declined the challenge, and Sweeny ordered a hostler to horse whip him. Unwilling to tarry in such rough company, Gay spurred his mount into a frantic getaway. But as he left [Gay reported] Sweeny yelled that he would 'shoot me the first time he caught me alone'.[41]

Whether Dodge was, as earlier mentioned, jealous of Sweeny's accomplishments and afraid he was stealing Dodge's thunder, cannot be established from this distance in time, but Sweeny's leadership from Wilson's Creek through Shiloh, Corinth, Resaca, to the outskirts of Atlanta, would seem to speak for itself. He found himself, however, in the closing months of this terrible war, entangled with his once and future enemy, and things would soon come to a head.

'Shockwaves of scandal reverberated throughout the Federal entrenchments facing Atlanta on July 25, 1864', writes Leslie Anders in a 1977 article in *Civil War Times Illustrated.* 'By sundown every private knew that Brigadier General Thomas W. Sweeny was being sent to Nashville under guard for striking his corps commander'.[42] Near Atlanta three days earlier, within a couple of miles of the shattered and besieged city, Sweeny's 16th had borne the brunt of a surprise Confederate counterattack in which Major General McPherson, the commander of the Union Army of the Tennessee, was killed. Sweeny's division had scrambled to get into formation, and the Battle of Atlanta ensued.

> Soon the whole rebel column burst upon them . . . the rebel column was now overlapping Dodge's command, and threatened to turn his flank. General Sweeny knew that in a great measure the fate of the day depended on his division; unless he could check the rebel advance long enough for the troops to take up position, [the rebels] would overwhelm them . . . [Sweeny] dashed from point to point, and if he saw any part of the lines wavering, there he was, regardless of shot and shell.[43]

During the mêlée, Dodge, as he had done before, issued orders directly to several officers in Sweeny's command – this time in combat.[44] Dodge's corps had always been a small one, and Sherman had borrowed Sweeny's division to fill a hole in the line. When the rebel attack commenced, Dodge was dining with General Fuller, and the two at first thought the troops were shooting hogs. Finally realizing what was happening, and with few real troops of his own to command, Dodge headed for where Sweeny was already engaged in battle and – outrageously as Sweeny saw it – began issuing orders. 'Grenville Dodge', Albert Castle notes, 'was dashing about and cutting across command channels to act as a colonel, brigadier general, and division commander, all in one'. He was undercutting Sweeny now in the very midst of the battle.[45]

The Confederate assault was driven back, and a post-battle gloom prevailed. The casualties had to be tended to; and word of General McPherson's death spread through the ranks. Fuller, Sweeny felt, had not done his part during the fight, and 'the more [Sweeny] brooded over Dodge's bypassing him to order the 2d Division's regiments about, the angrier he became. A withering note of protest to the corps commander was ignored . . . Sweeny was left to seethe all weekend'.[46] Three days after the engagement, on the morning of 25 July 1864, General Dodge and his staff rode out to assess the state of the lines should there be another counterattack. When they were in the area of Sweeny's headquarters tent, he hailed the pair and invited them in out of the sun, but hospitality was the last thing on his mind. He began a heated denunciation of 'damned political generals' and of the inefficiency of the Army of the Tennessee overall – he had received no reports of enemy presence in the area, for example, and had been in the right place only by accident. As he became angrier, the court-martial records indicate, his wrath began to turn toward present company. When he declared that Fuller's forces had broken during the battle, jeopardizing Sweeny's adjoining division, Dodge came to Fuller's defence. Furious, Sweeny now confronted Dodge, and, before long, had unleashed the dogs of war beyond recall – he was cursing Dodge to his face, calling him a liar. 'You are a God damned cowardly son of a bitch', he shouted. 'You are a God damned inefficient son of a bitch'. Dodge finally slapped him in the face, and Sweeny returned the favour. Staff officers leaped over one another to separate the two.

When Fuller put his hand on Sweeny's shoulder, Sweeny turned on him, and the two were now rolling on the tent floor, Sweeny having the upper hand momentarily, but the stocky Fuller ending up on top, chocking his one-armed opponent. When they were separated, Sweeny's artillery officer, Captain Frederick Welker, attempted to restrain him, but he again broke loose, shouting at Dodge, 'Mr. Dodge of Iowa, you can fire a pistol – and so can I'. Ultimately, Dodge ordered a subordinate officer to place Sweeny under arrest, but Sweeny, ever the stickler for military etiquette, shouted at the aide, 'You don't know *how* to arrest an officer!' – the man was not, as required, wearing his sword. As Dodge rode off from his camp, Sweeny yelled after him, again calling for a duel, 'Go, Mr. Dodge of Iowa, you God-damned political general. I shall expect a note from you, sir!'[47]

Sweeny was in trouble. No note pertaining to a duel would be forthcoming, but a court martial was. Fuller brought charges and carried them forward vigorously. There was no reference to Sweeny having been drinking at the time of the altercation, but Dodge would in fact later in life refer to Sweeny's having been, on one occasion at least, too inebriated to mount his horse.[48] But if so, Sweeny would be far from the only Civil War general given, or driven, to drink, Grant being the most obvious example. The war's end was in sight, however, and General Sherman had long harboured his own distrust of 'political officers' like Dodge, and both considerations probably worked in Sweeny's favour. In a communication to General Logan, commander of the Army of the Tennessee at this juncture, Sherman appears loath to press the matter:

> I beg you to see that no injustice is done to General Sweeny. I have noticed for some time a growing dissatisfaction on the part of General Dodge with General Sweeny. It may be personal . . . You can see how cruel it would be to a brave and sensitive gentleman and officer to be arrested, deprived of his command, and sent to the rear at this time . . . but still you are the one to judge. I fear that General Sweeny will feel that even I am influenced against him . . . but it is not so.[49]

The prosecution went ahead, however, and Sweeny was exiled to Nashville to await a military trial that would be five months in coming. When General Oliver Howard took command of the Army of the Tennessee in July, he requested a postponement because, with the battle for Atlanta still in progress, witnesses could not be spared from duty to make the trip to the trial.[50]

The court martial finally convened in Louisville on 5 December 1864, however, with Sweeny being charged on six counts of conduct unbecoming an officer and gentleman including striking a superior and commanding officer. Remarkably enough, when all was said and done, on 2 January 1865 he was acquitted on all counts. Officers testifying had tended to support the assertion that underlay Sweeny's original angry confrontation with Dodge and Fuller – that Fuller's sector of the front had indeed caved in, jeopardizing Sweeny's regiment. But the acquittal, three months before Lee's capitulation at Appomattox, was in effect only a legal one; Sweeny had insulted superior officers and was now getting the cold shoulder from Howard, the new commander of the Army of the Tennessee, who was adamant, declaring to Sherman that 'Sweeny has been cleared, but I don't want him . . . [He] might be mustered out, with a view to the interest of the service'.[51] Howard ordered Sweeny to New York on standby status. His 25 July farewell to his troops, delivered when the orders against him were first served, would turn out to be Sweeny's permanent farewell to them:

> Your General has been deprived of his command and ordered to Nashville in arrest. Before leaving he is constrained to express to you his admiration at the heroic manner in which you repulsed the terrific assault of the enemy upon your lines on the 22d instant . . . He had looked for the displaying by you of the ordinary fortitude of soldiers . . . but you did more than this . . . Your General confesses to you freely that the evening of the 22nd was the proudest of his life . . . and it was his desire to lead your victorious banner into the doomed city in our front: but this is not to be. It is only left with him to request of you to extend to your future commanders the confidence and cheerful obedience that you have always shown to him.[52]

Sweeny was relieved of command and reverted to the regular-army rank of major, which would change, in August of 1865, to a brevet rank of colonel. But his assignments would be marginal ones despite his appeals to return to combat duty. He was assigned again to St Louis and then to garrison duty at Nashville. From the latter post, on 12 October, he requested a twenty-day leave of absence to attend to business in New York. This business would define his direction for the near future – a preoccupation with the endeavour many Irish participants in the American Civil War, as earlier noted, had all along considered the conflict a training ground for – the liberation of Ireland from Britain.[53]

Three weeks earlier, on 26 September 1865, Sweeny had presided over a Fenian rally in St Louis. The *Missouri Democrat* of the following day headlined: 'GREAT FENIAN MEETING – THE COMING REVOLUTION – IRELAND TO BE FREE – THE

CONTEST NEAR AT HAND', and reported: 'The Fenian demonstration last evening was a grand affair. The crowd was immense. The rotunda of the Courthouse was packed with men, women, and children. There was also an immense crowd outside unable to gain admittance . . . General Sweeny, on assuming the chair, spoke as follows:

> "We are assembled here tonight to take into consideration the means by which we can render aide to our countrymen in Ireland who are now, from the indications I have seen in the foreign papers, about to strike one more blow for Irish independence. We . . . have in the last 600 years endeavored to throw off the yoke that has bound us down as serfs, not to a superior people, but to a more powerful nation, and whenever we have had strength in our arms to strike a blow we have struck that blow, and we are going to strike another . . . The spirit of independence is bound to succeed in the end . . . Now my friends, we who have borne so much; we who have been driven from our native land as exiles, into this – thank God – this generous land, that has received us all as children and brothers; we who have fought for our adopted country, will fight for our native land . . ."[54]

NOTES

1. Shouted by General Sweeny to the departing General Grenville Dodge after their scuffle at Sweeny's camp near Atlanta, 25 July 1864. Leslie Anders, 'Fisticuffs at Headquarters: Sweeny vs. Dodge', *Civil War Times Illustrated*, 15, 10 (1977), pp.8–15.
2. TWS Report to Adjutant, 1873, W. Sweeny, *Memoir*, p.15.
3. Thomas William Sweeny Papers, Huntington Library, San Marino, California.
4. TWS Report to Adjutant,1873, W. Sweeny, *Memoir*, p.16.
5. Ibid., pp.16–17.
6. Digging in the sense of erecting breastworks and so forth, it is true, became a commonplace of military strategy only later in the war as it became clear that the old romantic–chivalric battlefield models no longer applied. See Danto,'Gettysburg', pp.98–116.
7. TWS Report to Adjutant, 1873, W. Sweeny, *Memoir*, p.19. Sweeny's report details the battle as his unit experienced it, pp.17–19.
8. Quoted in William Sweeny, 'Brigadier-General TWS', *JAIHS,* (1928), p.262.
9. Albert D. Richardson *The Secret Service, the Field, the Dungeon, and the Escape* (Hartford, CT, 1865), p.239. Richardson mentions that he later met a Confederate soldier who had been there when Sweeny mistakenly rode up to the Rebel battery and that the man 'described with great vividness the impression which Sweeny's gallantry made upon him'. Richardson observes of Sweeny: 'His coolness and marvelous escapes were talked of before many campfires throughout the army'. Regarding Sweeny's wounding at Shiloh he writes that following upon his horse being killed, 'almost fainting with loss of blood, he was lifted upon another horse, and remained on the field through the entire day'.
10. Ambrose Bierce, 'What I Saw at Shiloh', *Ambrose Bierce Civil War Stories* (New York, 1994), p.5.
11. Ibid. pp.7–8.
12. Kelly, TWS Interview, January 1886.
13. Quoted in William Sweeny, 'Brigadier-General TWS', *JAIHS,* (1928), pp.271–2. The author of the poem is the American sculptor and artist, James Edward Kelly, elsewhere cited with reference to his January 1886 interview with General Sweeny.

14. Ibid., p.263.
15. Bierce, *Civil War Stories*, p.2.
16. *OR*, 1.17, pp.271–7617. From Corinth, 13 October 1862. Thomas William Sweeny Papers, Huntington Library, San Marino, California.
17. To Sarah Sweeny from Corinth, 13 October 1862, ibid.
18. Dodge to Grant, 13 and 14 December, *OR,* 17, pp.541–2.
19. Thomas William Sweeny Papers, Huntington Library, San Marino, California.
20. Ibid.
21. Quoted. in Coyer, 'Hero of the Armless Sleeve', p.238.
22. *OR*, 17, p.2.
23. Ibid.
24. Leslie Anders, 'Fisticuffs at Headquarters: Sweeny vs. Dodge', *Civil War Times Illustrated,* 15, 10, (1977), pp.8–9.
25. Coyer, 'Hero of the Armless Sleeve', p.243.
26. *OR,* 30, pp.735–8.
27. *OR,* 30, p.331.
28. *OR,* 30, pp.378–9.
29. Thomas William Sweeny Papers, Huntington Library, San Marino, California.
30. Castel, *Decision in the West*, p.137.
31. W.H. Chamberlain, 'Hood's Second Sortie at Atlanta – Battle of Bald Hill', in Johnson and Buel (eds), Vol. I, *Battles and Leaders of the Civil War, 1887*, p.327.
32. Castel, *Decision*, pp.162–3.
33. Ibid.
34. *OR,* 38, p.196–7.
35. Ibid.
36. William Tecumseh Sherman, *Home Letters of General Sherman*, (ed.) M.A. DeWolf Howe (New York, 1909), p.293.
37. *OR*, 38, p.196.
38. Ibid., p.378.
39. Anders, 'Fisticuffs', pp.11–2
40. Castel, *Decision in the West*, p.162
41. Anders, 'Fisticuffs', p.11.
42. Ibid., p.8.
43. David P. Conyngham, *Sherman's March through the South* (New York, 1865), pp.170–1.
44. Anders, 'Fisticuffs', pp.12–13.
45. Castel, *Decision in the West*, pp.418–19.
46. Anders, 'Fisticuffs', p.13.
47. Castle, *Decision in the West*, pp.418–19. Anders, 'Fisticuffs', pp.13–15. 'Court-Martial Proceedings Dec. 5, 1864, Pertaining to Thomas W. Sweeny', (LL–2995) Office of Judge Advocate General, National Archives, Washington, DC.
48. Anders, 'Fisticuffs', p.15.
49. *OR,* 38, pp.252–3.
50. Anders, 'Fisticuffs', p.15.
51. Ezra W. Warner, *Generals in Blue: Lives of the Union Commanders* (Baton Rouge, LA, 1964), p.492.
52. *OR*, 38, pp.253–4.
53. Granted that this devotion was in many cases cynically taken advantage of: Kerby Miller cites Thomas Francis Meagher as culpable in this regard, the eloquent Meagher having served as an enthusiastic recruiter of Irish immigrants for service in the war. See

Emigrants and Exiles: Ireland and the Irish Exodus to North America (New York, 1985), p.338. (Sweeny, of course, recruited too, but on a more modest level and not as an orator.) By mid-1863, Miller notes, 'even William B. West, the American consul at Galway, admitted that the Irish countryside was filled with thousands of bereaved households, bitterly "bewailing the loss of Brothers, sons and Husbands in our disastrous war" (p.359). And there were concerted Union efforts to recruit within Ireland itself as well as corresponding Confederate efforts to discourage Irish enlistments in the Union army, *see* Charles P. Cullop, 'An Unequal Duel: Union Recruiting in Ireland, 1863–64', *Civil War History*, 13 (1967), pp.101–13. Bishop Hughes of New York was reportedly one of those who went to Ireland in search of soldiers for the Northern cause, *see* John Rutherford's, *The Fenian Conspiracy*, Vol. 1 (London, 1877), p.286. As noted earlier, St. Louisan Father John Bannon was sent to campaign among the clergy in Ireland on behalf of the Confederate cause in the hope of diminishing Irish emigrant enlistment in the Union army.

54. *Missouri Democrat*, 26 September 1865, p.2.

6

Commanding the Armies of Ireland: The Fenian Invasion, 1866

> There was a Fenian meeting here last night . . . VIVE LA RÉPUBLIQUE IRLANDAISE.
>
> Sweeny, St Louis, 1865[1]

> Fenianism continues to be the all absorbing topic of the day. Nothing else is heard on any side.
>
> *Quebec Morning Chronicle*, 7 June 1866

Though his leave request read 'New York', Thomas Sweeny's destination was in reality Philadelphia where, on 16 October 1865, a convention of the Fenian Brotherhood was to convene. He attended as a delegate from Nashville.[2] At the bidding of the American Fenian leadership he now became involved with the task of coordinating and commanding the military forces of Fenianism as the designated Secretary of War of the Brotherhood and General Commanding the Armies of Ireland. That the Irish nationalist movement in the United States had long had its eye on him for a leadership role, is suggested by an article devoted to him in the *Irish-American* of 26 April 1862, which concluded:

> General Sweeny is an ardent lover of the land of his birth, and longs for the day and hour when, in her service, he may meet the common foe of his adopted as well as his native country. Even when lying disabled by his wounds in Mexico, he had made arrangements to cast himself into the then expected struggle for Irish independence. That opportunity was not afforded him; but his heart is still as warm as ever for the good cause, and the moment of action – if it come in his lifetime – will not find him wanting. Brave, generous, and confiding in an eminent degree, he is the true type of the Irish character – a representative man of whom our race may be proud in any comparison.[3]

As noted earlier, Sweeny was not one of the circle of founders of American Fenianism. The exact date on which he signed on officially with it is uncertain. His name does not appear in the Proceedings of the Chicago Fenian Convention of November 1863, for example, but his being in the midst of the war at the time would account for this. Given his interest in the military side of the Irish problem, however, he was unquestionably in contact with the extensive Fenian US Army network during the Civil War years; indeed, he could hardly have avoided it. During the war, US Army Fenianism developed virtually into an arm of the Brotherhood in its own right. Fenian networking even crossed Union–Confederate lines. In his *The Valiant Hours: An Irish-American in the Army of the Potomac*, Thomas Francis Galwey recalls meeting with a Fenian emissary travelling as a journalist; the man was in possession of passes signed by both Union and Confederate military authorities. Galwey describes a meeting held a few nights later in which Union and Confederate Fenian delegations were in attendance. He witnessed 'a joint meeting . . . held in a ravine not far from Falmouth. A sentry was posted at either end of the opening and the two delegations, one in gray and one in blue, after swearing . . . not to discuss the American Civil War, met in the center'.[4] During the Atlanta campaign Sweeny called a truce with his Confederate opposition, the likewise Irish-born General Patrick Cleburne, and sent the latter a message proposing that the two officers join in post-war operations to free Ireland.[5] Irish Republican Brotherhood (IRB) envoys and Fenian messengers crossed battle lines to deliver the latest news from Ireland as well and to collect money for 'The Cause'.[6] In his narrative Galwey describes another Fenian meeting in the ranks:

> Having made the acquaintance of some Irish officers who are Fenians, I have been introduced to the Circle. The Center of the Circle is Dr. Reynolds, Surgeon of the 63rd New York . . . The Secretary is Capt. John Rorty, a US artillery officer. The meeting begins at eight o'clock in the evening. A few minutes are enough for the dispatch of routine business, for the initiation of new members, and so forth. After this, an officer who has to go on duty is careful to steal away to his camp.[7]

Elsewhere Galwey records being invited to supper in an officer's tent: 'It was elegant even if it was a soldier's supper. A Mr. Froantree, lately from Ireland, who is an agent of the Fenian Brotherhood, with Captain Downing, Fitz Harris, and myself formed the party'.[8]

While participation in US Army Fenian activity was all to the good as far as those of the Sweeny persuasion were concerned – those who foresaw the United States as the place where the Fenian gathering was to be – among nationalists in Ireland there was strong resistance to Irish emigration to Civil War America. As R.V. Comerford notes, this resistance was not due to antipathy toward the Union cause, but to the fact that many Irish nationalists on both sides of the Atlantic feared that the exodus of young men to the United States stood to leave Ireland with diminished revolutionary manpower on the home front.[9] A Fenian envoy to Ireland wrote to John O'Mahony relative to an uprising there that 'it must be remembered, as you yourself told me, that we are running a race with emigration, and if we do not move soon, we will have no men in the country to move with'.[10] Joseph M. Hernon Jr cites the differing attitudes toward emigration-to-enlist evident in letters to the Cork *Examiner* from Myles O'Reilly and O'Donovan Rossa in 1863. O'Reilly, former commander of the Irish Papal Brigade, noted that he was receiving letters from soldiers who had served with him in Italy complaining of wretched conditions in the Union ranks, inadequate hospitals and 'useless and purposeless sacrifice of soldier's lives'. O'Rossa, on the other hand, while sharing O'Reilly's concern about the drain of Ireland's young men, argued in a letter of response that O'Reilly had bought into the 'English lie' that emigration from Ireland 'is attributable to the exertions of the American recruiting agent' rather than to the 'blighting effect . . . of landlord and English rule'.[11]

The attempt to stem the tide of emigration would prove to be for the most part a losing battle, however; Irish enlistments continued apace. O'Donovan Rossa's own family was thoroughly engaged in the conflict; his brother, John, along with his sister's husband, enlisted in the 69th Pennsylvania Infantry, and his brother, Conn, was in the US Navy.[12] At the 1863 Chicago Fenian convention 'it was reported that nearly every Irish regiment in the field sent its delegate, and at least one officer of high rank, Colonel J.G. Gleason of the Army of the Potomac, shared in the deliberations of the convention'.[13] The Fenians recruited openly in the Union Army throughout the war, and during his 1864 trip to the Chicago Fenian Fair, James Stephens, travelling incognito as 'Mr Daly', was able to visit and inspect Fenian circles within the Union Army thanks to enabling documents provided by Indiana Governor Morton and Brigadier General Grainger.[14] Kirby Miller notes that at war's end

> Fenianism had about 50,000 actual members, many of them trained soldiers, and hundreds of thousands of ardent sympathizers; in just seven years, and despite clerical condemnation, Fenianism had become the most popular and powerful ethnic organization in Irish-American history.[15]

This was probably the most formidable Irish power ever assembled. The question was how it might be effectively focused, and when and where.

That Sweeny was in significant contact with the Fenian network during the war is further suggested by, for instance, a letter from Colonel James Mulligan dated 29 July 1864, six months before Mulligan's death in battle in the Shenandoah Valley, among the Sweeny papers at the Huntington Library. Mulligan is responding to a letter inviting him to the Fenian 'Irish National Fair' in Chicago that year. The letter is from a fair official, but it is interesting that it should end up in Sweeny's collected correspondence. Mulligan enclosed 100 dollars and wrote:

> And if by the grace of God . . . we come to blows in support of this same holy cause . . . having first solidly settled this present question in favor of the Union – I devote all my heart – and all my strength – and whatsoever experience I possess 'to aid in establishing and maintaining the cause of Irish Nationality'.[16]

Prior association with the Fenian organization in the military ranks would account for Sweeny's appearing on the dais at the New York St Patrick's Day banquet of 1865 and at the Philadelphia convention in October of the same year

– in both cases sharing the platform with the likes of William Roberts and John O'Mahony.[17] It is unlikely that he was appointed Secretary of War by O'Mahony immediately thereafter, and confirmed by the senate, without already having built up some significant bona fides and constituency among the Fenian hierarchy and rank and file. Despite the historical image of them as a naive, quixotic lot, the Brotherhood of 1865 was made up of seasoned veterans from all walks of military life, possessed of abundant practical experience in warfare, and O'Mahony, a veteran himself, had an impressive group of former Civil War officers to counsel him.

One reservation that did come to the fore concerning Sweeny, however, was that his military experience had been largely in regimental, field command as opposed to the kind of broader tactical experience his new position would call for. Sweeny was himself cognizant of this criticism and, as noted previously, early on urged O'Mahony to make overtures to General Philip Sheridan – whose reputation and staff command experience were greater than Sweeny's – to accept the Secretary of War position.[18] But if O'Mahony did so it was to no avail, and the cautious Sheridan would remain in the wings, a rumoured military messiah for the Fenians throughout the 1860s – his name coming up again when Sweeny finally resigned the Secretary of War position.

Sweeny probably benefited in fact from not being a long-time inner-circle Fenian and not having a background in the cause in Ireland such as Stephans, Doheney, DeVoy, O'Mahony, et al. had. His more Americanized profile may have worked in his favour, holding out to the membership, much of which was interested in new leadership, the promise of a necessary element of new blood and new thinking in the Brotherhood hierarchy and a break with the older alliances, antagonisms and cliques. Sweeny, and his ally William Randall Roberts were, however, regarded as something of a breed apart among some of the Fenian old guard. Roberts was a businessman and widely considered to be a theatrical New York politico. John O'Leary wrote of him, for instance: 'John O'Mahony was not, indeed, an ideal leader, but he was an ideal Irishman while Colonel Roberts . . . and most of the Senators, were men of whom we knew little and for whom we cared less'. John Devoy described Roberts as 'a successful dry goods merchant who was vain and shallow but showy'. O'Donovan Rossa wrote to his wife from prison: 'You say that in America the party that befriended you most, of the factions, was the Roberts party. I must tell you Mr. Roberts did not make the most favorable impression on me.'[19]

It was not long after O'Mahony appointed him that it became clear, much to O'Mahony's displeasure, that Sweeny's allegiances lay with the activist senate faction of the Brotherhood. He aligned himself with those Fenian elements who were impatient with O'Mahony and Stephens and that pair's endlessly projected revolution in Ireland, a revolution that appeared to be taking far too long to materialize.[20] Particularly distressing was the fear that the Irish investment in the American Civil War would be for nothing, the Brotherhood's cohesive Union Army network dissolving and the war-weary Irish troops drifting off after their own pursuits, making any later attempt at gathering them together difficult. The Fenian direct-action wing felt these trained and seasoned soldiers needed to be rallied and brought to bear against Britain in short order – the trouble the Brotherhood would ultimately encounter in trying to muster these veterans arguably did stem in part from the dissolution of the Brotherhood's disciplined, US Army-based structure all too quickly after Appomattox.

The organization's senate faction had in 1864 called for a Grand Army to be raised and sent forth 'by the shortest route to meet the common enemy of Ireland and the United States'.[21] The 'common enemy' assumption was based on American resentment of British aid to the Confederacy. The 'shortest route' referred to making Canada the target. This idea of striking the British Empire at the point of its closest proximity to the United States seemed to many Fenians a promising strategy, and General Sweeny was reputed to have a detailed and credible plan for just such an undertaking. Sweeny wrote to Roberts in October 1865:

> The most reliable accounts from Ireland have convinced me that our friends there are totally unprepared for the martial means necessary to contend, with any show of success, against the British troops, and that to incite an insurrection, at present, would be but to provide a wholesale massacre in which thousands of brave lives would be sacrificed in a useless struggle. The Canadian frontier, extending from north of the St Lawrence to Lake Huron, a distance of more than 1,300 miles, is assailable at all points.[22]

Roberts and Sweeny, the leaders of the senate faction, were of somewhat similar backgrounds; both having immigrated to America from Cork before the Famine, and both having achieved a degree of fame – in Robert's case fortune as well – in their adopted country. Neither shared O'Mahony's and Stephens's Young Ireland background, 1848 exile experience, exposure to French and Italian revolutionary action, and so on. The two, along with the other members of the Fenian senate wing in America, tended to resent and to be impatient with the way in which a small group had early on defined Irish nationalist efforts in America – the impolitic John Mitchel, for instance, had gone out of his way to alienate the powerful American Catholic leadership.[23] Nor was the senate happy with the hold on power, the mutually reinforcing authority, that Stephens and O'Mahony together exercised over the whole nationalist scene on both sides of the Atlantic.[24] As early as 1850, the *Irish American* had written of the Young Ireland cohort:

> Previously to the arrival of the first 'refugee' in Philadelphia in the autumn of 1848, there had been a remarkable unanimity among the sons of Erin on these shores; but ever since that ill-fated moment it has been, with the Irish in America a regular succession of gales of anger, bitterness, passion and dissension.[25]

Whatever its cause, however, the dissension that characterized Irish-American affairs mid-century would soon take in General Sweeny; indeed, for a time he would find himself at the centre of the storm. A wholesale schism in American Fenianism, one that would never heal, began in earnest when O'Mahony and the senate appropriated $56,000 for Sweeny's war department just after the Philadelphia Convention, O'Mahony assuming the money would go toward preparations for military action organized by Stephens and the IRB in Ireland itself, the senate group knowing better. When O'Mahony, whose authority had been significantly curbed by the Philadelphia Convention, discovered that the funds were in fact earmarked for a Canadian invasion, he had Bernard Doran Killian, his treasurer, block payment. The senate faction led by Roberts retaliated by charging O'Mahony with financial irregularities in the issuance of Fenian bonds.[26] Fenian circles lined up with one or the other faction in the dispute – not a good omen for Sweeny, who was all the while working on an invasion plan that would presuppose extraordinary Irish unity if it were to have a prayer of success.

There was a brief transitional period during the autumn of 1865 when Fenian documents would be undersigned by both Sweeny and O'Mahony. The November appointment of Charles Carroll Tevis, a Sweeny-appointed West-Pointer, to be Fenian adjutant general, for example, was signed by Sweeny and further signed 'Approved' by O'Mahony. The appointment stated that 'all communications on military matters will be addressed to these Headquarters' (Sweeny's). Subsequent documents carrying Sweeny's orders related to preparations for an invasion are for the most part set forth through Tevis and with no reference to O'Mahony's approval. Things were under way. The Fenian organizational structure began to be defined by Sweeny and became more overtly military. Two weeks after Tevis' designation as adjutant, there was issued 'General Orders No.1' from Sweeny via the 'War Department, F.B.':

> I. In compliance with Special Orders No.1, War Department F.B., the undersigned [Tevis] assumes the direction of the Adjutant General's Office of the Fenian Brotherhood.
>
> II. All military officers belonging to the organization will report immediately their addresses in writing . . . giving a full history of their past services, stating the period of time served, in what arm of the service, in what corps, division, brigade, and regiment or battery; if on the staff and in what capacity; the battles engaged in . . . what military books studied; if wounded state how far incapacitated . . .
>
> III. Every report must be forwarded through the assistant inspector general of each State, or in his absence the Head Centre . . .
>
> IV. Any change of address will be immediately notified to this Headquarters; a non-compliance with this order will be considered as an evidence of insubordination and of an unwillingness to render service to the cause of Ireland . . .
>
> V. Tri-monthly reports will be furnished to these Headquarters by each Centre on the tenth, twentieth, and last day of each month stating the number of men prepared to go into the field at a week's notice; their

efficiency as soldiers; their arms and ammunition and equipments in their possession or at the disposal of the Circles.

VI. Centres will make such necessary remarks as will enable the War Department to distinguish the most reliable men.

By order of the Sec. of War, F.B. [Sweeny][27]

The attempt was to arrange in a short time for the kind of sophisticated and complex logistical system necessary to see to it that at the crucial moment 'the pikes would be together' – no small task, nor could Sweeny have foreseen how little time there would ultimately be available.

The two Fenian factions began gathering apart from one another and passing conflicting resolutions. An O'Mahony wing meeting in January 1866, for instance, emphatically refused to entertain any notion of a Canadian venture, even a diversionary raid, and called unanimously for war in Ireland itself. The faction further initiated publication of the *Irish People* as its newspaper voice, an event that, as William D'Arcy notes, 'marked the beginning of a campaign of vituperation, recrimination, and ridicule which continued unabated for years, even after both wings had lost the majority of their members'.[28]

In the hope of diminishing the animosity, Sweeny addressed remarks, dated 2 January 1866, to the Fenian Membership, ones pleading for the unity without which the cause would be lost:

> Our situation at present is that of two armies whose chiefs, although with the same great ends in view, cannot agree upon the lines of operation to be adopted. But this difference of opinion does not involve the necessity of a brawl which will be their mutual ruin. If they cannot act in concert, why not act separately?
>
> Out of our difficulties I can see but one way to escape. It is to call in each state a convention of delegates from the different circles, who, with a calm, dispassionate examination of the subject, will decide in whom they will repose their confidence, and then, in silence, without wrangling and without dangerous publicity, allow Colonel O'Mahony and myself to work out his respective plan for the freedom of Ireland.[29]

Later that same month, Sweeny and Roberts undertook a tour of some major American cities – Newark, Brooklyn, Hartford, Albany, Buffalo – to rally support for their cause, Sweeny's speeches often getting front-page newspaper coverage. In his Newark address on 19 January he defended his Canadian strategy:

> I am ready to fight, and, if need be, to die for Ireland, but it must be in connection with plans that hold out a fair chance of success. I never will ask my countrymen to follow me in a movement which can result only in their defeat. I will be no party to useless slaughter. Too much Irish blood has already been shed in vain and ill-considered projects . . . As a military man I believe we can strike the power of England effectively in Canada; and I

> believe a . . . rising in Ireland would be a mad endeavor. If any half a dozen generals of high professional repute, men who have characters to lose, will say that an insurrection in Ireland, with such assistance as we could render from America, would have any chance of succeeding, I will embark on it; but my own military knowledge and experience convince me that no such men would pronounce such an opinion. On the other hand, I know that they consider my Canadian plans realizable, if the Irish population in America will but give me a fair share of support.[30]

By this time it had become clear to Stephens in Dublin that the O'Mahony wing was losing out and that he, Stephens, would probably not be able to heal the split in the American Brotherhood. What was worse, to his mind, was that a new faction outside his sphere of influence and entirely committed to a Canadian rather than an Irish military strike had come to power in the United States. He was appalled and outraged, as is evident in a communication he sent from Dublin on 23 December in which he tried to reinstall O'Mahony and preserve his own plan for nationalist action:

> To the Members of the Fenian Brotherhood, and the friends of Ireland generally in the US of America, Canada, etc. . . .
> Countrymen and Friends: Aware that certain members of the Fenian Brotherhood, and notoriously the 'Senate' of that association, have, madly and traitorously, moved to a mad and traitorous end, raise the cry of 'to Canada!' instead of the cry 'to Ireland!' and aware that John O'Mahony, known as Head Centre and President of the Fenian Brotherhood, has wisely and firmly, as in duty bound, opposed this mad and traitorous diversion from the right path – the only path that could possibly save our country and our race, I . . . hereby appoint the said John O'Mahony Representative and financial agent of the Irish Republic in the United States . . . with ample and unquestionable authority to enroll men, raise money, and fit out an expedition to sail for Ireland and reach Ireland on the earliest possible day.[31]

In the meantime, Sweeny was still in the US Army while at the same time openly campaigning on behalf of the Brotherhood. He had written to his friend, William Bodge, on 26 September 1865, for example, describing the previously mentioned Fenian rally in St Louis: 'We had an immense Fenian demonstration here last night, at which I presided. There were 20,000 people present, and great enthusiasm, and the most perfect order prevailed. VIVE LA RÉPUBLIQUE IRLANDAISE'.[32] Questions began to be raised by some unsympathetic newspapers, however, as to how, as a commissioned officer in the US Army, Sweeny could be delivering such speeches. Even greater controversy was stirred up when he became the publicly avowed Secretary of War in a radical political organization. Only a Celt would presume to attempt such a thing, the *Chicago Tribune* asserted, 'A German would be considered insane'. *The Nation*, similarly indignant, wrote that 'General Sweeny was probably surprised to find that the President intends to decide himself when Canada had better be invaded . . .'.

Opposition continuing to mount, the *Cleveland Leader* editorialized: 'We protest against his holding this double position. It seems to us that a proper regard for its own dignity and constancy will compel our government to demand the resignation of General Sweeny'.[33] The same paper on St Patrick's Day, 1866, argued editorially that the Fenian project violated the neutrality laws and that the laws should be enforced. The specific law whose enforcement they called for read:

> If any person shall within the territory or jurisdiction of the United States begin or set on foot or provide or prepare for, any military expedition or enterprise, to be carried on from thence against the territory or the dominion of any foreign prince or state, or any colony, district or people with whom the United States is at peace, every person so offending shall be deemed guilty of a high misdemeanor and shall be fined not exceeding $3,000 or imprisoned more than three years.[34]

Under such newspaper editorial pressure, Sweeny's Army superiors refused his request for a three-month extension of his leave from duty in Nashville.[35] He appealed and was again refused, but still remained in New York. Finally, on 25 December 1865, President Johnson issued orders whereby Sweeny was dismissed from the Army for being absent without leave. His commission and his pension, the fruits of a lifetime of US military service, were now probably gone – sacrificed to the cause of Irish independence.

Some two months later, at the Pittsburg Fenian convention of 19 February 1866, he delivered the keynote address in which the imminence of action was not disguised:

> We have made large purchases of arms and war material. If you are prepared to stand by us, we promise that before the summer sun kisses the hilltops of Ireland, a ray of hope will gladden every true Irish heart, for by that time we shall have conquered and got hostages for our brave patriots at home. The green flag will be flying independently to freedom's breeze, and we will have a base of operations from which we can not only emancipate Ireland, but also annihilate England.[36]

He would not undertake such an invasion, Sweeny had insisted, with anything less than 10,000 men – this was premised on a winter invasion when the lakes and rivers would be frozen and crossable; in any other season 20,000 men would be the minimum. Each gun would be supplied with 500 rounds of ammunition, each man provided 200 rounds. He emphasized the advantage winter would afford:

> The fortifications of Quebec and Kingston are the only ones admitted by the British military engineers to be in a good state of defense, and preparations have been made to strengthen them by earthworks and entrenched camps at London, Stratford, Hamilton, Ottawa City, Prescott and Montreal. The severity of the winter, however, has interrupted their construction, which will be resumed with great activity as soon as the spring shall have set in. It is,

> therefore, of vital importance to our success that we attack this winter, while principal towns are comparatively defenseless and when the frozen rivers will prevent the operation of the enemy's gunboats against us.[37]

Another emphatic requirement would be three batteries of artillery. The funds called for would be $450,000. Sweeny's design was, as William D'Arcy termed it, 'a thorough one'.[38] Whether it would be realized in anything like all its detail, was another matter.

The plan was not, as Sweeny's son noted in a letter to a New York newspaper thirty years later,

> gotten up to suit the exigencies of the moment; but was the result of many years of careful study . . . and to which he devoted the knowledge of military life he had acquired in the Mexican war, among the Indians of the West and in the War of the Rebellion.[39]

The planning involved went back, William Sweeny noted, at least as far as his father's previously mentioned 1858 meeting with James Stephens and Michael Doheny.

Sweeny's plan would not lack for its supporters even outside the immediate ranks of the Irish ethnic population in the United States. At mid-century the American newspaper support for Irish nationalism was remarkably vigorous, as was a general romantic sympathy for Ireland and the eloquence with which she had traditionally, insistently, affirmed her identity as a nation. We sometimes forget that the Irish were then the pre-eminent instance in the American mind of a people occupied by force; Irish writers and orators – O'Connell, Tone, Sheridan, Emmet – represented the pre-eminent voices of national liberation. Frederick Douglas, for instance, the great American liberation orator, in his *Narrative of the Life of Frederick Douglas, an American Slave*, recalled the inspiration he drew, reading them as a slave, from the speeches of Richard Sheridan. Abolitionist leader William Lloyd Garrison, in his introduction to Douglas' narrative, quotes from a recent speech delivered by Daniel O'Connell in Dublin and describes him as a 'champion of prostrate but not conquered Ireland'.[40] Walt Whitman's 1861 poem 'Old Ireland' portrayed Ireland through a familiar trope, but one that, particularly in the wake of the recent Great Famine, resonated in America at the time:

> Far hence amid an isle of wondrous beauty,
> Crouching over a grave an ancient sorrowful mother,
> Once a Queen, now lean and tatter'd seated on the ground,
> . . .
> At her feet fallen an unused royal harp
> Long silent, she too long silent . . .[41]

Editorials sympathetic to Fenianism, such as the following one from the *Missouri Democrat* of 24 September 1865, headlined 'Ireland and the Fenians', were also common. The sceptical references to Catholicism in the editorial no doubt have in mind St Louis's own Archbishop Kenrick, arguably the most devoutly anti-Fenian figure in the American Church hierarchy:

> It is impossible to repress an emotion of sympathy with 'old Ireland' whenever her case is mentioned. That she has been grievously wronged by her conqueror, few will question . . . No movement can therefore be projected, having for its object the enfranchisement of the Irish people, which will not compel some respect from all who love freedom and hate despotism . . . Whether residents of the United States can, with strict propriety, organize to make war upon [a] government . . . holding friendly relations with our own may be very questionable, but it must be remembered in extenuation of the Fenian movement that, although living upon American soil, Irishmen cannot forget the land which gave them birth nor . . . the kindred whom they have left behind.
>
> Another circumstance which must operate to produce a favorable feeling towards the 'brotherhood' . . . is the remarkable . . . opposition it is encountering from the Catholic clergy . . . In America we must confess that we were surprised when we discovered that such was to be the policy of men holding high rank in the church.

The editorial made the further point that the Church's apparent devotion to the integrity of established government in the British Isles was nowhere in evidence – certainly not in St Louis in 1861 they might have added – in the course of the American Civil War: 'The men who now have so boldly taken up the gauntlet, when thrown down by Fenianism, were silent as the grave when our own free nationality was in her mortal struggle'.[42] This kind of backing, along with a great deal of expressed US Congressional support, was a great encouragement to Fenian assessments of their chances of success in anti-British undertakings such as the projected Canadian assault. Outright seductive, on the other hand, was American rhetoric at its most extreme which allowed for no fundamental British rights in North America, a rhetoric suggesting an open door to the north for a Fenian army.

The Canada of the middle of the nineteenth century, in which Thomas D'Arcy McGee chose to settle, was, as William G. Davis points out, 'by no means the same as the country which bears the name today'. People in the United States looking north perceived not the fully realized nation that is in place presently but rather a mostly uninhabited frontier, much of it untrammelled and quasi-arctic, to which a distant England had, to Americans, only dubious and anachronistic claims.

> It consisted only of the modern provinces of Ontario and Quebec, which had been united under the name of the Province of Canada in 1841. The four Atlantic provinces of Nova Scotia, New Brunswick, Prince Edward Island

and Newfoundland had their own separate governments and had little trade and other connections with Canada. The immense territories of British North America west of the Great Lakes were still held, in theory, by the great fur trading corporation known as the Hudson's Bay Company. But in actual fact, there were only a handful of white people in the Company's domain and the Indian tribes still hunted and roamed as they had always done. On the Pacific coast, separated from the nearest Canadian settlements by thousands of miles of wilderness, were two tiny British colonies which grew into the province of British Columbia . . .

The conflict between the French majority in Quebec and the English majority in Ontario . . . was already much in evidence. The two races regarded each other with hostility and suspicion and their representatives in the Legislature were in a state of perpetual deadlock.

The English speaking element was divided by a conflict of its own between the Protestants and the Catholics who were predominately of Irish origin. The kind of religious intolerance that was dying out in Europe still flourished in Canada, poisoning the life of many communities and sometimes leading to riots and bloodshed. This strife made stable governments difficult. In a legislature divided along racial and religious lines, it was impossible for any party to hold together an effective majority.[43]

Nor was the idea of invading Canada the exotic thing it would be today, especially given the earlier mentioned anti-British sentiment in the United States over England's aid to the Confederacy during the Civil War, which aid cost US shipping heavily, $15,500,000 being the post-war bill presented the British by the American government. Calls for the taking of Canada – quite aside from those issuing from Fenian quarters – were thus not uncommon immediately after the war. The mistake the Fenians made, though, was to equate the American variety of anti-Britishness, no matter how strident for a time, with the much deeper-seated and enduring Irish variety. At this point, however, there was still a real enough carry over of anti-English sentiment in the United States from the revolution, and, perhaps even more so, from the war of 1812. During the latter war the American poet, Philip Freneau, in response to the British burning of Washington in 1814, predicted an eventual blow delivered against the King via Canada, a blow

That, with a vengeance, will repay
The mischiefs we lament this day . . .

Will give him an eternal check
That breaks his heart or breaks his neck,
And plants our standard in Quebec.[44]

In 1861 the US Steamer *San Jacinto* had intercepted the British ship *Trent* on the high seas and arrested two Confederate envoys bound for Europe, conveying them to Boston where they were imprisoned. The British were outraged, and Lincoln, almost two months after the arrest, acceded to the Crown's demand for the release of the prisoners.[45] The Irish, however, drew encouragement, more indeed than was good for them, from such evidence of antagonism between America and England. Furthermore, in the prevailing American mindset then, United States borders were fluid – in the US's favour. America and Britain had been at loggerheads for decades over where the border should be drawn in the Oregon territory, and the United States had declared a provisional government in Canadian Oregon in 1843. Americans had moved into Spanish Texas as well and declared a portion of that state independent of Mexico. A 'Bear Flag Republic' had been declared by Fremont and his group in Spanish California in 1846. James Polk campaigned in 1844 on the slogan 'Fifty-Four Forty or Fight', and, in the face of this threat of military force being brought to bear, England in 1846 gave up a portion of what had been British Canada and agreed to the border being defined further north, at latitude 54°4'N. Many Americans, however presumptuously, assumed there would be further British yielding until Canada was finally US territory.

The opinion in the US was fairly widespread that: 'Even if England had both history and law on her side, it was our manifest destiny to overspread and to possess the whole of the continent which Providence has given us for the development of the great experiment of liberty'.[46] A communication addressed to the Canadian government in 1862 by the Duke of Newcastle – a document quoted by General Sweeny in presenting his invasion apologia to the Pittsburgh Fenian Convention – suggested that the British at that point considered an American attack on Canada likely. 'In the event of war with the United States', the Duke had written,

> Canada will naturally become a point of attack from those zealous advocates of increased sovereignty, which they term the 'Monroe Doctrine', and no body of troops which England can send to her American Colonies will suffice to make Canada safe, without the hearty concurrence of the Canadians themselves.

He went on to propose a much more robust Canadian military structure than was in place, but, as Sweeny noted, a bill introduced to accomplish such an upgrading received little support in the Canadian parliament and only a watered-down version was finally acted upon.[47]

The US's hard feelings toward England and Canada rekindled during and after the Civil War, especially along the border itself, were thus not something the Fenians imagined. Despite Britain's proclaimed Civil War neutrality, the Canadian Govenment had turned a blind eye toward the actions of Confederate agents based in Canadian cities.

> American grievances against the British were increased by the number of Southerners, including paid agents for the Confederacy, who were harbored on Canadian soil . . . In Canadian cities, especially in St Catherine's near

> Niagara, they met with Peace Democrats from the States, subsidized Peace Democrat journalists, financed the seizure of a Union gunboat on Lake Erie, rescued Confederate prisoners from Johnson Island off the Ohio coast and from a camp in Lake Michigan, and sent volunteer arson squads into the North. On the afternoon of 19 October 1864, a group of twenty-one Confederate raiders crossed the unguarded border into the United States and robbed three banks in St Albans, Vermont, of over $200,000. The *Chicago Tribune*, like other papers, called upon the American government 'to march a sufficient body of troops to Montreal, Quebec, or any other place where the St Albans pillagers may have taken refuge'.[48]

David Owen quotes from a Canadian woman's diary at the time with the observation that 'there appears to be a great probability of war with the Yankees'.[49]

The keenest sore point, however, had to do with the clandestine operation whereby Britain had afforded the Confederate States aid in building warships such as the *Florida*, the *Shenandoah* and the *Alabama*. In collusion with the Confederate military, England had constructed and outfitted these ships as commerce raiders under the pretense of their being merchant vessels. But the war sloop, CSS *Alabama*, for example, launched in 1862, set out on a career devoted to raiding American ships of commerce on the high seas, right away capturing and burning nearly a dozen Union merchant vessels. By the end of 1863 this Confederate raider had captured another forty ships, burning most of them. Before being sunk in June 1864, the *Alabama* had done great damage to the US merchant marine fleet and British perfidy in this destruction was not forgotten in the North when the war ended. Demands that Britain pay reparations for the damage the *Alabama* had caused to US interests were vigorously forwarded. (The 1872 reparation payment, $15,500,000, would be the largest that had ever been negotiated by an international court. England would pay the sum arrived at by a Geneva tribunal in order to mollify US ire and put an end to the worrisome anti-British sentiment that still tended to fuel American sympathy for the Fenian cause.) The *New York Times* in May of 1865 declared with reference to the war: 'The language and conduct of the British Ministry were expressly adapted to aid and comfort a rebellion which was striking at our national life'.[50] Michigan Senator Chandler, recalling the raids of the *Alabama* and other British-built ships, set forth a plan to seize Canada with an army of 200,000, a hybrid force that would utilize Northern and Southern troops from the war equally as a single army whose united cause, he maintained, would help bring the country together again. 'He argued that the United States had a right to seize Canada in payment for the damages . . .'.[51] Referencing British support of the Confederacy, the *New York Herald* editorialized:

> Let them remember . . . when the termination of our evil conflict shall have arrived, it may be the turn of our foreign enemies to suffer the consequences of the mischiefs they are attempting to do us. Four hundred thousand thoroughly disciplined troops will ask no better occupation than to destroy the

> last vestiges of British rule on the American continent, and annex Canada to the United States.[52]

This was the atmosphere in which Sweeny was operating in the United States of 1866. But while music to Fenian ears, this kind of American rhetoric would prove to be a siren call. Britain was counting on reconstruction to succeed soon and allow for a new group of Southern senators and congressmen to come to Washington, ones who would ameliorate Northern anti-British sentiment. And even the disunifying influences that had beset Canada up to this time were beginning – thanks to former Young Irelander D'Arcy McGee as much as to any other single individual – to show signs they might take a turn for the better. McGee's main preoccupation had become by now Canadian nationalism rather than Irish and his anti-Fenian influence had already diminished somewhat Canada's formerly robust Fenian organization.

The invasion Sweeny designed and presented in its main features to the Philadelphia convention entailed three regional offensives launched against British Canada. The westernmost wing of the invasion, involving 3,000 men to muster in the Chicago area, would be under the command of Brigadier General Charles Tevis, Fenian Adjutant General. This wing would advance east from Illinois, across lakes Michigan and Huron. After capturing the western terminal of the Buffalo and Lake Huron Railway, a force would land near Stratford and proceed to London, imperiling the capital, Toronto. The centre wing, involving a force of 5,000 under the command of Brigadier General William F. Lynch would occupy a line from Cleveland to Buffalo along the south shore of Lake Erie. From Cleveland one column would take Port Stanley and then link up with Tevis' force near London, Ontario. A second central column would cross the Niagara River from Buffalo, ultimately to also threaten Toronto.

The Ontario assaults envisioned here, while they were meant to be powerful, were in the nature of diversionary feints toward Toronto designed to draw Canadian regular units commanded by Sir John Michell, away from Canada east to west of Toronto. Sweeny's plan had as its goal the establishment of an Irish government in exile in the eastern townships of Quebec. The eastern wing of the attack, the major offensive, would include 16,800 assembled at St Albans, Vermont, and would drive into the Missiquoi frontier with the goal of capturing Quebec. This force, including five cavalry regiments commanded by Brigadier General Michael C. Murphy, would be under the command of Samuel P. Spear, in whom Sweeny placed great confidence, and who had, like Sweeny, risen from the enlisted ranks during the Mexican and Civil Wars to the brevet rank of Brigadier General. Smaller detachments would at the same time cross the Canadian border from Ogdenburg, Cleveland, Detroit and Buffalo targetting the Welland Canal and the eastern terminus of the Buffalo and Lake Huron Railway.[53] As Canadian forces moved to the defence of Toronto, Canadian

Fenian and French-Canadian elements would destroy the bridge at Ste. Anne-de-Bellvue at the confluence of the St Lawrence and Ottowa rivers. Sweeny was confident of a Canadian Irish and radical French alliance in Canada East, noting that: '[The French Canadians] were positively neutral during the invasions of 1775 and 1812, and the arrogance of the British troops had only embittered the aversion which, as Frenchmen, they have always felt toward the conquerors of their forefathers'.[54]

St Anne's bridge destroyed, Spear's force would be committed:

> Spear expected to be assisted by both the Montreal Irish and the Republican Parti Rouge, whose French-Canadian members had already negotiated with the Fenians. Spear's army was to follow the line of the Grand Trunk Railroad and capture Port Levis opposite Quebec City. This point had been designated as the Fenian's port to the Atlantic Ocean. Once this facility was in Fenian hands, three Fenian war ships, purchased from the US Navy, were to sail from Brooklyn Navy Yard and blockade the St Lawrence to prevent British convoys from coming to the assistance of the beleaguered British Army in Ontario. In the event that Quebec and Montreal could not be secured, Spear had been ordered by Sweeny to concentrate his force between the St Francis and Richelieu Rivers on and around Sherbrooke which would become the capital of the exiled Irish Republic.[55]

A letter written two years earlier from James Stephens to O'Mahony from Chicago, however, contained a foreboding note of the kind of thing that would come to haunt Sweeny despite his dedicated planning. On a tour of Fenian centres, Stephens was shocked to discover Fenian numbers at a mere fraction of what he had been led to believe they were: 'the Fenian Brotherhood was but 10,000 strong . . . I had given the Brotherhood credit for some 50,000 men'.[56] Such willful optimism, known as 'sunburstry' at the time – a reference to the sunburst on the Fenian flag – may have had its place in keeping spirits up, but it was pernicious when influential upon real political-military planning. In the limited time Sweeny had available to him, for example, he had to make plans based on the troop strength figures sent to him by the various Fenian centres.[57]

The Fenians/IRB had had their occasional spectacular successes such as the McManus funeral and James Stephen's escape from Richmond Prison, successful retreat underground and eventual escape to Europe. But Sweeny's sophisticated invasion plan perhaps failed to take into account the fact that the American-Irish were, after all, essentially a displaced post-colonial people who lacked the organizational skills required to coordinate military activities in the comparatively vast spaces of the United States, which was not their native ground. The Fenians tried to hew as closely as possible to the US Army organizational structure – Section 8 of the Brotherhood's military organizational statement, for example, read: 'The revised Army Regulations of the U.S., so far as the same can be made applicable, is hereby adopted for the government of the military . . . of the F.B. in America'.[58] But in the last analysis only the letter, not the spirit of the US Army structure could be adopted. It would seem that at the critical moment for the invasion in fact, many members reverted to the notoriously loose 'Irish time' and were appallingly late off the mark. Likewise, the kind of misrepresentation Stephens noted on the part of the leadership of various Fenian centres regarding their troop strength would go unchecked and would be a major factor undercutting Sweeny's Canadian venture.

Stephens was also often distressed by the lack of radical edge, of high political seriousness, in Irish-American circles, the picnicking and exuberant rhetoric associated with Irish nationalist get-togethers in the United States. O'Mahony had expressed an impatience similar to Stephens' with the faltering Irish-nationalist efforts in the United States of 1856, noting the lack of rigorous discipline and comparing Irish-American political conviction unfavourably to the more concerted and radical French and Italian variety of the time in Europe: 'I am sick of Yankee-doodle twaddle, Yankee-doodle selfishness and all Yankee doodledum! . . . It is refreshing . . . to turn to the stern front and untiring constancy of the continental apostles of liberty . . . '.[59]

Stephens blamed this general organizational looseness on the carry over of pernicious Young Ireland habits into the American context. He would write in his *Reminiscences* of the Irish-American scene at its worst:

> It was a wind-bag, or a phantom, the laughing stock of sensible men and the El Dorado of fools. For what was the sum total of Irish-American [Irish] patriotism . . . Speeches of bayonets, gala days and jolly nights, banners and sashes . . . bunkum and fulsome filibustering . . . the oratory of the Young Irelanders was the immediate cause of this scandalous state of things. They introduced into the Irish-American arena the pompous phrases of the old nation suppers and the gilded harangues of Conciliation Hall . . . Irish patriots sang songs and responded in glowing language to glowing toasts on Irish National Independence.[60]

But despite their experience in the secret society model employed by radical movements in Europe, Stephens and O'Mahoney themselves had their shortcomings in another, related aspect of Fenian undiscipline. Even in the small, insular context of Ireland, they were still unable to maintain a spy-proof IRB system. The hard-core radicals of the continent would surely have made short work of spies such as John Joseph Corydon, Pierce Nagle, or the nefarious, probably psychopathic, James 'Red Jim' McDermott who hung around the Fenian community in Ireland and the United States for decades, from the early 1860s through the 1880s, spying and informing virtually without hindrance.[61] McDermott ingratiated himself with O'Mahony and was scheduled to undertake a Fenian lecture tour, no less, in 1864 when Stephens wrote to O'Mahony from Louisville, Kentucky, expressing his suspicions of the man and remarking with reference to McDermott's projected lecture tour, 'I cannot believe it has your sanction'.[62] McDermott's boisterousness and flamboyance – contrary to the usual image of the spy – probably deflected suspicion from him generally; even Stephen's warning to O'Mahony is based more on a sense of McDermott as unstable and of dubious moral character than on his being flat out, as he was, an aggressive British paid informant who would communicate to Crown authorities information on various Fenian activities including the Sweeny invasion. McDermott's boldness is evident in his, for instance, appearing – probably self-appointed – as a pro-O'Mahony agitator at a speech by Sweeny in Newark in February 1866, where he shouted abuse at the general from the floor leading to his being ejected from the hall.[63] Yet McDermott, who among other things had been tried for murder in New York, was still plying his informer's trade in Ireland in the 1880s, visiting, all ears, at the bidding of Dublin Castle, imprisoned Irish leaders in Kilmainham with treacherous, hail-fellow-well-met exuberance.[64]

Stephens, while alive to O'Mahony's carelessness regarding Red Jim, was himself victimized by the British agents, Pierce Nagle and John Joseph Corydon; the former found employment in the offices of the *Irish People* with the result that the 1865 uprising was compromised and broken up. In February 1867 another insurrection in Ireland, one coordinated by Irish-American former Civil War officers, would fall apart due to Corydon delivering the plans to the British authorities in advance.[65] In the United States secrecy was arguably even harder to maintain since the Irish were dispersed without regard to their county-town origins so important in Ireland, making informant activity comparatively easy. In 1868, for example, John O'Neill's attempt at a Canadian incursion would fail miserably in part, at least, because O'Neill, expansive by nature and hard-drinking, gave away critical Fenian plans to Henri Le Caron, a perceived friend and Nashville, Tennessee, neighbour, who was in fact a British sympathizer ultimately recruited as a secret agent.[66] That British ears might be listening to his talk over drinks in a Nashville bar probably seemed a far-fetched worry to O'Neill who would not have been so sanguine in a Dublin or Wexford pub that year.

The work of British spies was accommodated, of course, by the unfortunate reckless Fenian tendency to noise their plans about as O'Neill would do in the late 1860s. Mark Twain remarked around that time of Fenian decline that 'no news travels so freely or so fast as the "secret" doings of the Fenian Brotherhood'.

> First we have the portentous mystery that precedes [the invasion] for six months, when all the air is filled with stage whisperings; when councils meet every night with awful secrecy, and the membership try to see who can get up first in the morning and tell the proceedings. [I]n solemn whisperings in the dead of night they secretly plan a Canadian raid, and publish it in the 'World' next morning.[67]

The Crown had agents such as Thomas Doyle surveilling Irish-America as early as the 1850s.[68] And the Canadian government was increasingly concerned as Fenian activity increased and louder invasion rhetoric emanated from south of their border. As early as November 1865, the now anti-Fenian Thomas D'Arcy McGee was urging Canadian authorities to establish spies in New York – 'a constant agency . . . filled with the very best men we can get' – to keep tabs on anti-Canadian Fenian activity. Edward Archibald, British consul in New York, closely monitored Fenian actions and sent hundreds of letters to Canadian officials throughout the period of the threat. He had spies infiltrate Fenian meetings and worked with people seeking to sell strategic information. Nor, as mentioned, would the Sweeny military operation, necessarily having to take on the karma of previous Fenian years, be exempt from likewise significant spy infiltration. One of Archibald's letters to Canada, written on 23 October 1865, reveals a serious breach of secrecy in the Fenian inner circle offices:

> About a week ago a confidential clerk of O'Mahony's who is also employed in the Office of the Secretary of War, F.B.[Sweeny], came to me and offered to sell me most important information . . . [S]eeing that he was entrusted with the correspondence of the War Department . . . I determined to offer him a sum on account . . . Having accordingly come to terms with him today, he communicated to me today a copy of a cipher letter addressed to Patrick Butler, Esq., Montreal . . . At the same time he communicated and explained to me the cipher in use by O'Mahony and Sweeny with its key, which you will find herewith enclosed . . . On two occasions when he called on me he had just come from the Post Office holding in his hand a score or more of letters for O'Mahony and Sweeny, with post-marks of various places in the West. He tells me he has . . . obtained some information respecting Canadian movements which he prefers to communicate to me verbally. General Sweeny has associated with himself a Brig. General Tevis . . . a West Point graduate and an able man . . . I enclose two printed circulars of Sweeny and Tevis which, at all events, show that they have commenced their move in a business like manner.[69]

The unnamed 'confidential clerk' is probably the ubiquitous McDermott or else Rudolf Fitzpatrick, the Fenian assistant secretary at this time, who was also a spy.[70]

Alexander McLeod, a bookkeeper at the Buffalo, New York, auction house run by the Fenian leader, Patrick O'Day, was another spy and agent of the Canadian government. O'Day's business was a centre of Fenian activity. McLeod wrote to Canadian authorities:

> The owner of the premises is Pat O'Day an auctioneer. He is an ignorant little Irishman, pretty well-off . . . The auction room today is full of Irishmen, a number of officers late of the US Volunteers, are there just now. The discussion I am told is all about the intended attack on Canada. Their talk is not *soto voce* for I can almost hear them, although my door is shut and they near 50 feet from it.

In a subsequent communication McLeod was reporting things more in detail and the invasion more imminent:

> There are now about 1,000 stand of muskets here, – and revolvers. They . . . are busy loading cases of arms into the cellar . . . Ammunition, military accoutrements and wagons are now ready in the city for an invading force of 5,000 men which is the contingent to move from Buffalo very soon . . . These people are in earnest. 100 men of the US Reserve Corps arrived last night.[71]

The *New York Times* of 21 May 1866, a time when Sweeny's invasion preparations were in progress, reported that a Fenian official in New York was reporting 'regular and minute information regarding the projects of the Brotherhood'. New York Fenians discounted the report, especially given its publication in an anti-Fenian newspaper, but, as William D'Arcy notes, the report is verified in a communication of 7 August 1866 between British officials:

> With a view to obtain authentic information relative to the Fenian Brotherhood and their plans I have employed since the spring of the year a person who was an officer in the . . . Confederate army, but is now reduced to a state of utmost poverty. He has been of great service to myself and to the Canadian Government, and I have in the course of the past few months given him on account of his traveling expenses at different times sums of money amounting to 105 pounds . . . I have found the information he supplies, trustworthy.[72]

The official – according to D'Arcy, the only one who fitted the description – was a man named Wheeler, a former Confederate colonel. This was not, apparently, the well-known Confederate General Joseph Wheeler, however. But these security breaches cannot be discounted as having contributed, along with the many other exigencies that were to come, to the ultimate Fenian disappointment in 1866.

Not that Sweeny lacked for his own intelligence network. In submitting his invasion plan to the Brotherhood he noted that:

> In order to project the plan of campaign, a full and accurate knowledge of the enemy's strength, position and resources is indispensable, and of this information I have been put in possession by the reports of my own secret agents and by those made by British officials to their government.[73]

The following letter suggests the intelligence reports he was getting from such agents. On the single US steamer, *Michigan*, plying the Great Lakes and ultimately to undertake anti-Fenian patrols, there was a Fenian circle of seventeen members coordinated by mate William E. Leonard. Leonard wrote to General Sweeny from port in Buffalo on 9 April 1866:

> Sir:
> William M. Andrew being over the Welland Canal, on the 6th of this month, reports as follows: Total number of men stationed there is 75, consisting of some cavalry, infantry and rifles; ten regulars in all. Arms rifles and six

> pounders placed on the dock. That is all the force of his knowledge on the Canal . . .
>
> The length of the canal is 28 miles, with 26 locks. Your point is the guard lock. By destroying this lock and the one below you destroy the whole canal The feeder runs into this lock; the feeder is 18 feet high; the highest one there is. There is no lock on the feeder and the force of the water from it will burst the best of the locks, as there is a great fall from this point to Lake Ontario There are also two railroad bridges that cross the canal; one at Port Colburn and the other at Thirrell. Both are wooden bridges and swing in the centre Port Colburn is 24 miles from Buffalo and 18 by railroad.[74]

An atmosphere of crisis prevailed in Brotherhood circles in America due to the sudden severe pressure brought to bear on Fenians in the Ireland of 1865–66 – Dublin Castle was coming down full force on the Irish rebel community. There was a sense of emergency and of the need for immediate action, even if risky, which would provoke first a Killian–O'Mahony imprudent adventure, and Sweeny's perforce premature military expedition following upon that.

> The autumn of 1865 was a time of grim reckoning for the Fenian Brotherhood in Dublin. In mid-September most of its leadership was arrested and jailed in a well-planned and coordinated police sweep. Although not entirely unanticipated, the speed and thoroughness of the action 'struck the Brotherhood like a thunderbolt'. Among those arrested were Thomas Clarke Luby, John O'Leary, and Jeremiah O'Donovan Rossa, the principle editors and agents of the journalistic voice of Fenianism in Ireland, the *Irish People*.[75]

On 18 February 1866, the Habeas Corpus Act was suspended in Ireland; IRB arms plants and arsenals were raided, suspected revolutionists, including naturalized American-Irish, had been rounded up en masse and imprisoned; James Stephens was in hiding and would be forced to flee once again to Paris.[76] Sweeny told an audience in a speech on 3 March 1866:

> The hand of the oppressor has fallen heavily upon our native land. The writ of habeas corpus has been suspended in Ireland by the British Parliament with a haste that betokens the terror our preparations have stricken to the hearts of our foes. This act of tyranny means deeper wrongs to our race . . . Now is our time to strike.[77]

The suspension of habeas corpus underscored the problems inherent in taking even the first steps toward revolt in Ireland – a stone's throw from London; the uprising in Ireland that had seemed imminent would again have to be postponed. This, and the emergency atmosphere, tended to lend credence to the Roberts–Sweeny position, one that was already being strengthened by the pair's touring and politicking. The charismatic, one-armed war hero, Sweeny, and the grandiose orator, Roberts, were making great headway with their direct-action message among the Fenian rank-and-file against the more scholarly and aristocratic O'Mahony whom many viewed as given to temporizing. It was in an attempt to regain the upper hand, to steal Sweeny's thunder, that O'Mahony and Bernard Killian conceived the idea of seizing Campobello Island at the mouth of the St Croix River, New Brunswick, an island that would one day be famous as Franklin Roosevelt's summer retreat.

Their argument for doing so was based in part, as Hereward Senior points out, on thinking borrowed from the Roberts–Sweeny Wing – the need to seize a piece of territory and thereby gain belligerent status. 'We must have a place to raise a flag, build ships, and issue letters of marque', Roberts had argued. Without such status any aggression carried out against British shipping, for instance, would have to be regarded by the United States as simple piracy.[78] In terms of satisfying the need for a geographical base to work from, Killian's plan had, in the abstract, much to recommend it. Its scale was considerably more modest than what Sweeny had in mind, seemingly more realizable. Campobello was of debatable nationality, as Oregon territory had been in the 1840s, with Britain and the United States both having their eye on it. If the united agreement of the whole American Fenian organization had been brought to bear – no small if – as well as patient, careful planning, the island site might have been well chosen. But Killian's Campobello plan was hastily formulated and poorly executed, and the Canadian maritime command, thanks again to the spy Red McDermott, was aware of the planning in advance.[79] The Fenians mustered at Eastport, Maine, were thus under the scrutiny of both Canadian and US authorities. Michael Murphy, the Toronto Fenian leader, and several others, were arrested on the train while headed for the Campobello gathering. Before any hostilities could get underway, the Fenian steamer, *Ocean Spray*, a revamped Confederate vessel, loaded with arms, was seized.

> At Calais, Maine, an exchange of fire developed between Fenians and British soldiers from St Stephens, New Brunswick. US citizens joined with the Fenians in the fight and drove the redcoats back over the bridge to Canada. There were no other Fenian triumphs. The US government was reacting slowly to British anger, but decided at last to prevent an international incident by sending three ships north. The 'border scare' ended on 19 April, with the arrival of Union General Meade in Eastport. The next day 200 disappointed Fenians, their arms confiscated by details of the United States Army, departed the scene aboard the steamer *New Brunswick*.[80]

This did not bode well for Sweeny, since his invasion planning was based on the assumption of US non-interference, but the Sweeny faction continued to act on best-case assumptions – arguably they had to or opt again for postponement. Killian had sounded out President Johnson and his secretary of state right after the Philadelphia Fenian Convention as to what the United States might do in the event the Fenians were to seize territory in Canada. Johnson's answer was ambiguous and politic, given with an eye toward the significant Irish Democratic vote. He declared that the US 'would acknowledge accomplished facts' in that event. Fenians of both factions put the most positive possible face on the administration's answer, taking it pretty much as a pledge that the US would take no strong hand in preventing Fenian military ventures into Canada.[8] The Roberts–Sweeny Wing continued to act on this cherished false assumption going forward with their invasion plan, a much more elaborate one than Killian had tried, even after the Campobello failure. Sweeny's scheme sought not just to nip off a piece of territory to satisfy international law requirements, but to strike a much more powerful blow against the British Empire by seizing the very heart of Canada.

The Campobello misadventure led not only to the collapse of O'Mahony's faction. To Sweeny's disadvantage it peaked Canadian and American surveillance of the border as well as threatening to bring ridicule upon the name of Fenianism generally and discouragement in the ranks. On 11 May 1866, James Stephens accepted O'Mahony's resignation in a formal letter observing: 'No man worth the name questions your honor and devotion to Ireland; but the united action we desire so much . . . would be impossible while you directed activities here'.[82] The Brotherhood's credibility was now at stake, and the ball was in the court of the senate faction. Stephens made a last-ditch effort to act as an intermediary to unite the American wings, setting out for the United States in the hope of achieving that aim. O'Mahony, now left with little power, was receptive to compromise proposals, but Sweeny and Roberts, riding comparatively high now after Killian's failure at Eastport, rejected O'Mahony's overtures when they were brought to them through William G. Halpine. Halpine wrote to Roberts: 'I see no difficulty in the way of carrying out General Sweeny's programme if we have a perfect understanding . . . Mr. Stephens will soon be here, and I think prudence would dictate a suspension of operations until he arrives'. The letter was addressed to Roberts as a private individual, however, at which he took umbrage, stating that any communications would have to be addressed to him as President of the Brotherhood. Halpine then wrote to Sweeny, informing him that Stephens would arrive on the next French steamer with the intention of undertaking reconciliation of the two Fenian wings in the United States. Sweeny, however, already under pressure to act and undo the Campobello humiliation, informed Halpine that an appeal for reconciliation would have to come directly from O'Mahony.[83]

There would be no meeting of minds; there were hard feelings that would not be overcome. When the senate faction had first confronted the O'Mahony establishment, some people in the O'Mahony camp, Red McDermott among them, had tended to go too far in the direction of political mayhem – disrupting speeches and meetings, and so on. At the Philadelphia convention in January 1866, Bernard Killian had mockingly walked around the hall with his arm out of its sleeve, imitating Sweeny's handicap, until irate delegates demanded he apologize.[84] Sweeny now went forward without a reconciliation, and the debilitating split would carry on into the forthcoming Canadian action. Roberts summoned him to a fateful emergency meeting in New York at which Sweeny was urged upon the desperate, unpromising course of immediate implementation of his plan:

> On the 16th of April I appeared before the Senate, when a resolution was passed urging me to immediate action; every member voting in the affirmative. Taking this action into consideration with the reckless pressure brought to bear upon me by the several Circles to hasten me into premature action, and the assurances of almost the entire organization that unless I took the field at once, the dissolution of the Brotherhood would be inevitable, I reluctantly yielded.[85]

The requirements he had set forth from the beginning as the minimum ones for the invasion now went by the board – the invasion would be initiated well before winter; rather than $450,000, $100,000 would be hastily raised; rather than the three batteries of artillery he had called for, he would have none at all and would have, instead, to count on capturing enemy artillery pieces. The attack would have to be initiated months prematurely – the all-important details of who was to be where and when would have to remain less than fine-tuned. Sweeny would be forced to go forward with something that was a mere shadow of what he had originally proposed. It would have to be a catch-as-catch-can, irregular operation, and the participants would have to do their best with a bad situation. If they were, as so many were, veterans of the American Civil War, they would in this operation by no means find the logistical and communications standards the US government had been able to provide, much as Sweeny and the Fenian leadership had hoped to duplicate that.

The invasion was initiated on 1 June. Something of the intrigue of the affair and the complexity of what Sweeny had to oversee is well captured by the historian, Benedict Maryniak, as he describes the travel of the O'Neill column toward its mission at Ridgeway, having more than the Canadian Army to be concerned about:

> The force was now only a few miles west of Buffalo, having left drab mercantile Cleveland before dawn, and continued all morning . . . John O'Neill was starting here. He and 150 men, comprising the Irish Republican Army's 13th Regiment, had left Nashville early on Monday. Colonel George Owen Starr and 150 members of his 17th IRA Regiment came aboard to join Colonel O'Neill's party. Another stop brought James B. Haggerty and a hundred more Fenian troops. This trainload of 'railroad laborers'—they had been instructed to wear work clothes – had pulled into Cleveland late in the evening on May 28. O'Neill and Starr had expected to find boats [at Cleveland] to carry them to Canada . . . But there had been no boats . . .
>
> Rolling through the outskirts of Buffalo, O'Neill's train slowed so men could jump off along the tracks. An earlier wire had warned Fenians that city police were awaiting their arrival at the Exchange Street station. As Buffalo Circle members led these Irish soldiers to halls, warehouses, and barns

> throughout South Buffalo, the gunboat USS *Michigan* steamed into Buffalo harbor with her Marine guard on deck. Later that day, ammunition was surreptitiously loaded into furniture wagons from a train in the Buffalo freight yard. Fenians were said to be on the move all over New England and along the Great Lakes, and US officials were attempting to confirm such reports. Fenian commander Sweeny later explained that he had sent forces on several contradictory paths, hoping to confuse US and British spies. Groups of Fenians left Cleveland by train . . . wearing conspicuously-uniform green caps and other emerald-tinted accessories.[86]

The lack of boats constituted one point of critical breakdown from the outset. General Lynch seems to have dropped the ball entirely as regards his obligations in the central, Buffalo–Cleveland, sector of the campaign. Indeed, he seems not even to have been there, mysteriously enough, at the crucial time: 'Brig. Gen. Lynch did not', Sweeny writes in his Official Report, 'in accordance with orders, establish his Headquarters at Cleveland, Ohio, and superintend the movement on Lake Erie'. Another serious failure occurred at Chicago where there was no transportation, so that, Sweeny wrote, 'one half of the column I had assurance of could not be mustered'.[87] As earlier remarked, had Sweeny had added months of preparation time, glitches of this sort might have been overcome or minimized by practice exercises, drills, and dry-runs, but the time was not there.

Absent the transportation that was to have been available for 4–5,000 men at Cleveland, Sweeny was left with only John O'Neill and the Fenians at Buffalo able to get troops across the Niagara River. Buffalo became the stepping-off point for the attack on Ontario and hundreds of Fenians converged on the city.[88] In the early morning of 1 June, a contingent of approximately 800 Fenian soldiers, under the command of O'Neill, crossed the Niagara River and occupied Fort Erie, Ontario, a small Canadian town of 600. Here they commandeered provisions, burned bridges, cut telegraph wires and secured some horses. Later in the day they marched north, distributing a proclamation from General Sweeny addressed to the Provincial citizenry and reading in part:

> We come among you as the foes of British rule in Ireland . . . We have no issue with the people of these Provinces . . . Our weapons are for the oppressors of Ireland. Our blows shall be directed only against the power of England; her privileges alone shall we invade, not yours . . . We are here as an Irish army of liberation . . . our war is with the armed power of England . . . not with these Provinces . . . To Irishmen throughout these Provinces we appeal in the name of seven centuries of British iniquity and Irish misery . . . our desolate homes . . . our millions of famine graves, our insulted name and race – to stretch forth the hand of brotherhood . . . and smite the tyrant where we can.[89]

The Fenian force that had crossed to Fort Erie marched three miles down river on the morning of 2 June, turning west to the Black Creek where they deployed. Here O'Neill learned that two columns of troops, one under Colonel

Booker and the other under Colonel Peacocke, were marching towards his own, planning to join at Ridgeway. He set out to engage Booker's forces near Ridgeway before Peacocke's arrived. At Limestone Ridge the Fenians encountered a militia force of 840 on the march, the 'Queen's Own' detachment in the lead. A battle ensued – Fenian forces charging forward, bearing their IRA banner and wearing IRA buttons, and ultimately putting the Canadian units, which had suffered ten killed and thirty-seven wounded, to full and disorderly flight. It was the kind of coup Sweeny envisaged occurring at key locations all along the extensive frontier from Detroit to Vermont, the incursions causing the inexperienced and less committed Canadian military to spread itself thin and become ineffective.[90]

Despite the abundant problems, the campaign appeared to begin promisingly enough. The *New York Herald* report of 1 June was encouraging from the Fenian point of view:

> The Fenians have drawn their first blood on the enemy's soil. They have had their first battle, advancing to the work with the steadiness of veterans and driving the enemy before them. They have shown that upon anything like equal terms the Canadian volunteers are no match for them and that the Roberts-Sweeny organization are resolved at least to give the Saxon some convincing proofs that they mean to strike him where they can most conveniently find him.[91]

The other major US and Canadian newspapers also devoted headlines to the invasion for days. GREAT NORTHWARD MOVEMENT OF THE F.B. was a 1 June headline in the *Chicago Tribune*. On the second of June, THE FENIANS IN CANADA, RAILROAD TORN UP AND TELEGRAPH LINES DESTROYED, appeared on page one. On 3 June: FENIAN CONCENTRATIONS AT ST. ALBAN'S AND MALONE, ENGAGEMENTS YESTERDAY AT RIDGEWAY AND FORT ERIE.[92]

Despite O'Neill's early qualified victory, however, the invasion's left wing was in a vulnerable position, an enemy column of some 1,400 threatening to flank it, so O'Neill returned to Fort Erie where another encounter ensued with Canadian troops who had moved upon that site. At this point, direct US interference entered in. O'Neill dug in at an old fort in the area anticipating the arrival of the second and larger Canadian column, this one a regular army unit reports had put at 1,400. He called for reinforcements from Buffalo where 3,000 Fenians were awaiting the call to march. On 1 June Sweeny had relayed orders to reinforce O'Neill's position at all costs, 'if he cannot hold his position let him fall back; send him and his men to Malone as rapidly as possible by the Rome and Watertown roads'.[93] O'Neill could not be reinforced, however, the steamer *Michigan* was blocking Fenian attempts to aid his garrison. He and his troops had to retreat to river scow boats on the morning of 3 June, and when midstream in the Niagara River, were forced to yield to the *Michigan*'s guns. A month later O'Neill remarked in a speech:

> I know that many of our Irish friends say we violated the neutrality laws and that the United States could not have done otherwise than it did . . . But I

> think that the United States was not bound to let the organization go on for years or to sell the leaders of the movement lots of arms and ammunition . . . No, the government had our hard earned money and then seized our purchases. It has acted toward us in bad faith.[94]

Ridgeway, and to a lesser extent Samuel Spear's foray in the east, would prove to be the only arguable successes of the campaign and about the only source of bragging rights the Brotherhood would be able to salvage. Mostly due to Spear's strike west from St Alban's still being in progress, however, it took a while for things to become clear to the public in the States. As late as 6 June a *Chicago Tribune* headline read: MOVEMENT NORTHWARD OF ST ALBAN'S FORCES. But after that the headlines told a sadder tale: ENTIRE LEFT WING OF THE GRAND ARM CAPTURED OR DISPERSED, CAPTURE OF $200,000 WORTH OF FENIAN WAR MATERIAL, ARREST OF ROBERTS AND SWEENY.[95]

General Meade had received orders to place Sweeny and his officers under arrest. 'This he did, reporting meanwhile the seizure of more carloads of arms at Watertown and DeKalb junction. The following day eleven Fenian officers were arrested at Malone and acknowledged the project to be a failure'. Sweeny had by now sent a telegram to Roberts in New York asking him to be certain to have funds deposited in a bank so that transportation, food and so on would be on hand to return the troops to their homes with some display of order and dignity. Roberts did not see to this task, and the Fenian soldiers were left ingloriously stranded. Meade reported 1,500 stranded and suggested it would be judicious for the government in Washington to pay their fares as a means of getting the whole matter over with. By 10 June Meade reported 1,200 Fenians transported home. He then moved his headquarters to St Alban's in the Canada East sphere of the action, where things had not yet concluded, to oversee US procedures there. By 11 June, he had sent home 1,200 soldiers from the St Alban's area and arrested eleven officers and 150 regular soldiers.[96]

The coordination had not been there nor were the troop numbers sufficient; the assault dwindled and stalled. Things went as badly with the Canada East prong of the attack as they did with the central one regarding which, referring to O'Neill's capture, Sweeny later wrote, 'the campaign opened under the most discouraging circumstances', and went on to detail his own misfortunes on the St Lawrence frontier:

> Nor did the prospect brighten when I arrived at Potsdam, Malone and St Albans. This was the most important division of the army . . . I here ordered seventeen regiments of infantry and five of cavalry. The average number of men in each regiment according to the latest report was 800. This would give me a force of 16,800 men, but I calculated that not more than 8,000 would arrive in time to take part in the first movement. I gave ample time for these regiments to arrive on the second of June in order to cross into Canada on that day. But judge of my surprise on arriving at the front on the 4th, to find that scarcely 1,000 men had reported to the General commanding the right wing of the army.[97]

Only a fraction of the Irish potential in the United States had been successfully brought to bear. People arrived late. Others, rendered cynical after years of mere oration, could only take the thing seriously when they read the headlines proclaiming that a Fenian army was indeed fighting on British soil to the north – many then attempted to get to the front. A small note in the *Chicago Tribune* of 5 June reported from the St Louis-Alton, Illinois, area:

> It was announced that Captain Richard T. Brophy, who was all through the Crimean War and has seen three years with the US regulars during the rebellion, sent in his resignation this morning as a member of the Metropolitan Police, to take command of a full company of Fenians for the seat of war.[98]

Brophy and his men, like so many others, though no doubt fully sincere, were far too late for the action. Again, perhaps the years of projected revolution and false alarm had thrown the Irish in America off. Very belatedly, on 9 June the *Irish-American* was still inaccurately reporting 'the whole border from Maine to Michigan bristling with Irish bayonets'.[99]

Sweeny, despite everything, had still been prepared to cross into Canada on 7 June with what he had. But on the midnight of 6 June he and his engineer and chief of staff, John Mechan, were arrested at St Albans and their arms stores seized. Unable to come up with the $20,000 bail, Sweeny was jailed, though after a few days he was allowed out within the confines of the town. Meanwhile, an anti-Fenian round-up was undertaken almost immediately in the United States by government authorities:

> Prominent Fenian leaders, who had remained at home, were arrested in various sections. Among those arrested in St Louis were P.J. Harmon, Doctor O'Reilly, Doctor John Finn, General Curley, Sam Erskin, Coroner Quail, James McGrath, and even some O'Mahony Fenians who were bitterly opposed to a Canadian invasion. In Chicago [John] Scanlon . . . [was] arrested and held to bail. In Cleveland, Thomas Levin, state center for Ohio, Thomas Quinlin, and Philip O'Neil were taken into custody.[100]

General Spear, commander of the invasion's right wing, had evaded arrest in Vermont and carried out Sweeny's orders despite things looking unpromising. He crossed the frontier, and by 10 a.m. on 7 June, his men had raised the Irish colours near the village of Pigeon Hill and had won a skirmish near Frelighsburg.[101] In a communication to Mechan sent from 'Headquarters Right Wing I.R.A.' on 8 June, Spear was still confident: 'I find many patriotic Irishmen here . . . mostly farmers, who give me all the information in their power; they even loan me horses, and the first one I received was tendered to me by one of this class; this gives me new life'. As O'Neill had done in the west, Spear now dug in and awaited, in vain, for his scheduled reinforcements. Unaware that Mechan and Sweeny had already been arrested, he declared himself, in a letter to Mechan, '. . . in the most excellent spirits . . . if I can hold my own until the 500 muskets and 100,000 rounds arrive, I shall have no doubt of success.'[102] Nothing would arrive, of course; although Spear did not know it, the Fenian invasion of Canada was over, and it had failed.

NOTES

1. Letter to William B. Bodge from St. Louis, 26 September 1865. Thomas William Sweeny Papers, Huntington Library, San Marino, California.
2. Coyer, 'Hero of the Armless Sleeve', p.293.
3. The *Irish-American* (New York), 26 April 1862. Thomas William Sweeny Papers, Huntington Library, San Marino, California.
4. Thomas Francis Galwey, *The Valiant Hours: An Irish-American in the Army of the Potomac* (Harrisburg, PA, 1961), p.245.
5. Castel, *Decision in the West*, p.216. See also Bill Goble, 'On to Canada! . . . Again?' *Military Images*, 16, 5 (1995), pp.22–5.
6. John Rutherford, *The Secret History of the Fenian Conspiracy*, Vol. I. (London, 1877), pp.24–5.
7. Galwey, *Valiant Hours*, p.74.
8. Ibid., p.79.
9. R.V. Comerford, *The Fenians in Context: Irish Politics and Society, 1848–82* (Dublin, 1985), p.114.
10. Quoted in D'Arcy, *The Fenian Movement*, p.59.
11. Hernon Jr., *Celts, Catholics and Copperheads*, pp.28–9.
12. Ibid.
13. Walker, *Fenian Movement*, p.22.
14. Ibid., p.34.
15. Miller, *Emigrants and Exiles*, p.336.
16. Thomas William Sweeny Papers, Huntington Library, San Marino, California.
17. *New York Tribune*, 18 March 1865, p.8; and 21 October 1865, p.1.
18. D'Arcy, *The Fenian Movement*, p.108. Brigadier–General Thomas Smyth of the Army of the Cumberland, an active Fenian, would have been another likely figure for a command position had he not been killed in action at the very end of the war in 1865.
19. O'Leary, O'Mahony, DeVoy, and Rossa quoted in *Devoy's Post Bag*, Vol. 1, *1871–1928* (eds), William O'Brien and Desmond Ryan (Dublin, 1948), p.8.
20. See, for instance, Comerford, *The Fenians in Context*, ch.3, pp.67–9. Comerford details the way in which Stephens and O'Mahony buttressed one another's authority.
21. Quoted in Walker, *The Fenian Movement*, p.52.
22. Quoted in Terry Golway, *Irish Rebel: John Devoy and America's Fight for Ireland's Freedom* (New York, 1998), p.51.
23. D'Arcy, *The Fenian Movement*, pp.3–4.
24. Roberts and Sweeny were a pair for political purposes only, however, they were very different personally and they ultimately had a harsh falling out.
25. George W. Potter, *To the Golden Door: The Story of the Irish in Ireland and America* (Boston, MA, 1960), p.556.
26. Walker, *The Fenian Movement*, pp.61–3.
27. Denieffe, *Personal Narrative*, pp.198–200.
28. D'Arcy, *The Fenian Movement*, p.110
29. *New York Herald*, 3 January 1866, p.8.

30. Denieffe, *Personal Narrative* (Appendix), p.274.
31. Idid., pp.207–8.
32. Thomas William Sweeny Papers, Huntington Library, San Marino, California. Sweeny's papers include a number of letters to 'Friend Bodge'. The content of the letters suggests that William B. Bodge was one of those civilian allies of the kind Army officers commonly depended upon to work politically on their behalf – contacting politicians and newspaper editors, for example.
33. Quoted in Walker, *The Fenian Movement*, p.73.
34. Ibid. p.78
35. *New York Times*, 9 January 1866, p.4
36. Quoted in D'Arcy, *The Fenian Movement*, p.114.
37. 'The Invasion of Canada', in Denieffe, *Personal Narrative* (Appendix), p.268.
38. D'Arcy, *The Fenian Movement*, p.144.
39. Letter printed in Denieffe, *Personal Narrative* (Appendix), pp.266–72.
40. Frederick Douglas, *Narrative of the Life of Frederick Douglas, an American Slave*, with a preface by W.L. Garrison (Garden City, NY, 1963), pp.xiii and 42.
41. *The Works of Walt Whitman*, The Deathbed Edition in Two Volumes, Vol. 1 (New York: 1969), pp.328–9.
42. *Missouri Democrat*, 24 September 1865, p.4.
43. William G. Davis, 'Thomas D'Arcy McGee: Irish Founder of the Canadian Nation. members.tripod.com/gail25/Mcgee/htm. (2 September 2004).
44. 'On the Conflagrations at Washington', in *American Poetry: The Nineteenth Century*, 2 vols., John Hollander (ed) Vol. 1 (New York, 1993), pp.8–11. And as late as 1869, no less than Charles Sumner, then chairman of the Senate Foreign Relations Committee, was proposing that Britain turn Canada over to the United States as Civil War reparation. See Irving S. and Nell M. Kull, *An Encyclopedia of American History* (New York, 1965), p.238.
45. D'Arcy, *The Fenian Movement*, p.21.
46. Richard Hofstadter, William Miller and Daniel Aaron, *The United States: The History of a Republic* (Englewood Cliffs, NJ, 1963), p.274.
47. Denieffe, *Personal Narrative* (Appendix), pp.268–9.
48. Keneally, *Great Shame*, p.438.
49. David Owen, *Year of the Fenians* (Buffalo, NY, 1990), p.53.
50. Quoted in Brian Jenkins, *Fenians and Anglo-American Relations during Reconstruction* (Ithaca, NY, 1969), p.41.
51. Walker, *The Fenian Movement,* p.35.
52. Quoted in Owen, *Year of the Fenians*, p.53. Congressman Ignatius Donnelly of Minnesota argued – a further example of Fenian support – for the 'by no means unpopular idea that American policy towards the Fenians should be identical to that pursued by the British in their relations with the Confederacy . . . that the necessary legislation be brought forward enabling the President to extend at his discretion belligerent rights to the Irish rebels'. Jenkins, *Fenians and Anglo-American Relations*, p.225.
53. Owen, *Year of the Fenians*, p.61; *see also* W.S. Neidhardt, *Fenianism in North America* (University Park, PA, 1975), pp.33–4; Senior, *Last Invasion*, p.64.
54. Denieffe, *Personal Narrative* (Appendix), p.270.
55. Owen, *Year of the Fenians*, p.61.
56. Quoted in D'Arcy, *The Fenian Movement*, pp.42, 56. Sweeny would, like Stephens, ultimately be shocked to discover the discrepancy between what he had been led to believe would be the numbers available and what those numbers – in his case at St Alban's – turned out to be.
57. The terminology involving 'centres', 'circles', 'sisterhood', and so forth, was originally John O'Mahony's. D'Arcy McGee claimed these terms reflected O'Mahony's

spiritualist interests and derived from spiritualist vocabulary. (McGee was quoted to this effect in the Burlington Vermont *Free Press* of 24 January 1866.)

58. Denieffe, *Personal Narrative* (Appendix), pp.198–9.
59. Quoted in Robert Kee, *The Bold Fenian Men*, Vol. 2 (London, 1972), p.11.
60. Ibid.
61. Regarding the British agent, Pierce Nagle, see D'Arcy, *The Fenian Movement*, pp.65–6.
62. Denieffe, *Personal Narrative* (Appendix), pp.185–6.
63. D'Arcy, *The Fenian Movement*, p.110.
64. T.M. Healy, *Letters and Leaders of My Day* (Dublin, 1883). See chapter 3, 'A Triple Imprisonment', available at 'Chapters of Dublin History' indigo.ie/~kfinlay/ index.htm (6 August 2004).
65. Corydon served as a lieutenant in the Union Army during the Civil War, after which he was a confidante of Stephens' and a Fenian courier between New York and Dublin. Regarding the failure of the February 1867 Fenian venture in Ireland and the role of the spies Nagle and Corydon in the British prosecution, see Denieffe, *Personal Narrative* pp.138–45. Michael Davitt would spend fifteen years in prison based on Corydon's 1870 testimony.
66. Senior, *Last Invasion*, p.133.
67. 'Unburlesquable Things', *Mark Twain: Collected Tales, Sketches, Speeches and Essays, 1852–1890*, Louis J. Budd (ed.) (New York, 1992), p.423.
68. Miller, *Emigrants and Exiles*, p.335.
69. Quoted in D'Arcy, *The Fenian Movement*, p.96.
70. Neidhardt, *Fenianism in North America*, p.26.
71. Quoted in D'Arcy, *The Fenian Movement*, pp.148–9.
72. Quoted in ibid., pp.151–2.
73. Denieffe's *Personal Narrative* (Appendix), p.268.
74. Ibid., p.228.
75. R.W. Kostal, 'Rebels in the Dock: The Prosecution of Dublin Fenians, 1865–66', *Eire-Ireland*, 34, (1999), 70–96.
76. The ramifications of this for US Fenianism were profound – the Stephens–O'Mahony position was essentially devestated at one fell swoop.
77. *New York Herald*, 4 March 1866, p.1.
78. Senior, *Last Invasion*, p.48. The extent of Fenian plans to attack British shipping and naval operations is evident in the fact that the Fenian, John Philip Holland, with Brotherhood funding, developed plans for a practicable submarine in the 1870s. *See* John Keegan, *The Price of Admiralty: The Evolution of Naval Warfare*, (New York, 1990), pp.215–16.
79. Senior, *Last Invasion*, p.188.
80. Keneally, *Great Shame*, pp.438–39.
81. D'Arcy, *The Fenian Movement*, p.84.
82. Quoted in Ruddy, 'An Irish Army in America', p.39, from *Philadelphia Inquirer*, 12 May 1866.
83. Halpine exchange of letters with Roberts and Sweeny in Denieffe, *Personal Narrative* (Appendix), pp.229–32.
84. *New York Tribune*, 11 January 1866, p.4.
85. Quoted in D'Arcy, *The Fenian Movement*, p.145.
86. Benedict Maryniak, 'The Fenian Raid and Battle of Ridgeway'. www.acsu.buffalo.edu/ ~dbertuca/g/FenianRaid.html (12 September 2004), pp.4–5.
87. Sweeny official report on the Fenian Invasion in 'The Fenian Invasion of Canada 1866', *Journal of the American Irish Historical Society*, 23 (1924), p.200. Hereafter TWS, 'Official Report', *JAIHS* (1924).

88. D'Arcy, *The Fenian Movement*, p.157.
89. *New York Times*, 5 June 1866, p.8.
90. In this regard Sweeny perhaps fell victim to the American tendency, especially in the nineteenth century, to patronize Canada and assume Canadian indifference regarding the integrity of their borders. A number of Canadian historians – notably Charles P. Stacey and later W.S. Neidhardt, and Hereward Senior – have pointed out that the Fenian incursions had an historic effect on Canada's self-image, stimulating Canadian nationalism and diminishing any sentiment there had been there in favour of annexation. This held true for the Campobello Fenian venture as well as for the mainland one: 'The attempted [Campobello] raid . . . moved New Brunswick to vote in favor of joining the Confederation of British North America, later Canada, and also stimulated greater efficiency in military organization'. www.campobello.com/history.html (30 July 2004). And the assassination of D'Arcy McGee by a Fenian in Ottowa in 1868 contributed greatly to the spirit of confederation and Canadianism. An 1870 issue of the Canadian *Weekly Globe* observed that: 'Canadians have gained more in national character during the last six years than in any previous twenty . . . the outrageous proceedings of the Fenians and their abettors have been among the chief agencies'. Quoted in Owen, *Year of the Fenians*, p.90.
91. Quoted in D'Arcy, *The Fenian Movement*, p.162.
92. *Chicago Tribune*, 1–3 June, 1866, p.1
93. TWS, 'Official Report', *JAIHS*, 23, 1924, p.200.
94. Quoted in Walker, *Fenian Movement*, p.116.
95. *Chicago Tribune*, 6–8 June 1866.
96. D'Arcy, *The Fenian Movement*, p.163–65.
97. TWS, 'Official Report', *JAIHS* p.201.
98. *Chicago Tribune*, 5 June 1866, p.2.
99. Quoted in D'Arcy, *The Fenian Movement*, p.166.
100. Walker, *Fenian Movement*, p.105.
101. Neidhardt, *Fenianism in North America*, p.79.
102. Denieffe, *Personal Narrative* (Appendix), pp.252–53.

7

Canada Aftermath, The Later Years

> If I had done this in some other country, I would be a hero. But here . . . I am just one of the boys, prowling the night with other highwaymen.
>
> Sweeny[1]

In a telegram from his besieged position on 1 June, Fenian Captain Hynes appealed to General Sweeny: 'Our men isolated. Enemy marching in force from Toronto. What shall we do?'[2] This might have served as a forlorn epigraph for the whole undertaking, as might one of Samuel Spears's early communications referring to the failure of supplies to arrive: 'the men hungry and most of them begging to go to the destination promised them – Canada'.[3] As mentioned earlier just before his arrest, Sweeny sent an equally melancholy dispatch via courier to Fenian Headquarters in New York urging Roberts to deposit money immediately into a New York bank account for the purpose of getting soldiers transported back to their homes from the front.[4] The depth of Sweeny's misery virtually alone in a small town in northern Vermont, having to see to aftermath details, the whole endeavour collapsed around him, is difficult to imagine. The standard wisdom that success has many fathers, but failure only one, would hold mercilessly true. He had laid everything on the line – the prestige and rank hard-earned on many battlefields as well as the pension he would need to support his family in the coming years. He had invested all his energy, all his knowledge and know-how, in the Canadian invasion plan in the belief or hope that sufficient numbers of others would do the same. Not enough others did. United States interference was a catastrophic factor in the invasion's failure, but the miserable turn out at some of the gathering points along the border, the insufficient number of boots on the ground, was a great disappointment as well. There is a strong tendency in revolutionary projects for people to wait to see signs of success before throwing their lot into the effort. The invasion would have had to have shown striking early success at major points in order to draw thousands of fence-sitters to the front and to have any hope of provoking a robust uprising among the Canadian Irish and French.

The scene was a sad one at some of the mustering locations as soldiers ready to attack had to be told the invasion had already broken down. Fenians formed at the Chicago headquarters were clamouring to be sent forward, but the expected word to go was not forthcoming. When the government, hoping to defuse a dangerous situation, offered transportation for the soldiers out of the city and back to their homes, Chicago leader Michael Scanlon urged them to refuse and to stay put in the hope the neutrality laws might yet be repealed and belligerent rights granted by Washington in response to Irish pressure. General Sweeny, however, sent word advising the soldiers 'to accept the government's terms and return to their homes. He said the stringent measures adopted by the army officials had rendered Fenian success impossible at the present time'.[5]

The *Army and Navy Journal* of 16 June 1866 articulated the bitterness felt from the Fenian side of things regarding US government perfidy. 'We assume, of course that it was the United States which demolished Fenianism, not Great Britain', the journal declared. It asserted that the inadequacy of even the best of the Canadian volunteer troops was manifest in the skirmishes that had occurred and that there were few regular regiments in reserve – 'very few for so enormous a [border]line'. Had the United States maintained neutrality in the matter, the editorial argued, and the Fenians been allowed to get ordnance and supplies to the front and had their line of communication from the rear not been interfered with, 'Sweeny could have flung his columns over the border wherever he liked'.[6]

In his official report of September 1866, Sweeny identified the same primary cause for the failure – seizure of arms and ammunition by the US authorities – the secondary cause being 'the misrepresentations made by the colonels of the regiments respecting their effective force'.[7] The two causes were probably, in fact, equally devastating. In this report, however, he did not reference, as he might have, the way in which the O'Mahony wing of the organization had at best dragged its heels and at worst worked actively to subvert his effort. A Dublin newspaper, however, was more outspoken regarding the responsibility of the O'Mahony people in the invasion's failure. The paper first recapitulated the disagreement between the factions, justifying Sweeny's plan, even now in retrospect, as sound:

> At war with the English power in Canada, [the Fenians] could claim from the American Government recognition as belligerents; in the harbors of Canada they would be able to equip privateers for such a game against English commerce as the *Alabama* played against the commerce of America.

The Stephens–O'Mahoney alternative remained a non-starter in the editor's view:

> England, being at peace with the world, could throw her whole force upon the neighboring island, which, of all places on the face of the earth, is that in which she could carry on hostilities with the greatest convenience to herself. Nowhere else could she send so large an army – nowhere else could she supply that army with every requisite so readily and so cheaply.

Quoting from some of Sweeny's speeches, the piece argued that 'the stamp of honesty and common sense was upon them', but that the O'Mahony group resented being superseded.

> They gave every possible opposition to the General's project; they denounced it at public meetings and in the press; they broke in with rowdyism upon the meetings which were being held to support it; they interrupted the speakers with shouts and cries . . . They put into circulation . . . a whole flight of falsehoods . . . These they set afloat for the purpose of diverting the minds of the Brotherhood from the plan proposed by General Sweeny . . . This opposition retarded considerably the preparations being made by the Senate Party, but did not stop them. The month of April came on; the time fixed by General Sweeny for the commencement of his operations . . . when, to the great surprise of the public, news arrived that the O'Mahony party themselves were demonstrating along the British frontier! Astonishing reports of all they were preparing to do were borne on the wings of the press. Mr. Doran Killian, who, it seems, has suddenly acquired the title of 'General', was reported massing his men and holding a convention at Eastport, and a rush into New Brunswick was reported as imminent . . .
>
> The organs of the Senate branch of the Brotherhood state that the [Killian] demonstrations were got up by the O'Mahonyites for the purpose of hastening the repressive interference of the American Government . . . They hoped to provoke the interposition in time to prevent the Sweeny party from crossing the frontier! . . . Such is the patriotism, such is the Fenianism, of Mr. O'Mahony and his men. They will suffer no attack, if they can help it, to be made by an Irish force on the British power unless under their auspices.[8]

The editors would seem to be correct in viewing Sweeny's tack as more realistic than the one Stephens and company adhered to which visualized a high-seas expedition from America to Ireland in the face of Britannia's naval might. A serious underestimation of the enemy would seem to have resided in that strategy rather than in Sweeny's. When John O'Mahony writes to John Mitchel from New York on 10 November 1865, for example, asking Mitchel to convey to him 'reliable information . . . of the amount of land and marine force of our enemies available for the defense of their domination in Ireland', one wonders if O'Mahony realizes what he is asking; can he seriously be requesting that Mitchel, in his spare time, draw up a summary of the totality of British military wherewithal?[9]

Sweeny forwent recriminations against the O'Mahony faction at this point, however; putting too fine a point on the matter would only have inflamed things further, to no useful purpose now. His expressed indignation was directed toward the Johnson administration, whose behaviour, he felt, suggested nothing less than entrapment:

> The muskets were purchased at Bridesburg Arsenal, Philadelphia, and the ammunition at Watervelt Arsenal, Troy. The United States Government, in selling these stores to my agents, was perfectly well aware of the purpose for which they were intended, and their willingness in allowing these sales to be made, together with the sympathy expressed for us by individuals in eminent positions at Washington, caused me to be totally unprepared for the

> treacherous seizure of our arms and ammunition . . . I submit the action of the Executive [President Johnson] to the liberty loving people of the United States, and I am mistaken in their character and generous and manly sentiments, if they award their approval to the Government having permitted its marshals and other civil officials to play the role of British detectives.[10]

And he was not alone in his suspicion of a conscious plot to entrap. General John A. Logan, Republican candidate for congressman-at-large, speaking to a Fenian audience in Chicago later that year, accused President Johnson of having duped Irish labourers and servant-girls into donating half their wages to buy military equipment and to field an Irish army in order that [Johnson] 'might confiscate those arms and equipment and imprison these patriots'. Schulyer Colfax, the speaker of the House of Representatives and soon to be vice president in the Grant administration, told the same audience that he was 'unutterably humiliated' by the US action against the Fenians, affirming that 'Congress has been wholly on the side of Ireland's independence, and my whole heart is with you'.[11]

There were numerous Fenian prisoners in Canada, many facing possible death sentences. As noted, Robert B. Lynch and Father John McMahon were in fact so sentenced, but a commutation was issued two weeks before their scheduled executions. A tendency to back off from severe retribution began to be evident in Canada as well as in the United States. The British government feared the reaction of French Canadians should a Catholic priest be executed and was concerned as well about Orange versus Catholic animosity, common in Canada, being exacerbated by such an event. In the United States, once Irish political power and organization was mustered and brought to bear, Roberts' and Sweeny's indictments for violation of the neutrality laws were never carried through. Nor were the Fenian leaders arrested in various US cities ultimately brought to trial. In July the Congress adopted a resolution calling for the prosecution of Fenians related to the Canada affair to be discontinued. In ninety-seven Canadian trials initiated, only twenty-one Fenians were convicted, and, over a period of three years even these men had their sentences commuted.[12] The dynamic involved in Canada, however, was arguably different from the one that prevailed south of the border; it was not based on Irish political clout. Luckily for Lynch and McMahon in particular, the British strategy that came into play, even disregarding the priest issue, was incompatible with executions.

London carefully avoided at this juncture the mistake it would make in 1916 – that of a Draconian response and the creation of martyrs. British propaganda was instead addressed toward controlling the matrix of memory that would surround the event; they would emphasize the farcical character of Sweeny's invasion, denying the Fenians the status of revolutionaries and preventing the attack from taking its place within any sustained and dignified narrative of nationalist struggle.[13] Before the invasion occurred, in fact, *Harper's Weekly* was satirizing the Fenians as though taking a note from the practice of the

Illustrated London News and *Punch* in England. Though Fenianism, as many historians have noted, caused considerable trepidation in England and arguably led to the comparatively liberal policies of the Gladstone years, the Irish once again fell victim to being perceived through alien media; the ineptness of the Fenian adventure was taken full advantage of and broadly caricatured in order to deny it any romantic–symbolic power. And unfortunately, as time went on Canadian invasions became an *idée fixe* among Fenians. Civil War animosity toward Canada quickly waned, but, thanks to John O'Neill and others, *truly* ill-conceived and redundant forays were undertaken in the later 1860s, ones that wore away sympathy for the cause.

By the time of O'Neill's ventures into Canada, in fact, the Canadian government no longer suffered much anxiety regarding the Fenians; so well-informed were Canadian officials by the informer LeCaron, that they could easily and humiliatingly intercept Fenian incursions. Such raids now merely provided grist for the mills even of humourists not necessarily interested in serving the ends of British colonial preservation. In 1870, Mark Twain, for example, published an essay referred to previously in which he satirized what had been by then a long series of *faux* invasions:

> First we have the portentous mystery that precedes [the invasion] for six months, when all the air is filled with stage whisperings; when councils meet every night with awful secrecy, and the membership try to see who can get up first in the morning and tell the proceedings. Next the expatriated Nation struggles with a travail of national squabbles and political splits, and is finally delivered of a litter of 'Governments', and Presidents McThis, and Generals O'That . . . [I]n solemn whisperings in the dead of night they secretly plan a Canadian raid, and publish it in the 'World' next morning; they begin to refer significantly to 'Ridgeway', and we reflect bodingly that there is no telling how soon the slaughter may be repeated. Presently the 'invasion' begins to take shape; and as no news travels so freely or so fast as the 'secret' doings of the Fenian Brotherhood, the land is shortly in a tumult of apprehension. The telegraph announces that 'last night, 400 men went north from Utica, but refused to disclose their destination.'[14]

Rather than being seen as exiles – many of them Famine refugees – attempting to strike a blow as best they could against the colonial power occupying their country, the most powerful empire on earth at the time, the Fenians were to be viewed as a joke and their efforts as comic opera. Not the disunifying effects of diaspora nor the maddeningly prohibitive distance from the heart of the matter, Ireland, were cited as the cause of revolutionary failure, but rather the flawed character of the Irish themselves. It was the scheme employed by the British to neutralize the 1848 Irish uprising at Ballingarry, and it worked very well in both cases. Although failed military adventures – to cite only fairly recent examples – the Bay of Pigs, the bumbling retreat from Saigon, the maladroit occupation of Iraq – are almost the rule rather than the exception historically, none of these events has been treated as an occasion for hilarity

Nor was, for instance, the abortive rescue attempt in Iran wherein the best intelligence and military-operational thinking in the US arsenal was brought to bear only to conclude with helicopters flying into one another or lying disabled by blowing sand, treated as a burlesque.

The 1866 Canadian invasion, on the other hand, was and is written about as if it were somehow uniquely silly, and historians have tended to embrace the British portrayal. Nor, of course, could Irish-American Catholic scholarship be counted upon to balance that portrayal, the Church at large being glad to be relieved of a troublesome element within its own ranks. Not until 1947 did a Catholic scholar address the issue well – William D'Arcy in his *The Fenian Movement in the United States*, which has been frequently referenced here. The 'comic opera' characterization has stuck, and Sweeny is often cited as the Fenian 'Secretary of War' (in quotes) as if such a designation were patently laughable. Blanche Touhill, in her *William Smith-O'Brien and His Revolutionary Companions in Exile* (1981), describes the same design, as earlier noted, carried out by British newspapers covering the 1848 insurrection: 'They would orchestrate the laughter. The battle at Ballingarry became known as a skirmish in Widow McCormack's cabbage patch, and O'Brien as leader of that skirmish was made out to be a fool'.[15] The allegedly bumbling Young Irelanders, for all their faults, ultimately had enough talent that afterwards one became Premier of New South Wales, two were Union Army generals, one was the territorial Governor of Montana, another the Governor General of Newfoundland, and yet another was one of the founding fathers of modern Canada. Likewise the officers who directed the Fenian attempt on Canada were mocked as so many Don Quixotes engaged in a nonsensical effort, though they were eminent military figures. In O'Neill, Spears, Starr, Mechan, Heffernan, Murphy, amongst others, Sweeny had in fact made excellent choices. Limerick-born Brigadier General Michael C. Murphy – to cite only one of them – who was in charge of Fenian Forces at Malone, New York, was a US Medal of Honor recipient for his leadership in the Civil War battle at North Anna River, Virginia, in 1864. As Lieutenant Colonel, 170th New York Regiment, he had kept his unit in position, calm and disciplined under enemy fire, and continued to hold for three full hours after his troops had run out of ammunition.[16]

The Fenian raid on Canada was, however, fitted into an ideological pattern already in place, the one just discussed, that whenever possible represented Irish nationalist efforts as emotionally superficial, fickle and probably drunken. The unquestioned Irish propensity for the gala, the field day, the dance, has been used to convict the nationality of a kind of primitive shallowness. Kevin Kenny has recently noted a related expression of this kind of prejudice in the context of Molly Maguire historiography. He points to the powerful and enduring myth that denied Irish perpetrators of violence all rationality and motivation, explaining their actions instead as a matter of natural depravity.[17] Nor was violence necessary for such neutralizing tropes to be employed. The honour the Irish bestowed on Terence McManus, for example, when his body was returned from San Francisco to Ireland by the Fenians for burial, when handled by some historians, even including some Irish ones, is caricatured beyond recognition. While it was one of the largest nationalist demonstrations in Irish history, R.F. Foster, for instance, allows only that the funeral was one of the Fenians' 'publicity coups'.[18] And R.V. Comerford sketches the event as devoid of any real significance, as not reflective of any real commitment on the part of the thousands of participants: 'Almost the only incontrovertible interpretation that can be put on the affair is that large numbers of people were in the mood for a public spectacle in Dublin on 10 November 1861'. The participants, as he would have it, were engaged in a recreational exercise; they were fair game for the apolitical stimulations of *any* congenial gathering; they were looking for 'an excuse for ovating'. It would be a 'grave error', he cautions, 'to assume that the crowd was giving assent to McManus's political doctrines'.[19] It is almost as if these Irish were so many puppies ready to follow anyone with some treats in their pocket; and the comic-opera narrative of Sweeny's Canadian invasion is disparagingly drawn along the same lines.

This is not of course a matter to be settled here, but Comerford's image of the nineteenth-century Irish is at variance with the witness of Stephen Crane, for example, who in the 1890s – if anything a less politically volatile time than the 1860s – was struck by exactly the opposite tendency in the Irish behaviour. Crane found in rural Ireland not a politically shallow and fickle population, but rather one fiercely resolute. He notes the treatment afforded the Royal Irish Constabulary – the 'stern tenant' that the Crown's representative not be acknowledged in any way:

> The natural custom of meeting a stranger or friend alike on the road with a cheery greeting like 'God Save You' is too kindly and human a trait not to be missed. But all through the South of Ireland one sees the peasant turn his eyes pretentiously to the side of the road at the sight of the constable . . . None looked, nodded, or gave sign. There was a line drawn so sternly that it reared like a fence . . . The mass of the Irish strictly obey the stern tenant.[20]

The testimony of the American Fenian priest Father Edmund O'Flaherty, based on his 1861 trip around Ireland, would also contradict Comerford's characterization of the contemporary Irish and ring truer to Crane's later evaluation:

> I have traveled through a large portion of the three provinces, Leinster, Munster, and Connaught, where I made the acquaintance not alone of many leaders of the movement, but also of no small number of the Rank and File. I found the men of the Irish Army (for by this name should we call it) neither noisy brawlers or enthusiasts; but on the contrary calm and collected patriots, doing their work quietly and surely . . . they are fully aware of the importance of the contest and of the great issues involved therein – the magnitude of the perils.[21]

Some of the sense of betrayal felt by the Fenians in the wake of the failure of the 1866 invasion is registered in these few stanzas from the Irish-American song, 'The Fenian Volunteer':

. . .
So I did hie to Mahoney
Where a phalanx was forming, O!
And to win fame, put down my name,
To leave on Tuesday Morning, O!
For Canada we shaped our way,
By General Sweeny's orders O!
To face the guns of Britain's sons,
Beyond the Northern Border, O!

. . .
Green Erin's years of bursting tears
Were near obliterated, O!
And vengeance black we'd soon pay back
To the cursed thieves we hated, O!
Our privateers would blanch the sneers
Upon their faces craven, O!
And many a ship, on a homeward trip
Would never reach a haven, O!

But we were sold for English gold,
By those who should befriend us, O!
McShawn indeed, and Seward and Meade
But then, the devil mend us, O!
. . .[22]

While under arrest in St Alban's, Sweeny had written, perhaps disingenuously, to the Fenian membership exhorting them not to be disheartened and to 'guard, cherish and protect our now really powerful organization'.[23] However, a good deal of discouragement did, understandably, set in. When Fenian correspondence urging a new start up of Fenian action began to circulate, not everyone was enthusiastic. The following letter, capturing the disillusionment felt by many formerly devoted Fenian activists, was sent from Louisville, Kentucky, by Brotherhood Centre Patrick Bannon to the Philadelphia Fenian, John Gibbons:

> I received your dispatch this morning to attend Senate meeting on Wednesday. Circumstances prevent my attending. I have dispatched to that effect, and, laying my resignation of Senator and State Centre before you, you will of course accept it, as I will no longer serve in that position. I will work at home for the Brotherhood, if anything can be done.
>
> . . . The people here have let down and are dispirited, and I decline to go in the dark. If anything turns up in the future, I may go again if it looks all right.
>
> I have not sold any bonds. I would not offer them for sale until something would be done that would look like a victory. The consequence is I have $10,000 worth of them and will return them when called upon.
>
> Your Senate should have met in Washington and hurled anathemas against those who deceived and betrayed us, and demand of them to pursue the dismissal of every Cabinet officer that made a cat's paw of us . . .

> Kentucky will now have a chance to stay home and leave the management of affairs to more able and wiser ones. Believe me your kind and affectionate friend, Bannon.[24]

At the Troy, New York, convention of 4 September Sweeny read his official report. There were calls for new military leadership, and even the invasion's two comparatively successful operations tended to be credited to the immediate field commanders involved, O'Neill and Spear, rather than to Sweeny. O'Neill particularly, as the hero of Ridgeway, became the new Fenian hope, but he would fare no better than Sweeny in the long run. In 1870, under arrest in Burlington, Vermont, he wrote an official report regarding the miserably failed attempt to invade Canada that occurred under his own command and direction on 25 May of that year. From that vantage point, he was able to identify with what Sweeny had faced in 1866:

> The movement of 1866, for two causes, either of which had been sufficient, resulted disastrously. The men failed to be on the ground in available numbers at the appointed time, and those who did arrive were unprovided with arms and ammunition; various reasons were assigned for these two mishaps . . . nearly all reflecting on the capacity and management of the then commanding general, T.W. Sweeny. The charges then made against General Sweeny have since been repeated, but with more bitterness, against myself. In a movement like ours, if unsuccessful, it seems inevitable that someone has to be made the victim.[25]

From the perspective of the present day, it is of course easy to second guess Sweeny's strategy. Given the way things turned out, it would probably have been better had he operated more in the asymmetrical vein of Michael Collins, Che Guevarra or Geronimo. A smaller, tighter, guerilla army could probably have functioned more effectively. But that model was not a significant part of the military vocabulary of 1866 except perhaps for the legendary guerilla-style exploits of Confederate Colonel John Mosby and his cavalry raiders during the Civil War.

American Fenian energies now moved to the political stage. The Johnson administration and the Democratic Party were put on notice that the Irish political clout would be brought to bear against them for their recent actions. At a Washington rally the Fenians passed a vehement anti-Johnson resolution:

> Whereas the [Fenian] military expedition . . . was fully capable of accomplishing its noble mission, were it not for the fact that the attempt was frustrated and its noble actors hunted down, crushed and malignantly persecuted by order of Andrew Johnson, President of the United States . . . therefore he merits . . . unqualified condemnation . . . The thanks of Irishmen are due to congressmen whose large hearted and comprehensive republicanism . . . revolted at the toadyism to English sentiment displayed by Andrew Johnson and . . . William H. Seward.[26]

But Sweeny, a soldier and not a politician, decided to leave the fray. Having addressed the Troy convention, he resigned his position in the Brotherhood – it would be taken by Spears – and, by way of a notice on page four of the *New York Tribune* of 28 September 1866, announced his desire to separate from the organization:

> In consequence of the numerous invitations which Gen. Sweeny is now receiving to attend Fenian picnics and other reunions of the Fenian Brotherhood, he wishes it to be understood that he resigned the position of Secretary of War at the Troy Congress, and declined the offer of the Commander-in-Chief of the Army of Ireland, which was tendered to him by that body. Being, therefore no longer connected with the organization of the Fenian Brotherhood, he does not intend to take any part at present in the proceedings of the Brotherhood, to whom he feels grateful for the continued confidence evinced toward him by these invitations.[27]

Sweeny's Fenian involvement was finished. It was a failure, but was as well historically significant in terms of, at the very least, its effect upon Canadian–US relations and as a demonstration before the world that Ireland was not resigned to its status as a colony, nor was Irish-America, though things would have to wait numerous decades more for the dream to be fulfilled. This was, to quote Thomas Keneally, 'a catastrophic period of reckless Fenian endeavour and failure, yet of gestures potent enough to set the tone of Anglo-Irish discourse for the remainder of the nineteenth and much of the twentieth centuries'.[28]

Sweeny's attempt to distance himself publicly from the Brotherhood was probably made with an eye to removing a possible hindrance to recovering his commission in the US Army and securing his pension – he had children to support – which he undertook to do immediately. There was as well the matter of his reputation, how he would be remembered. Now 46 years old, he had invested most of his life in the US military. Not wanting to let that career be recorded as having ended with a dismissal due to his being absent without leave, he wrote the President on 29 October 1866:

> Sir:
> I have the honor to request that I may be reinstated in the United States Army. I was dismissed . . . on the 29th of December 1865 for absence without leave, and as I presume the circumstances connected with it are well known to your Excellency, it would be unnecessary for me to relate all of them – At the time of my dismissal I had application for an extension of my leave of absence at the Headquarters of the Army and was awaiting an answer in this City believing it would certainly be granted.
>
> I am Sir,
> Very respectfully,
> Your Obdnt Serv.
> T.W. Sweeny [29]

This brief letter was of course not expected to do the trick itself, but was a matter of formality. The real appeals would be carried out by Sweeny's political allies. Retired General Thomas W. Egan, himself a veteran with heroic Civil War service to his credit, was one of those who undertook to work on Sweeny's behalf toward reinstatement. In a letter to the Secretary of the Treasury, H.M. McCullough, Egan appealed to McCulloch to use his influence toward restoring Sweeny's commission, citing the latter's service and sustained bravery over the years which, he argued, should outweigh the charges against him. He sought to explain that Sweeny's prolonged leave, self-granted though it was, had not been ignoble, that Sweeny had sincerely believed that Ireland could be liberated through the capture of British territory in Canada, and that obeying that call to duty was his only crime.[30]

As 1866 was an election year and, apparently in response to the efforts of Egan and others, President Johnson was loath to anger American-Irish voters any more than he had already done. He wrote a memo to the adjutant general's office urging that Sweeny's case be given special attention.[31] However, when the matter came before General Grant he rejected the proposal for reinstatement, arguing that the position in question had long since been filled and that 'to reinstate [Sweeny] would be unjust to officers who have remained in service and performed their duty'.[32] Even this was not enough to dissuade Johnson, however, and in the end he overrode Grant's denial of approval and ordered Secretary of War E.M. Stanton to revoke the order of December 1865 whereby Sweeny had been relieved of his duties. After some further bureaucratic snags were finally overcome, on 18 April 1866 the US Senate confirmed Sweeny's reinstatement and he was soon in Augusta, Georgia, serving as reconstruction military administrator. He wrote to his daughter, Fannie, from there on 30 December 1866:

> I arrived here on Christmas Day, and assumed command of this Post, which embraces several of the surrounding counties. I like the place very much; the climate is delightful, and the people are disposed to be friendly. Of course there is a great deal of bitterness still remaining . . . Col. Silbey gave me my choice of posts garrisoned by the 16th Infantry, and I selected this [Augusta] in preference to any other. The city has a population of nearly 30,000 inhabitants, is very beautiful, and resembles Savannah somewhat. The principle streets are very wide, and have double rows of trees, which entirely protect one from the sun in summer.
>
> I think you would like the place . . . and when you are well enough you must come down here and bring Mary Barnard with you. You can stay as long as you please and return when you get tired of the place. You can come to Savannah by water, where I could meet you, and from there to this place by R.R. is only 132 miles.[33]

But like U.S. Grant, Sweeny was not at his best during peace time. His self-discipline wavered – the profound disappointment of the Fenian episode on top of the stress associated with his wife's death and years of combat duty had worn him down – he had suffered from illness and exhaustion while under arrest at St

Alban's. He was not long at his post in Georgia before being caught up once again in an extended controversy leading to yet another court martial. His final three army years, in keeping with the years immediately preceding them, were controversial. As early as July of 1867 he found himself accused of interfering with the civil government in the area he was in charge of and, more humiliatingly, charged with drunk and disorderly conduct including urinating in public on St Patrick's Day 1867, and, finally, consorting with female visitors in his quarters on certain evenings during May and June of that year.

Once again Sweeny, in arguing his case, was able to blunt the edges of the main charges. His charm was still working, and local Georgia citizens supported him, writing letters testifying to his fairness and restraint as military administrator. After a judge advocate's hearing, he was sentenced on 24 September 1867 to confinement to the city limits of Augusta for six months and suspension of pay for the same period.[34] Perhaps resolved to turn over a new leaf, eleven days earlier he had married an Atlanta girl, Eugenia Reagan, a young woman less than half his age and only slightly older than his own eldest daughter, Sarah. Eugenia would be his wife for the remainder of his life and the mother of two of his sons.

But the affair in Augusta would not remain confined to that city. The *New York Times*, a newspaper that had long evidenced an anti-Fenian bias and a dislike for Sweeny personally, was outraged by the lightness of his sentence and took the opportunity to attack him with a vengeance in an editorial of 6 October 1867.

> Two years ago . . . Thomas W. Sweeny, while holding a commission in the US Army, undertook the formation of an independent military organization, under the style of the Irish Republican Army, taking a position at the same time in a concern that called itself the Irish Government, as Secretary of War. Sweeny, although not himself present at any of the skirmishes that the Fenian bush-wackers engaged in . . . was the organizer of these lawless expeditions . . .
>
> One might have supposed after a United States officer . . . had disgraced his uniform by taking a leading part in what turned out a heartless imposture that he would have been allowed to serve a short probationary term before being reinstated . . . But no: Fenian sympathizers backed his appeal, and he went back to duty . . . with the *prestige* of a man who could defy the rules of army discipline . . .
>
> Recent events have come to light respecting Sweeny which show that he has not failed to improve upon the immunities thus accorded him through political influence. At his post at Augusta, Georgia, he has been tried before a partial and friendly Court of military officers for acts of beastliness, dishonesty, and insubordination of the most flagrant kind . . . Here is a Fenian hero for you . . . [J]ust as he found influence a year ago sufficient to get reinstated . . . he seems to have had influence now to get clear of all but a fraction of the ordinary penalties attaching to his offence. . . .[35]

The editors would have been even more enraged had they known that after three months even his comparatively light sentence was set aside by President Johnson in response to appeals, including ones from the Augusta citizenry and the Augusta *Chronicle and Sentinel*.[36]

Sweeny was now transferred to a similar command in Atlanta, the city where he had been instrumental in foiling General Hardee's counterattack on the Union forces during the siege, but which city he never entered in victory because of the fracas with Dodge and the ensuing prosecution. He spent nine months in the Georgia capital during which time, on 14 July 1868, his wife gave birth to the couple's first child, Thomas Francis Sweeny.[37]

There was a military cutback in 1869–70 and Sweeny, having by then been transferred once again to Augusta, was retired at that time with the rank of brigadier general, his wounds from Churubusco, Wilson's Creek and Shiloh being cited as by now incapacitating him for further military service. With his wife and child he departed Augusta for New York, where on 11 May 1870 he recieved official orders of retirement. New York, and specifically Long Island, would be his base – a civilian one – from now on. A year later a second son, William Montgomery Sweeny, was born to him and his wife. William would become an historian and genealogist, particularly of the Virginia area, as well as a curator of his father's papers which he put at the disposal of William D'Arcy when the latter was writing and researching his book on the American Fenian movement. In retirement, Sweeny lived out the rest of his life with his family on Long Island, at 120 Franklin Street, enjoying the sidewalks of New York, stopping in pubs and visiting friends. He and Philip Sheridan, old men now, would exchange letters and pictures of their grandchildren.[38] A *New York Tribune* correspondent described the aging warrior in retirement: 'Sweeny is very domestic now, having a quiet, comfortable home in the suburbs, but he is often seen in the busy haunts downtown with his armless sleeve – fit emblem of a dauntless soldier'.[39]

He died at the age of 72 on 10 April 1892, leaving a widow and five children, and was buried in the family plot in Greenwood Cemetery, Brooklyn, the burrow of New York he had come to with his mother from Ireland as a boy of twelve. Gone was a man who, granted his many faults, was a spirited, tough and intrepid adventurer. The *Army and Navy Journal* called him 'as gallant, warmhearted, and impulsive an officer as ever wore the uniform'.[40] Margaret Fuller, writing on the Irish character in 1845, pointed to their 'truth to domestic ties . . . their indefatigable good humour . . . their ready wit, their elasticity of nature'.[41] Few Irishmen ever reflected those virtues more than Sweeny.

On a spring morning, as they banged the drums slowly, six batteries of artillery served as funeral escort. Francis E. Pinto who, as a lieutenant in Mexico, had helped Sweeny back to a medical tent and held him during the amputation of his arm, was one of the pallbearers. Father Walsh of St Raymond's Church conducted the service and delivered the eulogy. The variety of honorary delegations at the graveside – representing among others the Society of California Pioneers of 1849, the Veterans of the Mexican War, the 16th US Infantry, the 37th Irish Rifles, the Corcoran Legion and the Irish Brigade[42] – could barely suggest the extraordinary range of Tom Sweeny's journey from the day he left Brooklyn to this last return.

NOTES

1. Quoted in Maryniak, 'The Fenian Raid and Battle of Ridgeway'.
2. TWS, 'Official Report', *JAIHS,* (1924), p.200.
3. Denieffe, *Personal Narrative* (Appendix), p.251.
4. TWS, 'Official Report', *JAIHS,* (1924), p.202.
5. Walker, *The Fenian Movement*, p.103.
6. Quoted in TWS, 'Official Report', *JAIHS* (1924), p.194.
7. Ibid., p.203.
8. 'A Dublin Newspaper' is the only identification given in the Appendix to Denieffe's *Personal Narrative*, pp.273–6.
9. Quoted in ibid., pp.201–2.
10. Quoted in D'Arcy, *The Fenian Movement*, p.169. The extent of the US government's having earlier looked the other way is evident in the fact that the Fenians had purchased 4,220 Bridesburg rifle-muskets and had them converted to breech loaders at a US armory in Trenton, New Jersey. (See Goble,'On to Canada', p.22.) Quoted in Walker, *Fenian Movement* p.115.
11. Quoted in Walker, *Fenian Movement* p.115.
12. Arthur H. DeRosier, 'Importance in Failure: The Fenian Raids of 1866–71', *Southern Quarterly,* 3, 3, (1965), pp.181–97. The original adamant, prosecutorial attitude in Canada towards the arrested Fenians is reflected in D'Arcy McGee's response to a priest's appeal for him to help a person implicated in the raids. In a public letter, McGee responded emphatically that he would not intervene 'to whatever punishment the law hands him over, no word of mine can ever be spoken in mitigation; not even, under these circumstances, if he were my own brother'. See Robin B. Burns, 'D'Arcy McGee and the Fenians', in Maurice Harman (ed.), *Fenians and Fenianism* (Seattle, WA, 1970), p.88.
13. Historian Kevin Whelan notes the same kind of propaganda strategy brought to bear upon the 1798 rebellion in Ireland – the attempt (largely successful historically) to characterize the rebellion as an impromptu, amateurish and Catholic affair when it was in fact none of those things: 'For conservatives, the immediate task in the aftermath of the rebellion was to create an exclusively sectarian narrative of the origin and progress of radicalism in the 1790s. By doing so, the revolution could be stripped of its ostensibly secular mask, revealing instead its real (and ghastly) popish face . . . conservative rhetoric popularized this interpretation'. ''98 after '98: The Invention of Tradition', Paper delivered to the American Conference for Irish Studies, Queen's University Belfast, June 1995.
14. 'Unburlesquable Things', *Twain: Collected Tales, Sketches, Speeches and Essays*, p.423.
15. Blanche Touhill, *William Smith-O'Brien and His Revolutionary Companions in Exile* (Columbia, MO, 1981), p.12.
16. www.army.mil/cmh-pg/mohciv2.htm
17. Kevin Kenny, *Making Sense of the Molly Maguires* (New York, 1998), p.12.
18. R.F. Foster, *Modern Ireland, 1600–1972* (London, 1988), p.393.
19. Comerford, *The Fenians in Context*, pp.78–9.
20. Stephen Crane, *Tales, Sketches, and Reports*, (ed.) Fredson Bowers (Charlottesville, VA, 1973), pp.489–90.
21. Letter to John O'Mahony quoted in D'Arcy, *The Fenian Movement*, p.23. This kind of disconnection from the realities in Ireland arguably characterized the older Fenian leadership going as far back as the Brotherhood's New York incarnation as the Emmet Monument Association. Joseph Denieffe recounts how in June 1855, when he received

news of his father's serious illness, he booked passage for Ireland and went to see Michael Doheny before leaving New York. Denieffe had been led to understand that an insurrection in Ireland was set for that September, and, arriving at Doheny's, John O'Mahoney being present, he inquired to whom he should report when he arrived in Ireland. To Denieffe's amazement, Doheny replied that the organization had 'no one there as yet' and that Denieffe had 'carte blanche' to do what he could. 'I went with a cheerful heart', Denieffe wrote, having been reassured that September was indeed the time, 'although I had no one in Ireland to report to. Oh what a charming period is youth, when nothing seems impossible'. (Denieffe, *Personal Narrative*, pp.2–3). The Fenian movement in general, in fact, was never able to get over this colonized habit of cultivating and tolerating fantasies.

22. Printed on page 1 of the *Rolla Weekly*, Rolla, MO, Thursday, 2 September 1869.
23. *New York Tribune*, 6 July 1866, p.8.
24. Quoted by Maryniak, 'The Fenian Raid and the Battle of Ridgeway'.
25. John O'Neill, *Official Report of General John O'Neill, President of the Fenian Brotherhood, on the Attempt to Invade Canada* (New York, 1870).
26. Quoted in D'Arcy, *The Fenian Movement*, p.185.
27. *New York Tribune*, 28 September 1866, p.8.
28. Keneally, *Great Shame*, p.413.
29. Thomas William Sweeny Papers, Huntington Library, San Marino, California.
30. Thomas W. Egan to H.M. McCulloch, 25 September, 1866. Sweeny Service File, National Archives.
31. Quoted in Coyer, 'Hero of the Armless Sleeve', p.108.
32. Johnson to adjutant general, 29 September 1866. Sweeny Service File, National Archives.
33. Thomas William Sweeny Papers, Huntington Library, San Marino, California.
34. Sweeny Court Martial Records (00–2482) National Archives.
35. *New York Times*, 6 October 1866, p.2. A letter from Sweeny replying to the *Times* attack went unpublished but is included in the Sweeny court martial material cited above.
36. *Augusta Chronicle and Sentinel*, 13 November 1867, p.2.
37. Thomas William Sweeny Papers, Huntington Library, San Marino, California.
38. Ibid.
39. Quoted in William Sweeny, 'Brigadier-General TWS', *JAIHS,* (1928), p.267.
40. Ibid.
41. Margaret Fuller, 'The Irish Character' in *Margaret Fuller's New York Journalism*, Catherine C. Mitchell (ed.) (Knoxville, TN: 1995) p.166.
42. *New York Herald*, 14 April 1892, p.12.

Bibliography

Adams, Ephraim Douglas. *Great Britain and the American Civil War*, 2 Vols (New York, 1924).

Adams, George Rollie. *General William S. Harney: Prince of Dragoons* (Lincoln, NB, 2001).

American Poetry: The Nineteenth Century, 2 vols, (ed.) John Hollander (New York, 1993).

Anders, Leslie. 'Fisticuffs at Headquarters: Sweeny vs. Dodge', *Civil War Times Illustrated*, 15, 10 (1977), pp.8–15.

Athearn, Robert G. *Forts of the Upper Mississippi* (Englewood Cliffs, NJ, 1967).

Axelrod, Alan. *Chronicle of the Indian Wars: From Colonial Times to Wounded Knee* (New York, 1993).

Beiber, Ralph P. (ed.). *Southern Trails to California* (Glendale, CA, 1937).

Bierce, Ambrose. 'What I Saw at Shiloh', *Ambrose Bierce Civil War Stories* (New York, 1994), pp.1–17.

Billington, Ray Allen. *The Far Western Frontier: 1830–1860* (New York, 1962).

Blessing, Patrick J. *The Irish in America: A Guide to the Literature and the Manuscript Collections* (Washington, DC, 1992).

Boatner, Mark Mayo. *The Civil War Dictionary* (New York, 1988).

Brooksher, William Riley. *Bloody Hill: The Civil War Battle of Wilson's Creek* (Washington, DC, 1995).

Brown, Thomas N. *Irish-American Nationalism* (Philadelphia, PA, 1966).

Burns, Robin B. 'D'Arcy McGee and the Fenians', in Maurice Harman (ed.), *Fenians and Fenianism* (Seattle, WA, 1970), pp.77–92.

Captain Patrick Naughton: Fifth Iowa Volunteer Cavalry. scriptoum.org/c/p/naughton.html (2 October 2004).

Carter, Samuel. *The Siege of Atlanta*, 1864 (New York, 1973).

Castel, Albert. *General Sterling Price and the Civil War in the West* (Baton Rouge, LA, 1968).

—— *Decision in the West: The Atlanta Campaign of 1864* (Lawrence, KS, 1992).

Chamberlain, W.H. 'Hood's Second Sortie at Atlanta – Battle of Bald Hill', in Johnson and Buel (eds), *The Century War Series,* Vol. 1 (New York, 1978).

Cleland, Robert G. 'An Exile on the Colorado', *Westerners Brand Book*, 6 (1956), pp.17–29.

Cohen, Hennig (ed.). *The Battle Pieces of Herman Melville* (New York 1964).

Comerford, R.V. *The Fenians in Context: Irish Politics and Society, 1848–82* (Dublin, 1998).

Conynghan, David P. *Sherman's March Through the South* (New York, 1865).

Cowell, Josephine W. *History of Benicia Arsenal, Benecia California, January 1851–December 1962* (Berkeley, CA, 1963).

Coyer, Richard J. '"Hero of the armless sleeve": the military career of Thomas W. Sweeny", Master's Thesis, University of San Diego, CA, (1978).

Crane, Stephen. *Tales, Sketches, and Reports* (ed.) Fredson Bowers (Charlottesville, VA, 1973).

Cullop, Charles P. 'An unequal duel: Union Recruiting in Ireland, 1863–64, *Civil War History*, 13 (1967), pp.101–13.

Danto, Arthur C. 'Gettysburg', *Grand Street* 6,3 (1987), pp.98–116.

D'Arcy, William. *The Fenian Movement in the United States: 1858–1886* (Washington, DC, 1947).

DeKay, James Tertins, *The Rebel Raiders: The Astonishing History of the Confederacy's Secret Navy*. (New York, 2001).

DeKay, James Tertins, *The Rebel Raiders: The Astonishing History of the Conferacy's Secret Navy* (New York, 2002).

Denieffe, Joseph. *A Personal Narrative of the Irish Revolutionary Brotherhood*, ed. Stephen J. Richardson (New York, 1906).

DeRosier, Arthur H. 'Importance of Failure: The Fenian raids of 1866–1871', *Southern Quarterly*, 3,3 (1965), pp.181–97.

DeVoto, Bernard. *The Year of Decision 1846* (Boston, MA, 1943).

Devoy, John. *Devoy's Post Bag*, ed. William O'Brien and Desmond Ryan (Dublin, 1948).

Douglas, Frederick. *Narrative of the Life of Frederick Douglas, an American Slave* (Garden City, NY, 1963).

Drum, Richard C. 'Reminiscences of the Indian Fight at Ash Hollow'. *Collections of the Nebraska State Historical Society,* vol. 16 (1911), pp.143–51.

Engle, Stephen D. *Yankee Dutchman: The life of Franz Sigel* (Fayetteville, NC, 1993).

Englehardt, Zephyrin. *San Diego Mission* (San Francisco, CA, 1920).

Evans, William R. 'The Garra Uprising: conflict between San Diego Indians and settlers in 1851'. *California Historical Society Quarterly*, 45,4 (1866), pp.339–49.

Faherty, William B. *The St Louis Irish: An Unmatched Celtic Community* (St Louis, MO, 2001).

—— *Exile in Erin: A Confederate Chaplain's Story: The life of Father John B. Bannon* (St. Louis, MO, 2002).

Ó Fiaich, Tomás. 'The Clergy and Fenianism', *Irish Ecclesiastical Record*, (1968), pp.81–103.

Fiske, John. *The Mississippi Valley in the Civil War* (Boston, MA, 1900).

Fort Mojave Indian Tribe, 'Mojave Indian History to 1860' *www.nps.gov/moja/mojahtm3.htm* (15 August 2004).

Foster, R.F. *Modern Ireland 1600–1972* (London, 1989).

Frazer, Robert W. (ed.) 'Camp Yuma – 1852'. *Southern California Quarterly*, 52,2 (1970), pp.170–84.

—— (ed.). 'Military Posts in San Diego, 1852', *Journal of San Diego History*, 20, 3 (1974), pp.44–52.

Galwey, Thomas Francis. *The Valiant Hours: An Irish-American in the Army of the Potomac* (Harrisburg, PA, 1961).

Goble, Bill. 'On to Canada! . . . Again?' *Military Images*, 16, 5 (1995), pp.22–5.

Goetzmann, William H. *Army Exploration in the American West, 1804–1863* (New Haven, CT, 1959).

Golway, Terry. *Irish Rebel: John Devoy and America's Fight for Ireland's Freedom* (New York, 1998).

Harmon, Maurice (ed.). *Fenians and Fenianism* (Seattle, WA, 1970).

Healy, T.M. *Letters and Leaders of My Day* (Dublin, 1883).

Heintzelman, Samuel P. *The Papers of Samuel Peter Heintzelman* (microform) Washington, D.C. Library of Congress, 1977.

Heitman, Francis B. *Historical Register and Dictionary of the United States Army* (Urbana, IL, 1965).

Hernon, Joseph M. Jr. *Celts, Catholics and Copperheads: Ireland Views the American Civil War* (Columbus, OH, 1968).

Hirshson, Stanley P. *Grenville M. Dodge: Soldier, Politician, Railroad Pioneer* (Bloomington, IN, 1967).

Hofstadter, R., W. Miller and D. Aaron *The United States: The History of a Republic* (Englewood Cliffs, NJ, 1963).

Hogan, Michael. *The Irish Soldiers of Mexico* (Guadalajara, 1999).

Horn, Stanley F. *The Army of Tennessee* (New York, 1941).

Hunt, Roger D. and Jack R. Brown. *Brevet Brigadier Generals in Blue* (Gaithersburg, MD, 1990).

Irish in America. History Channel. www.historychannel.com

Jacobson, Matthew Frye. *Special Sorrows: The Diasporic Imagination of Irish, Polish, and Jewish Immigrants in the United States* (Cambridge, MA, 1995).

Jenkins, Brian. *Fenians and Anglo-American Relations during Reconstruction* (Ithaca, NY, 1969).

Johnson, Robert Underwood and Clarence Buel (eds). *Battles and Leaders of the Civil War, The Century War Series*, 4 Vols, *1884–88* (reprinted, Secaucus, NJ, 1982).

Johannsen, Robert W. *To the Halls of the Montezumas: The Mexican War in the American Imagination* (New York, 1985).

Jones, Gregory T. 'The Yuma Crossing'. *www.desertusa.com/mag99/jan/stories/crossing.html* (10 September 2004).

Kee, Robert. *The Most Distressful Country* (London, 1972).

—— *The Bold Fenian Men* (London, 1972).

Keegan, John. *The Price of Admiralty: The Evolution of Naval Warfare* (New York, 1990).

Kelly, James Edward. Interview with Thomas William Sweeny, 16 January 1886, Kelly Papers, New York Historical Society.

Keneally, Thomas. *The Great Shame and the Triumph of the Irish in the English-Speaking World* (New York, 1998).

Kenny, Kevin. *Making Sense of the Molly Maguires* (New York, 1998).

Kinchen, Oscar A. *Daredevils of the Confederate Army: The St Albans Raiders* (Boston, 1959).

Kostal, R.W. 'Rebels in the Dock: The Prosecution of Dublin Fenians, 1865–66', *Eire-Ireland*, 34 (1999), pp.70–96.

Kull, Irving S. and Nell M. *An Encyclopedia of American History* (New York, 1965).

Lamar, Howard R. (ed.). *New Encyclopedia of the American West* (New Haven, CT, 1998).

Larkin, Thomas O. *Letters to the Secretary of State about the Gold Discovery*. www.sfmuseum.org/hist6/larkin.html (25 August 2004).

Le Caron, Major Henri, *Twenty-Five Years in the Secret Service: The Recollections of a Spy* (London, 1892).

Loomis, Noel M. 'The Garra Uprising of 1851', *Westerners Brand Book, 2* (San Diego, 1971), pp.3–26

Love, Frank. 'Louis Jaeger Saw Opportunity in Yuma Ferry'. www.yumasun.com/artman/publish/articles/story_7065.shtml (7 September 2003).

Macdonald, John A. *Troublous Times in Canada: A History of the Fenian Raids of 1866 and 1870* (Toronto, 1910).

Maloney, Alice Bay (ed.). 'Some Oatman Documents', *California Historical Society Quarterly*, 21, 1 (1942), pp.107–11.

Maryniak, Benedict. 'The Fenian Raid and the Battle of Ridgeway' www.acsu.buffalo.edu/~dbertuca/g/FenianRaid.html (12 September 2004)

Mattison, Edward D. 'The Harney Expedition Against the Sioux: The Journal of Capt. John Todd', *Nebraska History*, 43, 2 (1962), pp.89–130.

McCann, Lloyd E. 'The Grattan Massacre', *Nebraska History*, 37, 1 (1956) pp.1–25.

McCarthy, Cormac. *Blood Meridian or the Evening Redness in the West* (New York, 1992).

McGee, Thomas D'Arcy. *The Irish Position in British and in Republican North America* (Montreal, 1866).

McGuire, Randy R., *St Louis Arsenal: Armory of the West* (Chicago, 2001).

McPherson, William (ed.). *From San Diego to the Colorado in 1849: The Journal and Maps of Cave J. Couts* (Los Angeles, CA, 1932).

Meade, George. *The Life and Letters of George Gordon Meade, Major General US Army*, 2 Vols (New York, 1913).

Meyler, David. '"To the Glory of Our Country": The Fenian Invasion of Canada, 1866', *Command Magazine*, March–April (1992), pp.30–5.

Miller, Kerby A. *Emigrants and Exiles: Ireland and the Irish Exodus to North America* (New York, 1985).

Miller, Robert Ryall. *Shamrock and Sword: The St Patrick's Battalion in the US–Mexican War* (Norman, OK, 1989).

Mills, John Stuart. *Autobiography*, (ed.) Jack Stillinger (Boston, MA, 1969).

Monaghan, Jay. *Civil War on the Western Border, 1854–1865* (Lincoln, NB, 1955).

Morgan, Jack. 'The Irish in John Ford's Seventh Cavalry Trilogy', *Melus,* 22, 2 (1997), pp.33–44.

—— '"The Dust of Maynooth": Fenian Funeral as Political Theater – St Louis, 1865', *New Hibernia Review*, 2, 4 (1998), pp.24–37.

Moriarty, James Edward. 'Fighting Tom Sweeny: The California Years', *Journal of San Diego History*, 26, 3 (1980), pp.206–17.

Moriarty, James Robert III. 'Soldiering at the Mission San Diego de Alcala, 1849–58', *Westerners Brand Book, 3* (San Diego, CA, 1972), pp.142–51.

Morris, Roy Jr. *Sheridan: The Life and Wars of General Phillip Sheridan* (New York, 1992).

Morrison, Lorrin. *Warner: The Man and the Ranch* (Los Angeles, CA, 1962).

Mulligan, James A. 'The siege of Lexington, Missouri', *Battles and Leaders of the Civil WarBased on the centuries War Series, 1884–87*, Vol. 1 (Rprint, Secaucus, NJ, 1982), pp.307–313.

Myers, Augustus. *Ten Years in the Ranks of the US Army* (New York, 1914).

Neidhardt, W.S. *Fenianism in North America* (University Park, PA, 1975).

North, Diane M.T. *Samuel Peter Heintzelman and the Sonora Exploring and Mining Company* (Tucson, AZ, 1980).

O'Broin, Leon. *Fenian Fever: An Anglo-American Dilemma* (New York, 1971).

O'Mahony, John. 'Fenianism – An Exposition', *Irish People* (25 January–18 July 1868).

O'Neill, John. *Official Report on the Attempt to Invade Canada, May 25, 1870'* (New York, 1870).

O'Reilly, Private Miles. *Baked Meats at the Funeral: A Collection of Essays, Poems, Speeches, Histories and Banquets* (New York, 1866).

Owen, David. *Year of the Fenians* (Buffalo, NY, 1990).

Parkman, Francis. *The Oregon Trail* (New York, 1996).

Parrish, William E. *Turbulent Partnership: Missouri and the Union, 1861–1865* (Columbia, MO, 1963).

Peckham, James. *General Nathaniel Lyon and Missouri in 1861* (New York, 1861).

Pettis, Edward S.J. (ed.). 'Olive Oatman's Lecture Notes', *San Bernadino County Museum Publications,* 16, 2 (1969).

Phillips, Christopher. *Damned Yankee: The Life of General Nathaniel Lyon* (Columbia, MO, 1990).

—— *Missouri's Confederate: Claiborne Fox Jackson and the Creation of Southern Identity in the Border West* (Columbia, MO, 2000).

Phillips, George Harwood. *Chiefs and Challengers: Indian Resistance and Cooperation in Southern California* (Berkeley, CA, 1975).

Piston, William Garrett and Richard W. Hatcher. *Wilson's Creek: The Second Battle of the Civil War and the Men who Fought It* (Chapel Hill, NC, 2000).

Potter, George. *To the Golden Door: The Story of the Irish in Ireland and America* (Boston, MA, 1960).

Richardson, Albert D. *The Secret Service, the Field, the Dungeon, and the Escape* (Hartford, CT, 1865).

Ruddy, Michael. 'An Irish Army in America', *Civil War Times,* 41 (2003) pp.32–40.

—— 'Here Comes that Damned Green Flag Again', *Civil War Times*, (2003), Vol. I, pp.32–40.

—— The Fenian Brotherhood. www.freepages.geneology.rootsweb.com/~mruddy/fenian/.htm (6 September 2004).

Rutherford, John. *The Secret History of the Fenian Conspiracy*, 2 Vols (London, 1985).

Sarbaugh, Timothy, 'Post Civil War Fever and Adjustment: Fenianism in the California Context', *Irish Studies Program Working Papers,* 91, 2–3 (Boston, MA, 1992).

Savage, John. *Fenian Heroes and Martyrs* (Boston, MA, 1868).

Senior, Hereward. *The Last Invasion of Canada: The Fenian Raids, 1866–1870* (Toronto, 1991).

Severance, Frank. 'The Fenian Raid of "66"', *Buffalo Historical Society Publications*, 25 (1922), pp.263–85.

Shannon, William. The American Irish (New York, 1963).

Shaw, Frederick B. *One Hundred and Forty Years of Service: A History of the Second Infantry U.S. Army* (Detroit, MI, 1930).

Sherman, William Tecumseh. *Home Letters of General Sherman*, (ed.) M.A. DeWolf Howe (New York, 1909).

Sifakis, Stewart. *Who Was Who in the Union Army: A Biographical Encylopedia of more than 1500 Participants* (New York, 1989).

Slaughter, Linda W. 'Fort Randall', *Collections: State Historical Society of North Dakota*, Vol. 1 (1906), pp.423–9.

Smith, Walter Gifford. *The Story of San Diego* (San Diego, CA, 1892).

Sowles, Edward A. 'Fenianism and the Fenian Raid in Vermont', *Magazine of History,* 7, 1 (1908), pp.32–47.

'"*Springfield is a Vast Hospital": Civil War Medicine at Wilson's Creek*' www.nps.gov/wicr/cwmedicine.html

Stacey, Charles P. 'Fenian Interlude: The Story of Michael Murphy', *Canadian Historical Review*, 15 (1931), pp.133–54.

—— 'Fenianism and the Rise of National feeling in Canada', *Canadian Historical Review*, XII, (1931), pp.238–61.

—— 'Garrison of Fort Wellington: A Military Dispute during the Fenian Troubles', *Canadian Historical Review*, 14 (1933), pp.161–76.

—— 'The Fenian Troubles and Canadian Military Development', *Canadian Historical Association Report,* (1935), pp.26–35.

Stratton, Royal B. *Life among the Indians: Narrative of the Captivity of the Oatman Girls* (San Francisco, CA, 1857).

Sweeny, Thomas W. 'Narrative of Army Service in the Mexican War and on the Plains, 1846–53', *Journal of the Military Service Institution of the United States*, 42, 151 (Januray–February 1908), pp.126–137.

—— 'Official Report of General Thomas W. Sweeny, Secretary of War, Fenian Brotherhood and Commander in Chief, Irish Republican Army, Headquarters, F.B., September, 1866', *Journal of the American Irish Historical Society*, 23 (1924), pp.193–203.

—— *Journal of Lt. Thomas W. Sweeny, 1849–1853,* (ed.) Arthur Woodward (Los Angeles, CA, 1956).

Sweeny, William M. 'Brigadier-General Thomas W. Sweeny, United States Army – A Biographical Sketch', *Journal of the American Irish Historical Society*, 2 (1899), pp.193–201.

——'A Biographical Memoir of Thomas W. Sweeny' (*c.* Privately Printed, 1907).

—— (ed.) TWS, 'The Fenian Invasion of Canada, 1866', *Journal of the American Irish Historical Society*, 23 (1924), pp.193–203.

—— 'Brigadier-General Thomas W. Sweeny, United States Army', *Journal of the American Irish Historical Society*, 22 (1928), pp.257–72.

Tamplain, Pamela. 'Philip Crosthwaite, San Diego Pioneer and Public Servant', *Journal of San Diego History*, 21, 3 (1975). sandiegohistory.org/journal/75summer/Crosthwaite.htm. (8 August 2004).

Thompson, Jerry. *Major Samuel Peter Heintzelman's Journal of Texas and the Cortina War* (Austin, TX, 1997).

Thompson, Mildred C. *Reconstruction in Georgia* (Savannah, GA, 1972).

Touhill, Blanche. *William Smith-O'Brien and His Revolutionary Companions in Exile* (Columbia, MO, 1981).

Tucker, Phillip Thomas. *The South's Finest: The First Missouri Confederate Brigade from Pea Ridge to Vicksburg* (Washington, DC, 1993).

—— *Westeners in Gray* (Jefferson, NC, 1995).

Twain, Mark. *Mark Twain: Collected Tales, Sketches, Speeches, and Essays, 1852–1890*, (ed.) Louis J. Budd (New York, 1992).

—— *Life on the Mississippi* (New York, 2001).

US War Department, *The War of the Rebellion: A Compilation of the Official Records of the Union and Confederate Armies*, 128 Vols (Washington, DC, 1881–1901).

Utley, Robert M. *Frontiersmen in Blue: The United States Army and the Indians, 1848–1865* (New York, 1967).

Walker, Mabel Gregory. *The Fenian Movement* (Colorado Springs, CO, 1969).

Ward, Francis J. 'Early Irish in St Louis, Missouri', *Journal of American Irish Historical Society*, 6 (1906), pp.46–50.

Ware, Eugene F. *The Lyon Campaign and the History of the 1st Iowa Infantry* (Topeka, KS, 1907).

Warner, Ezra. *Generals in Blue: Lives of the Union Commanders* (Baton Rouge, LA, 1996).

The Wild Geese Today. 'Tom Sweeny – The Didn't Call Him "Fighting Tom" for Nothing'. www.the wild geese.com/pages/sweent.html (5 October 2004).

Wilson, David A. 'The Fenians in Montreal, 1862–68: Invasion, Intrigue and Assassination', *Eire–Ireland: Journal of Irish Studies* (Fall–Winter 2003) pp.109–33.

Wilson, Frederick T. 'Fort Pierre and its Neighbors', *South Dakota Historical Collection*, 1 (1902), pp.263–379.

The Works of Walt Whitman, The Deathbed Edition in Two Volumes (New York 1969).

Woodward, Arthur. 'Oasis at Vallecito', *Desert Magazine,* 5,5 (1942), pp.22–6.

—— *Feud on the Colorado* (Los Angeles, CA, 1955).

—— Scofield DeLong and Leffler B. Miller, *The Missions of Northern Sonora: A 1935 Field Documentation* (Tuscon, AZ, 1993).

Index

[Throughout this index 'Sweeny' refers to Thomas Sweeny, except as otherwise shown, while 'son', 'daughter' and other such relationships are those of the people named to Thomas Sweeny.]